The Censorship Files

SUNY series in Latin American and Iberian Thought and Culture
Jorge J. E. Gracia and Rosemary Geisdorfer Feal, editors

The Censorship Files

Latin American Writers and Franco's Spain

Alejandro Herrero-Olaizola

❖

State University of New York Press

Published by
State University of New York Press, Albany

© 2007 State University of New York

All rights reserved

Printed in the United States of America

No part of this book may be used or reproduced in any manner whatsoever without written permission. No part of this book may be stored in a retrieval system or transmitted in any form or by any means including electronic, electrostatic, magnetic tape, mechanical, photocopying, recording, or otherwise without the prior permission in writing of the publisher.

For information, address State University of New York Press,
194 Washington Avenue, Suite 305, Albany, NY 12210-2384

Production by Kelli Williams
Marketing by Anne M. Valentine

Library of Congress Cataloging-in-Publication Data

Herrero-Olaizola, Alejandro.
 The censorship files : Latin American writers and Franco's Spain / Alejandro Herrero-Olaizola.
   p. cm. — (SUNY series in Latin American and Iberian thought and culture)
 Includes bibliographical references and index.
 ISBN-13: 978-0-7914-6985-9 (hardcover : alk. paper)
 1. Spanish American fiction—20th century—Publishing—Spain. 2. Censorship—Spain—History—20th century. I. Franco, Francisco, 1892-1975. II.Title. III. Series.

PQ7082.N7H47 2007
098'.120946—dc22

2006012826

10 9 8 7 6 5 4 3 2 1

For David

Contents

Illustrations   ix

Preface   THE CENSORSHIP FILES   xi

Acknowledgments   xxix

Chapter 1. PUBLISHING MATTERS: *The Boom and Its Players*   1
    The New Rules of Censorship   9
    The New Seix Barral   13
    Bitching about the Boom   22

Chapter 2. THE WRITER IN THE BARRACKS: *Mario Vargas Llosa Facing Censorship*   37
    Facing the Censors, Facing the Market   45
    The Marketing of Military Literature   58

Chapter 3. CUBAN NIGHTS FALLING: *The Revolutionary Silences of Guillermo Cabrera Infante*   71
    The Cuban Connection: Spain and the "Infantes of the Revolution"   79
    Silencing the Cuban Revolution: From "Vista del amanecer en el trópico" to *Tres tristes tigres*   89
    Censorship Remains: A Revolutionary's Career   103

Chapter 4. FROM MELQUÍADES TO VERNET: *How Gabriel García Márquez Escaped Spanish Censorship*   109
    Wise and Unwise Catalans   117
    García Márquez and His "Familiar" Censors   125
    A Citizen Censor   135

Chapter 5. BETRAYED BY CENSORSHIP: *Manuel Puig Declassified* 141
    Betrayed by the Marketplace 146
    Betrayed by Aunt Clara 155
    "Playing 'Toro'" Betrayed by Ms. Hayworth 165

Epilogue. LEGENDS OF THE BOOM: *Latin American Publishing Revisited* 173

Notes 185

Works Cited 203

Index 221

Illustrations

Fig. P.1: Censor's report on Manuel Puig's
La traición de Rita Hayworth (1966)   xxiv
Fig. P.2: Censor's report on José Lezama Lima's
Paradiso (1968)   xxv
Fig. P.3: Censor's report on Julio Cortázar's
Libro de Manuel (1973)   xxvi
Fig. P.4: Censor's report on Carlos Fuentes'
La región más transparente (1973)   xxvii
Fig. 1.1: Book cover. Adriano González León's
País portátil. 1st ed. (Seix Barral, 1968)   35
Fig. 1.2: Book cover. Nivaria Tejera's *Sonámbulo del sol*.
1st ed. (Seix Barral, 1972)   36
Fig. 2.1: Book cover. Mario Vargas Llosa's *Pantaleón y las
visitadoras* (censored cover; Seix Barral, 1973)   65
Fig. 2.2: Book cover. Mario Vargas Llosa's *Pantaleón y las
visitadoras* (replacement cover; Seix Barral, 1973)   66
Fig. 2.3: Book cover. Mario Vargas Llosa's *La ciudad y los
perros*. 4th ed. (Seix Barral, 1974)   67
Fig. 3.1: Photographs: "Lo que la censura no ve."
Lunes de Revolución (February 20, 1961)   82
Fig. 5.1: Book cover. Manuel Puig's *Boquitas pintadas*.
2nd reprint (Seix Barral, 1976)   145
Fig. 5.2: Book cover. Manuel Puig's *La traición de
Rita Hayworth*. 1st ed. (Seix Barral, 1971)   163
Fig. 5.3: Book cover. Manuel Puig's *La traición de
Rita Hayworth*. 1st ed. *Biblioteca Formentor* (Seix
Barral, 1982). [*edición completa*; uncensored version]   164

Preface
The Censorship Files

I am no stranger to censorship, since for years I was a censor myself. This confession is not out of place, I hope, in a book dealing with the Spanish-language publishing industry and the promotion of Latin American literature in the 1960s and 1970s. I would like to use my personal experience to frame a discussion of official censorship during the last phase of the dictatorial regime of Francisco Franco (1960–1975), and of the way it relates to the publishing of Latin American literature during that period. These are the years of the *apertura*, the political opening up of the Franco regime that started with a series of economic and political reforms designed to break down Spain's international isolation on the world scene.

Since I was born when the *apertura* was in full swing, I experienced the regime's "most liberal" side while growing up. Nevertheless I was trained in school to write and to read like a censor. My writing was censorious in its form and content in the same way the regime had been for years. I also read and thought censoriously, for I was constantly reminded of an authoritative and censorial entity poised to watch over my thinking process. Of course, growing up in Franco's Spain, I was not aware that I was a censor, that censorship existed, or that Latin American literature had been censored by the Franco regime. Nor was I privy to the economic and cultural expansion into Latin America on which the regime had embarked around 1960, or to the seemingly contradictory policies of the Franco regime as it overhauled the Spanish book trade and in pursuit of that goal simultaneously promoted and censored the works of many Latin American writers.

I became aware of this paradoxical relationship between censorship and book production when in 1997 I began to examine the official reports of the Franco regime. These reports include declassified documents on the Spanish book trade in the Americas and the censorship files on the Latin American novels that were considered for publication or published in Spain. Examining the official reports of the Franco regime has made me realize now that the success of Latin American literature in the 1960s and 1970s was, in part, due to censorship (or, more precisely, to the new rules of censorship implemented by the regime in the 1960s). But for me they also exemplify with particular clarity the way I was led to understand Latin America while growing up in Spain.

These official reports reveal the negotiations and behind-the-scenes maneuvering that went on among those involved in the Spanish publishing industry: censors, government officials of the Spanish Book Institute, publishers, literary agents, book exporters and importers, and Latin American writers. They are now housed in Spain's National Archive, the *Archivo General de la Administración*, in Alcalá de Henares, the birthplace of Miguel de Cervantes and now the headquarters of Spain's latest cultural enterprise overseas, the *Instituto Cervantes*. My current dossier of government documents (censors' reports, employee records, regulations, and letters exchanged between editors, government officials and censors) is about four thousand pages. For this book I have examined records concerning about thirty Latin American writers, whose work was at some point submitted to the Spanish censorship authorities, such as Reinaldo Arenas, Jorge Luis Borges, Mario Benedetti, Adolfo Bioy Casares, Alfredo Bryce Echenique, Alejo Carpentier, Guillermo Cabrera Infante, Julio Cortázar, José Donoso, Carlos Fuentes, Salvador Garmendia, Gabriel García Márquez, Adriano González León, Vicente Leñero, José Lezama Lima, Álvaro Mutis, Manuel Puig, Ernesto Sábato, Severo Sarduy, and Mario Vargas Llosa. These files offer abundant evidence concerning particular cases. But they also demonstrate the way the Spanish government officials reported on Latin America, and, even more importantly for my immediate purpose, they show which kind of Latin American literature the censors found suitable to play a role in the desired expansion of the Spanish publishing industry.

While these authors are not the only censored Latin American writers, their files are the most significant ones. In examining some of them here, I propose to explore a shift in the control of the Spanish-language publishing industry between 1960 and 1970, and to map out Spanish government policies for the marketing of books through tax breaks, subsidies for paper, and some leeway in the rules of censorship. In my view, the fiercely competitive publishing world of the 1960s and 1970s defined the marketing strategies that govern today's book trade. By the 1990s the strong (and often subsidized) publishing industry in Spain of the *apertura* had become a prime target of global investors, who sought to benefit from Spain's position as the leading publisher in the Spanish-language market. Nowadays, global alliances such as the Bertelsmann Group—which comprises well-established publishing houses such as Random House, Planeta, Plaza & Janés, and Sudamericana—have created a form of market-generated censorship for Spanish publishing, one that is particularly tough for new authors. My study implicitly addresses the relation between forms of censorship and book production, a phenomenon that has been neglected in recent studies on literary production and book markets (Epstein, Radway, and Schiffrin). The censorship files unintentionally epitomized in their reports this relation between censorship and book production and illustrated some of its more paradoxical aspects.

But, as I have mentioned, these are also the files that triggered many memories of my youth, particularly concerning how I envisioned Latin America. They have shown me how my own perception of Latin America was formed as an adolescent who lived through Franco's *apertura*, the period whose seemingly endless and agonic character was encapsulated by Chevy Chase, as I later learned, in his clever phrase "Generalissimo Franco is still dead." For that reason, I consider my own case exemplary of how the Spanish government promoted Latin American literature from 1960 onwards, and of how "we" read the publishing boom of Latin American literature at that time. My personal history provides a context for the way I read government's and censors' reports that I will discuss in this book.

In particular it accounts in great part for the expectations I had when I began to examine the censorship files of the Franco regime. For instance, I expected to find out (and I did) that the censors thought the works of Manuel Puig were "immoral," those of Guillermo Cabrera Infante, José Lezama Lima, and Álvaro Mutis "blasphemous" and "pornographic," and those of Julio Cortázar politically "dangerous" or "tending in the direction of the subversive leaflet" ["deriva hacia el panfleto subversivo"] (Expedientes de *La traición de Rita Hayworth* [*Betrayed by Rita Hayworth*], *Tres tristes tigres* [*Three Trapped Tigers*], *Summa de Maqroll* [*Maqroll's Summa*], *La casilla de los Morelli* [*The Morelli Box*], *Libro de Manuel* [*A Manual for Manuel*]). Others like Reinaldo Arenas were outright rejected without further explanation or were the object of scathing remarks for the "irreverent" nature of their work, as was the case also with Mario Benedetti (Expedientes de *El mundo alucinante* [*Hallucinations*], *Gracias por el fuego* [*Thanks for the Fire*]). These cases were somewhat predictable. What I did not expect to see, however, was that the censors focused so much on the command of the Spanish language displayed by Latin American writers, who were often the subject of praise or criticism for their handling of the language's resources. Nor did I initially have a sense that criticisms of Spain's colonial past bothered the censors as much as derogatory comments about the Franco regime.

For many censors, how Latin Americans used the Spanish language and talked about Spain's historical heritage in the Americas became a litmus test. For instance, they praised Jorge Luis Borges's *El Hacedor* [*The Maker*] because it "is a show-piece of his good and erudite literature" ["hace gala de su buena y erudita literatura"] (Expediente de *El hacedor*). Likewise, Adolfo Bioy Casares's works were commended for being "well crafted" and "pleasurable reading" ["la novela bien construida... se lee con gusto"] (Expediente de *Diario de la guerra*). On the other hand they gave mixed reviews to Ernesto Sábato's *Sobre héroes y tumbas* [*Of Heroes and Tombs*]: "está maravillosamente escrita, pese a la abundancia de jerga criolla y algunas incorreciones gramaticales" ["wonderfully written despite the abundance of Creole jargon and a few grammatical errors"] (Expediente de *Sobre héroes*); and they rejected Carlos Fuentes's *La región más transparente* [*Where the Air is Clear*] on the grounds that it was written in "incomprehensible language" ["un lenguaje incompresible"] (Expediente de *La región*).

Similarly, the censors did not tolerate any criticism of Spain's past or present history. They argued, for example, that Fuentes often made "derogatory remarks concerning Spain" ["un tono de repulsa hacia España"] (Expediente de *Los reinos originarios* [*Originary Kingdoms*]), and that Alejo Carpentier explicitly attacked Spain and its Catholic values: "Se aprovecha toda ocasión para denigrar a la Iglesia con irreverencia y a España por su catolicismo" ["It takes advantage of every opportunity to mock the Church irreverently and Spain for its Catholicism"] (Expediente de *El siglo de las luces* [*Century of Lights*]). And they rejected Carlos Fuentes for including in one of his novels a priest who reveals a secret learned in the confessional, thus breaking his vows (Expediente de *Las buenas conciencias* [*The Good Conscience*]).

The censorship files revealed to me the disturbing secret that I had been a censor. When I began to examine them, I quickly found myself revisiting my mandatory school book reports on the works of Vargas Llosa and García Márquez, and I began to think about how they shaped (or perhaps misshaped) my early understanding of Latin America. For instance, the censor's report on Mario Vargas Llosa's *Conversación en la catedral* [*Conversation in the Cathedral*] could easily be a direct quotation from one of my book reports: "a well-written novel, as is often the case with Vargas Llosa, even though there is an abundance of Anglicisms and Gallicisms, and too much Latin American vocabulary" ["novela escrita muy bien, como es habitual en Vargas Llosa, aunque abunden los anglicismos y galicismos y haya un exceso de vocabulario hispanoamericano"] (Expediente de *Conversación*). But not all the censors' reports resonate in this familiar way for me, since many Latin American writers never made the list of my mandatory readings in high school. Such is the case of Manuel Puig, whose novels were in fact published in Spain as early as 1971. Yet we never read any Puig text for our school assignments.

I now realize that my early readings of Latin American literature were tied to the culture of the *apertura*, and specifically to the Franco regime's attempts to promote Latin America as both a beneficial cultural endeavor and a profitable economic enterprise. This realization has led me to wonder why it was that I had to write reports, and more specifically, reports on Latin American novels for my Spanish literature courses; and why reporting of a certain censorious kind became a crucial writing exercise in most of my years of schooling. Comparing what I wrote back in school with what the censors wrote in their reports has helped me understand not only the extent of Franco's censorship, but also how it reached far beyond the official files and into daily life.

That said, my familiarization with Franco's *official* censorial practices began only when my research led me to the *Archivo*. This archive is known among scholars as the "Censorship Archive" [*Archivo de la censura*], which is a telling name for a supposedly general archive. At the *Archivo* the process of locating the censorship files (*expedientes*) is complex and time-consuming. When I first began my research there, a staff member would escort me to one of the darkest floors of the building, where I had limited time to look through some file cabinets. These contain the names of authors and works that were censored during the Franco regime (1939–75). Each author and work has a file number, which includes the last two digits of the year the censor's report was issued. This number is the first step in the research process. Back in the reading room, the researcher needs to locate the box containing the report with this number, and also the shelving area in which this box may be. Once all this information is gathered (report number, box number, and shelf number), the researcher has the illusion of having mastered the system, and, as it were, "broken the code." S/he may now request the boxes, assuming that they contain the reports (Fig. P.1–P.4). This, however, is not always the case. Many reports are missing or misplaced. There is an average wait of thirty to forty-five minutes before the coveted boxes arrive in the reading room. To make things more difficult, according to the archive's regulations, researchers can request only ten boxes at once, and a total of twenty-five per day.

I have many times wondered if in this way Spanish officialdom intended for researchers to get a firsthand feel for censorship at the *Archivo de la censura*. It is hard to believe that any Spanish government has ever been that creative. Nonetheless the possibility does cross the mind, and never more than when I consider these research procedures.

For my strategy to bypass some of these restrictions, I drew inspiration, therefore, from my early experience with the Franco regime. I spent my first few weeks at the *Archivo*, befriending the reading room supervisor and her assistants, always acknowledging that they had the authority to "censor" me if they pleased, for I was simply a college professor coming from the United States in need of their help. I gradually became their confidant and learned that the inner workings of the archive, in procedural matters, are astonishingly close to the inner workings of the Franco regime. As a result, I soon figured out that I could actually see thirty-five boxes in a given day, since there is an unwritten rule that allows researchers to hold up to ten boxes from the previous day in addition to the stipulated twenty-five per day.

Recently, in an effort to modernize its research facilities and procedures (there's now a detailed brochure titled "Researchers' Rights and Obligations" at each desk), the *Archivo* has opened a new room downstairs where researchers have access to what used to be the file cabinets, now transformed into an automated filing carousel with rotating shelves. One catch, though: the new equipment does not have enough shelves, so it stops after the letter "s," which has not been particularly helpful for my research on Mario Vargas Llosa. These difficulties may seem petty, but they are very illustrative of how regulations (censorship rules being no exception) were and are implemented in Spain. They also show that what the law says and the regulations designed to implement that law often differ. This was the case in spades for those affected by censorship under the Franco regime: the theory of censorship set forth by the regime often clashed with its implementation through written and unwritten regulations. In this book, I do focus somewhat, therefore, on the actual rules and regulations of censorship under the Franco regime in an attempt to define the relationship between these rules, the marketing of Latin American literature, and the expansion of Spanish publishing worldwide. But I am most interested in theorizing the actual practice of censorship through an examination of what the Spanish censors actually did in specific cases. My primary focus is therefore "regulatory censorship" (the official rules and the practical conventions), which is distinct from a broader "constitutive censorship"—the more abstract phenomenon that Sue Curry Jansen views as essential to any human community (6–13).

In this respect, my experience at the *Archivo* has been instructive. I learned that one has to become "like" a censor, or at least, one has to be able to put oneself in the position of a censor—to "think like a censor"—in order to research and report on censorship effectively; that is what I did. Perhaps I can illustrate this process of learning to be "like" a censor by looking briefly at one of the most incisive Latin American literary texts ever written about censorship, Luisa Valenzuela's "The Censors."

In "The Censors," the protagonist, Juan, after learning "from a confidential source" that his beloved (and possibly exiled) friend Mariana has not forgotten him, rushes to send her a letter at her address in Paris. Soon thereafter he realizes he has committed a faux pas. The letter "won't be a problem," he thinks, "it's irreproachable, harmless, but what about the rest?" (25). He knows that the censors "examine, sniff, feel and read between the lines of each and every letter, and check its tiniest comma and most accidental stain" (25). Overtaken by the fear that he and Mariana might be in danger, he decides to apply for a job at the Ministry of Communication's Censorship Division. His goal is clear and simple: to work hard and diligently as a censor, and hope for a promotion to the Post Office's Censorship Division. There he may eventually intercept his own letter before it reaches the "real" censors. But in order for his plan to be successful, he must excel as a strict censor, use lots of red ink, and, of course, learn all the nuances of coded language people use in their letters. By the end, the protagonist will have become such a great censor that, months later, when he is finally confronted with his own letter to Mariana, he cannot help himself and censors it "without regret" (31).

I, of course, never worked for Spain's Censorship Services, although for the last seven years it has almost seemed that way. Trying to understand the inner workings of censorship under Franco, I have often felt like the unfortunate protagonist in Valenzuela's short story. I, too, had to learn the coded language of censorship, the specific practices of the Spanish censors and the regulations under which they worked, as well as the government policies that hide behind their reports. So my greatest fear in writing this book has been that I may end up like Valenzuela's Juan, censoring the very documents I have been searching out and collecting for years. I now face the difficult task of reporting on censorship without being censorious in my turn, because I am trying to describe and explain the censorship practices of others with a view to effectively "un-censoring" the Latin American Boom.

Valenzuela's protagonist's mistaken belief that he can act like a censor without being or becoming a censor suggests very powerfully how censorship extends its reach even to those, like myself, who oppose or dare to challenge it. I never thought I was a censor, but I learned to write, read, and think "like" a censor, thus I was a censor. The process is comparable to the evolution of Valenzuela's protagonist. During his learning process as an official censor, he is "only pretending" to be a censor. But his successful career at the Censorship Services cannot be disregarded: as a great performance of censorship in its own right, it makes him a real censor. Moreover, since he was—like me—already acculturated to censorship prior to his working for the censorship authorities, he was actually a censor beforehand. How else could he have known that his letter was "irreproachable and harmless?" How did he figure out that the phrase "the weather's unsettled" might mean that someone secretly schemed to "overthrow the Government?" (31). Having been brought up under censorship, he reads every single line in each letter just as a censor would, looking for every possible double meaning or coded word. For the Nobel Prize-winning South African author J. M. Coetzee, writers under censorship often "involuntarily incorporate" a censor figure in their writing. Such writers, in effect, "familiarize" censorship and assimilate it despite their efforts to reject it. The "censor figure," in Coetzee's words, "produces a certain degree of intimacy with someone who does not love you, with whom you want no intimacy, but who presses himself upon you" (10–38). We shall see the relevance of these words to a number of Latin American writers, and Valenzuela's text too seems interested in fictionalizing this process by presenting the "letter writer" and the "censor figure" as one and the same. (Valenzuela claims that she has not herself been the "victim" of any real form of censorship, like burning books, but feels "censored" by the critics and by certain reviewers of her work [Magnarelli 205–6"].)

It is very easy, therefore, for me to take the lessons of "The Censors" to heart. The Censorship Division where Valenzuela's protagonist works resembles the building in which I conducted my research: "The building had a festive air on the outside that contrasted with its inner staidness" (27). Juan works for the Ministry of Communication, and I read the reports from the Spanish Ministry of Information (26); Juan's career as an official censor takes him from Section K to Section E, and then on to Section B, "where the job became more interesting," and "he could analyze the letter's content" (29). This reminds me of the various sections of the *Archivo* I had to learn about before reaching the "more interesting" stuff on censorship.

During my first year at the *Archivo* I exclusively researched the materials catalogued under *Cultura* [Culture], which contains the censorship files and the reports from the National Book Institute. As I became more familiar with the institution and its staff in the following years, I realized that an important part of the documentation I needed was catalogued under other rubrics. Under *Asuntos Exteriores* [Foreign Affairs], I found the reports on the economic, political, and cultural exchanges between Spain and Cuba; under *Educación* [Education], I saw the educational background of the censors and other government officials; and under *Comercio* [Commerce], I gathered information on the import and export of books and on other economic policies of the Franco regime. In this way I came to realize that there were additional censorship files on books that had been imported into Spain. These reports were not catalogued under *Cultura*, but under *Comercio*. I also learned that Spanish publishers often asked for permission to import small quantities of books from Latin America in an effort to "test" the authorities, to see how they would react to an already published work the publishers wished to acquire for a future Spanish edition.

The fact that Juan never reaches Section A also makes me wonder about the materials I might not have seen at the *Archivo*. I personally do not feel that my research was literally censored at the *Archivo*. Nevertheless, there are many indications that one cannot have full access to the censorship files of the Franco regime, given the restrictions in the reading room, the antiquated cataloguing system, the off-limits nature of the stacks, and the fact that many files "never made it to the archive" (that is the official phrase). Although I have concluded that these supposedly missing files may, in fact, just be misplaced (since the *Archivo* does not have any kind of computerized system and some handwritten registries are often hard to understand), this is not to say that the Spanish authorities are not hiding the "good stuff" elsewhere. It is just that I think it is unlikely in view of the significant number of confidential reports that *are* available at the *Archivo*. I did in fact find some of the "good stuff" on censorship there, although it has not been an easy task.

The process of initiation that I went through at the *Archivo* has been key, then, to my coming to understand how one "breaks the code" of censorship: as Valenzuela's story suggests, one has to appropriate censorship to oneself. Quite similarly, the evidence is that just such a "familiarization" process was a primary factor in the publication history of many Latin American novels in Franco's Spain. When one looks, as I did, at confidential letters written by Latin American writers to the Spanish censorship authorities, and becomes privy to the subsequent behind-the-scenes negotiations among publishers, censors, and these writers, one can see the writers learning how to be censors. But their familiarity with the institutions and processes of censorship shows up in another important way. Censorship practices are actually embedded in the works of many Latin American writers who, like Valenzuela, have used their fictions to present narratives that expose the intricacies of publishing. Such narratives often fictionalize writers under military regimes (think of the protagonist in Mario Vargas Llosa's *La ciudad y los perros* [*The Time of the Hero*]), agents and writers competing for success and prestige in the literary market (like Julio Méndez, Marcelo Chiriboga, and Núria Monclús in Donoso's *El jardín de al lado* [*The Garden Next Door*]), readers decoding manuscripts (such as the Buendías in García Márquez's *Cien años de soledad* [*One Hundred Years of Solitude*]), or secret police and military reports as in Manuel Puig's *The Buenos Aires Affair* and *El beso de la mujer araña* [*Kiss of the Spider Woman*], and Mario Vargas Llosa's *Pantaleón y las visitadoras* [*Captain Pantoja and the Special Service*]. These writers' obsession with the writing of reports and with the intrication of literary fiction and the publishing business reveals their deep familiarity, not only with censorship and with the economics of book publishing that they themselves faced in the 1960s and 1970s, but also with censorious societies other than that of Franco's Spain.

The way Franco officials reported on Latin America literature is clearly embedded in the history of Spain's cultural and economic dominance in the Americas. It is entirely consistent with that history that publishing in Spain was for many Latin American writers a matter of prestige and recognition, which they sought even if it meant publishing a censored version of their works. Recently, a series of *ediciones definitivas* [definitive editions] of many of these Latin American novels has appeared. These new editions confirm not only that the Boom novels that were published in Franco's Spain were censored, albeit with varying degrees of intervention, but also that their authors were willing to tolerate and even collaborate with the censors' work. The new editions of Vargas Llosa's and Fuentes's works by today's most important Spanish-language publishing house Alfaguara, and the 1999 Seix Barral's "final edition" of *Tres Tristes Tigres* attest in these ways to the reach of Franco's censorship.

Under his regime, censorship and economic policies became so entangled (particularly during the *apertura*) that while the censors often wanted to teach Latin Americans how to write, how to be truly Hispanic (read: Hispanophile), the government's policy makers pushed for significant relaxations of the censorship regulations and did so for reasons that were exclusively economic. Foreseeing the great marketing possibilities Latin America had to offer, they advocated a streamlining of censorship. The "new" economics of censorship that resulted produced an ambiguous shift in the historical codependency between Latin America and Spain. While the Latin American writers appeared to "invade" or "colonize" the Spanish book market with their best seller novels, their desire for the prestige of Spain's publishing houses ultimately reinforced their dependency on the former colonial power. Conversely, while the Franco regime should have opposed these writers, for example, for allying themselves with Castro's Cuba, the profits generated by the massive distribution of the Latin American Boom novels canceled out the negative effect of such open allegiances in the eyes of the authorities, since the revenues from the Spanish publishing industry made an important contribution to the regime's economic ambitions.

Most notably, the efforts of the avant-garde publishing house Seix Barral became crucial for both the promotion and the distribution of Latin American literature in the context of the new economic expansion proposed by the Franco regime and subserved by the publication in Spain of the Latin American Boom writers. This firm was located in Barcelona, which was then not only a cultural center and a bastion of political opposition to the Franco dictatorship, but also a major production site for many Latin American writers. So much so that when I first embarked on this project, my intention was to study the Latin American writers who lived and published in Barcelona in the 1960s and 1970s, and to explore the literary and artistic circles that flourished in and around the city at that time. Barcelona's architectural wonders had been a source of fascination for me since my adolescence. That fueled my interest in finding, perhaps, a common bond with the colony of Latin American writers who became familiar figures in the intellectual circles of Barcelona during the *apertura*. Barcelona was then seen as a cosmopolitan city, "very European," some would say, in a country that had been shut off from Europe and ruled by a Fascist dictator who was not particularly well versed in the arts. Avant-garde publishing houses, art galleries, theater, and architecture were among the significant components of the city's cultural life, while the Latin American colony in and around Barcelona included Gabriel García Márquez, José

Donoso, and Mario Vargas Llosa (together with frequent visitors such as Carlos Fuentes and Julio Cortázar), whose writing became widely available during my school years.

When I began my research for this book, I hoped to discover that these writers too were fascinated with Barcelona's architectural wonders, and I was intrigued by their dealings with Seix Barral. I read interviews and personal accounts (by Carlos Barral and José Donoso, among others), which confirmed that there was much to be said about the importance of Barcelona as a major publishing and production site for Latin American writers of the 1960s and 1970s.

But what then caught my attention was the following paradox about the Latin American colony of writers and Seix Barral: a group of what were deemed left-leaning writers had published their work in Barcelona under the censorship of a right-wing dictatorship. This, I was to discover, was a compelling example of how in Franco's Spain censorship and book production worked more often than not in complicity rather than in conflict. The regime not only allowed the publication and massive distribution in Spain of supposedly dangerous Latin American writers, but even caved in, on occasion, to the demands of publishers, to the extent of altering the censorship regulations where necessary. Meanwhile, in this process, publishers such as Seix Barral became involuntary proxy censors and agents of the Spanish government's policies in pursuit of a new colonial enterprise: the conquest of the Latin American book trade. The negotiations between writers, publishers, and censorship authorities that I became privy to make it clear that official censorship was not the only culprit when it came to producing the censored versions of Latin American literature that were published in Franco's Spain. The government, which had granted the book industry priority status in its program of economic expansion in 1959, the censors, who had their own ideological and aesthetic priorities, the publishing houses, concerned with international prestige coupled with profits, and finally the authors themselves, all had fingers in the pie that became the Boom. This complex of different interests, along with the many compromises and complicities their entwinement engendered, became the new focus of my research and constitutes the real subject of this book.

Annabel Patterson argues that "the economics of publication has itself a political dimension, and censorship has consistently been more intolerant of cheap editions to reach a large audience than specialized texts designed for an elite few" (902). But what happened under the Franco regime was somewhat different. A massive distribution of paperback editions invaded the Latin American market with inexpensive editions of distinguished writing that reached a very large audience. Publishers such as Seix Barral, as much as the government, were interested in the vast Latin American market, whose most avid consumers were the middle and upper classes. Confidential government reports insisted that the expansion of the Spanish book industry rested upon a successful incursion into the "Ibero-American markets" (Informe sobre el comercio 5). But such expanded sales opportunities also encouraged the complicity (tacit or otherwise) of Spanish publishers, many of whom (as well as many of the authors) were simultaneously at odds with the regime because of the many publishing restrictions they had faced for years.

Despite this mutuality of interests, however, the censorious attitude of the colonizer toward the (formerly) colonized continued to dominate the regime's attitude toward Latin American writing. Seix Barral itself—one of this book's principal protagonists—viewed Latin American literature as another register of Hispanic literature and part of "a mosaic of equidistant languages" (*Catálogo* 13). For this firm, therefore, the promotion of Latin American literature was not specifically a matter of cultural or economic dominance. Rather, such writing belonged to the "universality" of Hispanic literature, which, of course, the publisher was willing to promote and benefit from. Even though they did not argue in the same fashion, the official reports of the Franco regime often suggest likewise that Latin American literature was regarded as "our" literature. It was, after all, written in Spanish. Who could possibly know better than Spaniards about anything written in "our" language? This attitude meant that the literature was "ours" to censor, since it was "our" publishing houses that promoted the works of many Latin American authors. And similarly the Latin American book market was "ours" to exploit. This market had been in part lost to Argentinean and Mexican publishers in the aftermath of the Spanish Civil War (1936–39), mainly in the 1940s and 1950s, it was now seriously threatened (according to the official reports) by the new cultural institutions emerging in revolutionary Cuba (Ediciones R, *Casa de las Américas*, etc.). That it was "our" book market also implied its availability, therefore, to become one of the bastions of Spain's resurgent cultural and economic presence in the Americas.

But in the same breath, the official reports insist that Spain had a duty to preserve the Spanish language, "our" heritage in the Americas. So the government suggested in a 1963 report: "el libro es el principal vehículo para la presencia cultural de España en el mundo" ["books are the main vehicle for Spain's cultural presence in the world"] (Informe sobre el comercio 3). In this way, the ancient colonial relationship between Spain and the Americas—part economic exploitation and part cultural dominance—was revived. Latin Americans produced literature, Spain promoted and exported it, and in so doing generated not solely valuable economic returns for the home country and a new chapter in (post)colonial cultural history, but also a wealth of reports about the riches and the endless possibilities of the Latin American book market. These reports provide a necessary context for the studies that follow.

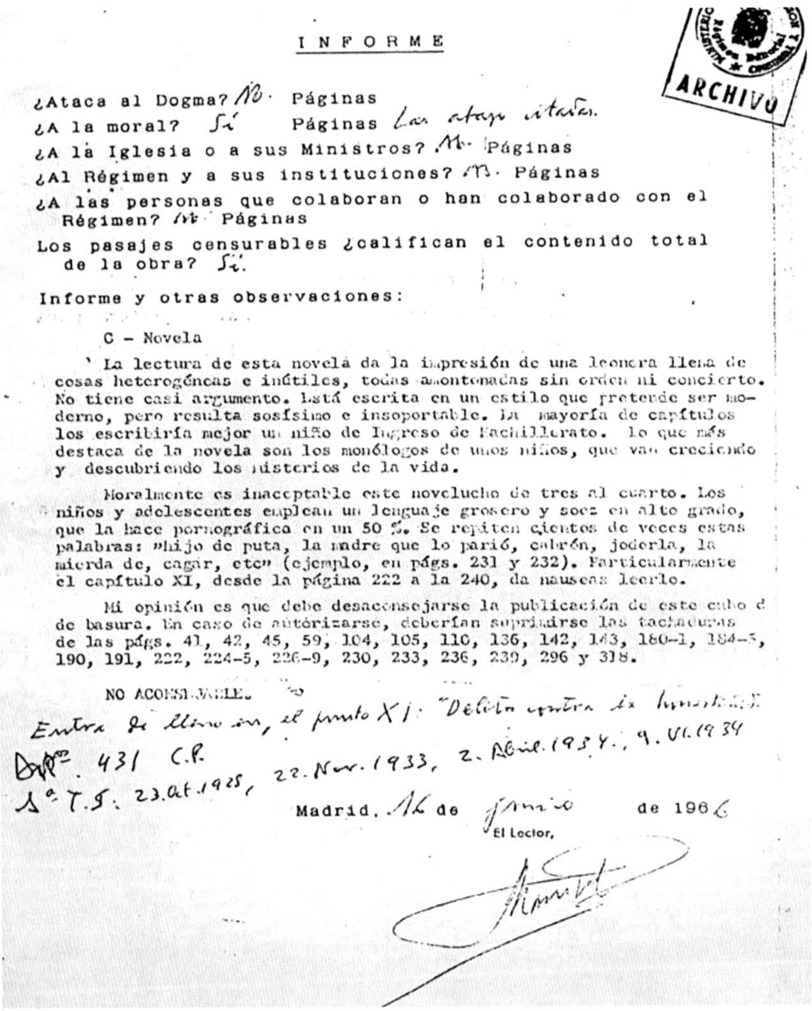

ARCHIVO

INFORME

¿Ataca al Dogma? No. Páginas

¿A la moral? Sí Páginas

¿A la Iglesia o a sus Ministros? No. Páginas

¿Al Régimen y a sus instituciones? No. Páginas

¿A las personas que colaboran o han colaborado con el Régimen? No. Páginas

Los pasajes censurables ¿califican el contenido total de la obra? Sí.

Informe y otras observaciones:

C – Novela

La lectura de esta novela da la impresión de una leonera llena de cosas heterogéneas e inútiles, todas amontonadas sin orden ni concierto. No tiene casi argumento. Está escrita en un estilo que pretende ser moderno, pero resulta sosísimo e insoportable. La mayoría de capítulos los escribiría mejor un niño de Ingreso de Bachillerato. Lo que más destaca de la novela son los monólogos de unos niños, que van creciendo y descubriendo los misterios de la vida.

Moralmente es inaceptable este novelucho de tres al cuarto. Los niños y adolescentes emplean un lenguaje grosero y soez en alto grado, que la hace pornográfica en un 50 %. Se repiten cientos de veces estas palabras: "hijo de puta, la madre que lo parió, cabrón, joderla, la mierda de, cagar, etc" (ejemplo, en págs. 231 y 232). Particularmente el capítulo XI, desde la página 222 a la 240, da nauseas leerlo.

Mi opinión es que debe desaconsejarse la publicación de este cubo de basura. En caso de autorizarse, deberían suprimirse las tachaduras de las págs. 41, 42, 45, 59, 104, 105, 110, 136, 142, 143, 180-1, 184-5, 190, 191, 222, 224-5, 226-9, 230, 233, 236, 239, 296 y 318.

NO ACONSEJABLE.

Madrid, 16 de junio de 1966

El Lector,

Fig. P.1: Censor's report on Manuel Puig's *La traición de Rita Hayworth* (1966). *Source: Ministerio de Cultura. Archivo General de la Administración.*

Preface   xxv

INFORME   22. 11-68

¿Ataca al Dogma?   Páginas
¿A la moral?   Páginas
¿A la Iglesia o a sus Ministros?   Páginas
¿Al Régimen y a sus instituciones?   Páginas
¿A las personas que colaboran o han colaborado con el Régimen?   Páginas
Los pasajes censurables ¿califican el contenido total de la obra?

Informe y otras observaciones:

> Novela de ambiente cubano. Muy compleja, muy rica en lenguaje y situaciones, muy bien escrita, aunque con un exceso de barroquismo, de disquisiciones y situaciones inconexas. El argumento es lo de menos; es un pretexto para pintar un ambiente y una postura mental y moral.
> Muestras de pornografía barroca: 224, 227-228, 228-229, 229, 230, 232-234, 234-235, 235-238, 239-241, 251, 252-253, 281-282, 282-283, 295-296, 311-312, 331-333, 364-365, 367-369, 397-398, 406-4o7, 472, 473-474, 475.
> Propongo que se tengan en cuenta antes de decidir.

Madrid, 18 de noviembre de 1968
El lector,

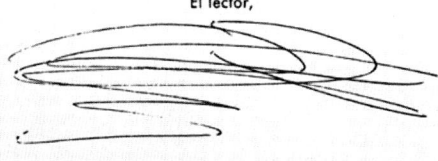

Fig. P.2: Censor's report on José Lezama Lima's *Paradiso* (1968). *Source: Ministerio de Cultura. Archivo General de la Administración.* Note: [underlining in the original]

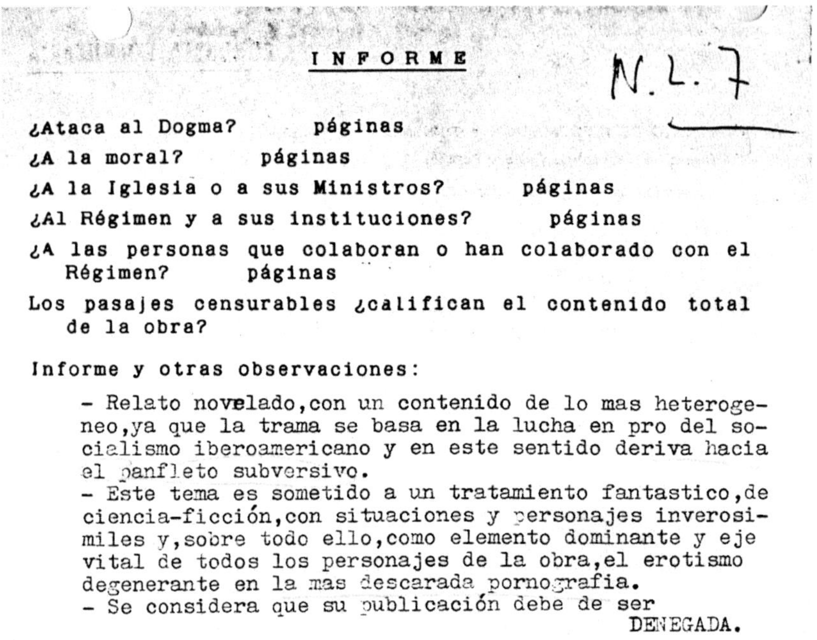

```
                    I N F O R M E           N.L.7

    ¿Ataca al Dogma?        páginas
    ¿A la moral?       páginas
    ¿A la Iglesia o a sus Ministros?      páginas
    ¿Al Régimen y a sus instituciones?       páginas
    ¿A las personas que colaboran o han colaborado con el
       Régimen?       páginas
    Los pasajes censurables ¿califican el contenido total
       de la obra?

    Informe y otras observaciones:

         - Relato novelado,con un contenido de lo mas heteroge-
         neo,ya que la trama se basa en la lucha en pro del so-
         cialismo iberoamericano y en este sentido deriva hacia
         el panfleto subversivo.
         - Este tema es sometido a un tratamiento fantastico,de
         ciencia-ficción,con situaciones y personajes inverosi-
         miles y,sobre todo ello,como elemento dominante y eje
         vital de todos los personajes de la obra,el erotismo
         degenerante en la mas descarada pornografia.
         - Se considera que su publicación debe de ser
                                                   DENEGADA.
```

Fig. P.3: Censor's report on Julio Cortázar's *Libro de Manuel* (1973). *Source*: Ministerio de Cultura. Archivo General de la Administración.

INFORME

M.L. 4

¿Ataca al Dogma?   Páginas
¿A la moral?   Páginas
¿A la Iglesia o a sus Ministros?   Páginas
¿Al Régimen y a sus instituciones? Páginas
¿A las personas que colaboran o han colaborado con el Régimen?   Páginas
Los pasajes censurables ¿califican el contenido total de la obra?

Informe y otras observaciones:
   - Novela en la que por el sistema de acciones paralelas se retrata el ambiente social de la ciudad de Méjico en todos sus estratos.
   - En la linea general de crudeza de la actual literatura hispano-americana y con su peculiar,y muchas veces incomprensible lenguaje pleno de modismos,quiere ser un testimonio vivo del Méjico de nustro tiempo.Algunos pasajes por su elevada carga de erotismo deben de ser suprimidos en las páginas 52,58,59,119,122,172,192,193,194,201,256, 277,293,301,302,303,307,310,323,324,340,350,427,428,438, 439,440,con las cuales su publicación puede ser
                                            AUTORIZADA.

52-192-193-194-256-
277-293-301-302-303-
307-324-427-438-440

Madrid, 21 de Mayo de 1973
El Lector,

F.F.Monzón.

Fig. P.4: Censor's report on Carlos Fuentes' *La región más transparente* (1973). Source: Ministerio de Cultura. Archivo General de la Administración. Note: [encircling and underlining in the original]

Acknowledgments

I am indebted to the National Endowment for the Humanities Fellowship Program and to the American Council of Learned Societies' Charles A. Ryskamp Research Fellowship Program for supporting my work. These fellowships allowed me to devote all my attention to this book. My gratitude also extends to the University of Michigan's Horace H. Rackham Faculty Fellowship and Research Grant, which provided me with travel funds for my first exploration of the "censorship files."

A number of friends and colleagues who guided me during the research and writing of this book also deserve my deepest gratitude. For his careful and incisive reading of my work I am immensely grateful to Ross Chambers, and for her unconditional support I owe many thanks to Lucille Kerr. Thanks as well to Juli Highill for always believing in this project; Jarrod Hayes for our many late-night conversations; Cristina Moreiras-Menor for being so enthusiastic about my work; Gareth Williams for his attentive reading of the final typescript; and David Caron for encouraging me from day one. Peggy McCracken, George Hoffmann, Bill Paulson, Catherine Nickel, and Frances Aparicio also helped me at various stages of the writing process. I thank my past and present colleagues at the University of Michigan for their support over the years.

I am also grateful to Marie-Hélène Huet, Ángel Loureiro, and Ricardo Krauel for facilitating my access to Princeton University. My friends Yolande Daniels and Sunil Bald in New York City were also very helpful in this respect. And I should not forget Guiomar Fages Casals for being my Catalan informant, or my valued friend Alain Martinossi for his many words of encouragement all along.

Several presentations of my work were particularly helpful for this book. I wish to thank the graduate students at the University of Toronto and at Michigan State University for inviting me as keynote speaker to talk about this book. I thank Rosa Sarabia and María Eugenia Mudrovcic respectively for suggesting my name.

I am also grateful for the comments I received from the press's anonymous readers, and for the work of Lisa Chesnel and her editorial team (especially Kelli Williams) that made this book possible.

For permission to reproduce Seix Barral's book covers, I am grateful to Elena Ramírez, *Editora Ejecutiva* of the publishing house. I also thank Spain's *Archivo General de la Administración* and *Ministerio de Cultura* for allowing the reproduction of several censor's reports; in particular, the staff members at the *Archivo* for handling the necessary paperwork and for making my research there a pleasant and unique experience.

Last, but not least, I thank my sister Teresa for her efficient assistance in obtaining all the necessary permissions for the images in this book, and my brother Juan for his complicity in all of this.

Sections of chapter 1 are a revised version of "Publishing Matters: The Latin American 'Boom' and the Rules of Censorship," *Arizona Journal of Hispanic Cultural Studies* 9 (2005): 193–205, and of "Consuming Aesthetics: Seix Barral and José Donoso in the Field of Latin American Literary Production," *MLN* 115 (2000): 323–339. An early version of section 1 of chapter 2 appeared as "Sujetos a la censura: Mario Vargas Llosa y el mundo literario de la España franquista" in the *Journal of Interdisciplinary Literary Studies* 9.1–2 (2003): 59–79. The epilogue was originally published as "Historias de papel: Latinoamérica en la memoria editorial" in *Salina: Revista de Lletres* 15 (2001): 221–228. I thank the editors of these journals for allowing me to republish.

Chapter 1

Publishing Matters

The Boom and Its Players

Shortly after the approval of the printing and publishing law of 1966, Manuel Fraga Iribarne, Spain's Minister of Information and Tourism, reportedly commented: "He dado orden de que los lápices rojos los dejen en el fondo del cajón" ["I have ordered that the red pencils be stored at the bottom of the drawer"] (Cisquella 19).[1] Fraga's pronouncement echoed not only the letter of the law—articles 1 and 50 allowed for freedom of publishing and article 3 eliminated official censorship—but also the government's claim that censorship no longer existed. Unfortunately, the red pencils nevertheless continued to be placed at the very top of the desk drawers of many Spanish censors. These "readers" (as they were officially called at the Ministry of Information) saw their censorial duties regulated but in no way eliminated by the new law's claim to recognize "the right to free expression of ideas" ["el derecho a la libertad de expresion de ideas"] (*Prensa e Imprenta* 79). Some subtle changes, however, did begin to appear in the censorship practices of the regime. Where before the *apertura*, the political "opening up" of the 1960s, these "readers" had worked for the coercive "Book Inspection Services," the new modernizing efforts of the regime now "transferred" them to the apparently inoffensive "Department for Editorial Orientation," also known as the "Department for Bibliographical Orientation."[2]

These ingenious euphemisms notwithstanding, then, Fraga's speech to a group of publishers made it clear that more red pencils would still be needed at the Ministry: "Ya tienen Ley de Prensa. Yo la he elaborado y yo voy a gobernar su cumplimiento. A mí, y no a ustedes, toca administrarla" ["Here you have your printing law. I drafted it, and I plan to enforce it. I, not you, will administer it"] (Cisquella 27). More precisely, Fraga was to administer the law in such a way as to alter, but not to end, the censorship practices of the regime, which were maintained by the controversial article 2 of the law. In this article, freedom of expression was circumscribed by a requirement that included, among other things, respect for truth and morals, allegiance to the Principles of the National Movement, due respect for the Institutions of the State, and the preservation of privacy and personal and family honor (*Prensa e Imprenta* 80). This article would not be repealed until 1977, two years after Franco's death (Abellán, *Censura* 117).

Indeed, article 2's list of limitations was a blank check for the government to continue its past censorship practices. The regime obviously did not present things in this way, or more accurately did not argue along such lines. Francisco Abella Martín, chair of the commission in charge of examining the law before parliament, defended it for its comprehensive understanding of what the U.N. Declaration of Human Rights and the European Council saw as "valid limitations of expression," such as respect for the freedom of others, respect for moral order, and for a society's welfare. Furthermore, Abella Martín hinted that the government was attempting to promote self-imposed censorship on the part of editors and publishers: "El proyecto de Ley, ante el dilema censura o responsabilidad, opta por la Segunda" ["Considering the dilemma of censorship vs. responsibility, the law opts for the Second Option"] (*Prensa e Imprenta* 26–7). What this formulation really meant seems obvious today, but it became a matter of debate among critics, publishers, and writers at that time. For Carlos Barral, the new law brought a "rationalization of censorship" and "easier ways" to exchange ideas with the censorship authorities (*Almanaque* 12); for Manuel Abellán, the law was "a judicial ploy" ["un montaje jurídico"] (*Censura* 119); and for Hans-Jörg Neuschäffer the law was designed to "influence the very process of creation" (49). In my view, the new rules of censorship paved the way for a strategic expansion of the book industry, an ambitious policy of the regime that culminated with the approval of a significant piece of legislation in 1975, the *Ley del Libro* [the Book Law]. My research at the *Archivo* indicates that this law had been drafted as early as 1969, was revised in 1972 and 1973, and was finally approved in 1975. The new legislation (incidentally, still on the books) encouraged not only the promotion, production, and distribution of books, but also provided a carefully designed structure intended to coordinate the government's efforts to pursue the expansion of the Spanish book industry through subsidies and tax credits. These measures took place under the Economic Plans for Development (*desarrollismo*) of the *apertura* years, when leading figures of the Franco regime such as López Rodó designed a series of economic and political reforms that would allow the regime to break down Spain's international isolation from the world scene, with one clear goal in mind. The idea was to:

> promover el crecimiento de la economía como vector generador de prosperidad y el bienestar material de la población, con la esperanza de que dicha prosperidad y bienestar cimentaran la paz social, suplieran la falta de libre participación democrática y dieran legitimidad de ejercicio a un régimen autoritorio pero también modernizador.
>
> To promote economic growth as the generating principle of prosperity and well-being for the population, in the hope that this prosperity and well-being would be the foundation for social peace, make up for the lack of free and democratic participation, and give legitimacy of exercise to an authoritarian yet modernizing regime. (Moradiellos 149)

For the book industry economic growth and prosperity implied some relaxation of the censorship regulations, together with the implementation of government-sponsored subsidies and reforms geared toward the modernization and expansion of what the regime saw as a somewhat out-of-date industry. With the 1966 law, the government was claiming to put an end to the censorship of printed materials under the banner of "censorship no longer exists" ["la censura ya no existe"], but despite this claim, all printed material still had to receive the seal of approval of the Ministry of Information, which meant that censorship continued. What the new law did change was the way in which censors evaluated manuscripts. And in the case of Latin American literature, the new law allowed for a wider distribution of Latin American texts, since many works by Latin American writers were authorized for printing as long as they were not distributed in Spain (Abellán, "La censura"). For instance, the 1973 submission of Salvador Garmendia's *Día de ceniza* [*Ash Day*] was done for "export" purposes only, and that pleased the censors who in 1968 had not approved Seix Barral's request to import the book due to its "eroticism." The authorities saw no objection to approving the 1973 petition since the book was to be marketed overseas (Expediente de *Día de ceniza*). Similarly, Barral

Editores submitted Alfredo Bryce Echenique's *Huerto cerrado* [*Closed Orchard*] "para exportar" ["for exportation"]. The censor authorized the "4,000 copies for exportation" but held the "1,000 copies to be distributed in Spain" until corrections were made on "pages 111 and 112" (Expediente de *Huerto cerrado*). This policy of exporting to Latin America was balanced by the many restrictions on importing books from abroad, particularly from Cuba and Argentina, two of Spain's most notable competitors in the literary distribution of the Latin American Boom.

It is no coincidence, then, that the debate leading to these reforms and to the approval of the 1966 and 1975 laws coincided with the successful penetration of José Donoso, Mario Vargas Llosa, Carlos Fuentes, Guillermo Cabrera Infante, and other Latin American writers into Spain's 1960s literary market. For the Franco regime, the publishing success of many of these writers was pivotal in its plans to take control of the Spanish-language book market. Furthermore, the new censorship practices of the *apertura* were crucial, not only for the Boom writers and the renovation of the Spanish book industry, but also and most importantly for the development of Spain's transition into democracy. For example, the "softening" of the many restrictions on the printing and distribution of books fit the government's plan to keep the Latin American book markets as one of Spain's main export markets, but it did so at the price of allowing the publication of Boom writers who sided with the Cuban Revolution of 1959 and were known to be on the side of the left. In this chapter, I use the double sense of the phrase "publishing matters" to summarize this apparent paradox: censorship worked hand in hand with a certain liberalization required by the desired expansion of the book trade. Thus, I read the new rules of censorship vis-à-vis the confidential government reports on the book industry, on the one hand, and, on the other, Seix Barral's publishing policies (the Boom's leading publishing house in Spain) as laid out in its 1969 *Catálogo General de Publicaciones*. I do this with a view to showing how censorship worked simultaneously in conflict and in complicity with the Franco regime, as well as with Seix Barral's publishing ambitions and the Boom writers' careers and literary production.

For the regime, the promotion of "Hispanic" culture in the Americas became the magic formula that resolved the conflict created by the successful incursion of pro-democracy Boom writers into the book market that the government sought to control. In a confidential report dated October 1963, the Spanish government framed the promotion of pan-Hispanic culture as a vital cultural endeavor that would—not coincidentally—generate important revenues for the regime: "El libro es el principal vehículo para la presencia cultural de España en el mundo... también tiene el libro considerable importancia para una economía como la española, que ha de esforzarse continuamente para incrementar un comercio exportador todavía precario" ["Books are the main vehicle for Spain's cultural presence in the world. Books are also of considerable importance for an economy that must constantly struggle to improve its still precarious commerce abroad"] (Informe sobre el comercio exterior del libro 3–5).

For the authors of this document, books could not be regarded as "mere merchandise," nor could they be "measured only in economic terms" ["meramente valorado mediante criterios económicos"]. Indeed, they viewed Spanish books (that is, books printed in Spain) as the "highest exponent of our culture" ["el más alto exponente de nuestra cultura"] and "of the ideological and moral principles that inform our country" ["de los principios ideológicos y morales que informan a nuestro país"] in the Spanish-speaking world (Informe sobre el comercio 3). So, in their eyes, the importance of the Latin American book market lay in the fact that it responded both to a cultural ambition, "books are the main vehicle for Spain's cultural presence," and to Spain's desire to become a modern economy through the massive exportation of books.

These anonymous bureaucrats probably did not imagine that their dull and often verbose reports on the book industry would illustrate today's debate about the value of the literary work, the contingencies that define it, and the economic and cultural capitals generated by it (Pierre Bourdieu, John Guillory, and Barbara H. Smith, among others). Yet they clearly show that a nexus between literary value and economic worth is paramount in understanding the workings of the Spanish book market between 1960 and 1975. At that time, the economic interests of the Spanish government conflicted as often as they converged with the defense of "national moral values" imposed by Franco's censorship. But for the regime, books ensured "Spain's cultural presence in the world"["la presencia cultural de España en el mundo"] (Informe sobre el comercio 3). For that reason, the "cleansing effect" of censorship was expected to make a positive contribution to the production of books, rather than to impede it.

Of course it is true that Latin America had been a traditional target of Spain's international policies, which had always favored economic and cultural exchanges with Ibero-American countries. It is also the case that the *apertura* failed to convince the European democracies of any substantial changes in the Franco regime. Nevertheless, for the Spanish government, publishing *did* matter, and in order to overcome the import/export imbalance Spain faced at the time, the regime granted priority status to certain industries (the so-called *industrias prioritarias*) under its new economic policies, including the tourist and the book industry, both supervised by Fraga's Ministry.

So government officials went on repeatedly interpreting Spain's "cultural presence" as part of a larger economic enterprise to reap profits in the Americas. As pointed out by a 1970 report from the National Book Institute (*Instituto Nacional del Libro Español*, INLE), in thirty years "the peoples of Spanish America will reach six hundred million inhabitants who will know how to read and write and will be consumers of books" ["los pueblos de Hispanoamérica dentro de 30 años sumarán seiscientos millones de habitantes que sabrán leer y que serán consumidores de libros"] (Conclusiones de la Primera Exposición Itinerante 15). Never mind that this prediction was wildly off the mark. (Today's estimates of potential readers in Latin America total just over three hundred million.) It is evident that the National Book Institute felt a need to beef up the numbers of "consumers of books" in support of governmental policies that had already been decided.

Still, and as inflated as these reports were, the statistics these officials had at hand were themselves quite promising. Between 1959 and 1975, the publication of literary works in Spain tripled—from about two thousand to over six thousand new titles per year. Meanwhile, two of Spain's most significant competitors, Argentina and Mexico, saw a significant drop in the numbers over the same period. There was a 50 percent reduction in Argentina—from two thousand to one thousand new titles—and in Mexico a stagnant production of fewer than eight hundred new titles in Mexico (Santana 46–47).[3] These data are consistent with the Spanish government's own "bookkeeping": the revenues generated by all these new titles were quite significant. In 1959 the total sales for Spanish books exported to Argentina, Chile, and Cuba amounted to roughly 557 million pesetas. By 1961, this amount had doubled, and in July 1962 it reached about 100 million pesetas a month (Datos de la Exportación de Libros).

It was the regime's view, remember, that this expansion was undertaken under the aegis of a historical call of duty to promote and protect Hispanic cultural heritage worldwide. As such, the government often appraised books simultaneously in terms of their economic and cultural value, stressing on occasion the concurrence of the regime's views in this respect with those of publishers:

> se han presentado...diversas peticiones del Instituto Nacional del Libro, Dirección General de Prensa, Gremio de Libreros...solicitando en las tarifas postales de impresos,

rebajas, con objeto de favorecer—dicen—la expansión y desarrollo del libro y, consecuentemente de la cultura.

Several petitions from the National Book Institute, General Department of the Press, and the Association of Booksellers request a reduction in the postal rates for printed matter in order—as they put it—to *expand and to develop the book industry, and thus culture.* (Nota-Informe sobre las tarifas 1; emphasis mine).

Accordingly, books were seen as *cultural commodities*: simultaneously merchandise for consumers in an expanding market and a staple of cultural exchange. This commercial-cum-cultural endeavor, legitimated as the honest promotion of Hispanism in the Americas, found a further raison d'être, and simultaneously a justification for the practices of censorship, in the idea of linguistic purity. In many censors' reports on the works of the Boom writers, language—more precisely, the preservation of what they defined to be the Spanish language—became the determining factor in the approval or rejection of a literary work. Needless to say, the claim of preserving the Spanish language provided cover for moral and political censorship of the writing of Latin American authors who happened to be regarded as profitable and were to be launched massively on the international scene.

The preservation of linguistic purity also masked another concern. The Franco regime feared that the success of established publishing houses in Mexico and Argentina (and the newly created *Casa de las Américas* in Cuba) might translate into a different linguistic and cultural approach (*their* versions, if you will, of the promotion of "Hispanism"), an approach whose success would result in losses for Spain in the book markets of Europe, Latin America, and the United States.

Particularly worrying, in the eyes of the Spanish government, were the advances of the book industry in Argentina and in Cuba: "El libro argentino se afirma, pues, en su propio mercado y se lanza a la conquista de otros nuevos, fundamentalmente Sudamérica, pero también en España" ["Argentinean books are strong in their home market, and they are being launched into new markets, especially in South America, but also in Spain"] (Informe sobre el comercio 5). In Cuba, "un peligro político-económico lo constituye el consorcio editor ruso-checo, que ha establecido su fase de operaciones en Cuba. Este peligro es realmente serio...los libros de origen soviético se venden en Sudamérica a precios que calificaríamos de nominales: alrededor de un tercio del precio del libro español" ["a political and economic danger is the Czech-Russian publishing consortium that has established operations in Cuba. This danger is really serious... Soviet-financed books are sold in South America at what we would call nominal prices, about a third of the price of Spanish books"] (Informe sobre el comercio 10).

Reports like these alerted the authorities to the emerging changes in the Spanish-language book trade and to Spain's most competitive rivals. They also drew attention to the expanding commercial possibilities presented by the United States' market for books in Spanish. In 1963, a confidential report mapped out the Rockefeller and Ford Foundations' subvention programs and their implications for Argentinean publishers (Planes de Estados Unidos 1–4). That same year another report drew attention to the importance of the United States market:

> Hemos de felicitarnos del interés creciente que manifiestan hacia nuestras publicaciones los países exteriores del área idiomática hispánica, singularmente en Estados Unidos y la Europa occidental... EL PORVENIR DE LA EXPANSIÓN EDITORIAL ESPAÑOLA depende esencialmente de la situación de los mercados ibero-americanos, que es donde se encuentra amenazada precisamente.
>
> We must congratulate ourselves on the increasing interest in our publications in countries outside the Hispanic world, particularly in the United States and Western Europe... THE FUTURE OF THE EXPANSION OF THE SPANISH BOOK INDUSTRY rests upon the Ibero-American market, precisely where it is threatened. (Informe sobre el comercio 5)

Note the emphatic capitals. The twin tools of this government-sponsored commercial and cultural expansion in the direction of Latin America were competition and production, on the one hand, and censorship, on the other. That is why the government reexamined the 1943 decree that established the rules and regulations for Spain's National Book Institute, which was now supposed (at least in theory) to "guard and make a difference for the Spanish Book in Spain and in the world" ["vigilar e impulsar la diferencia del Libro Español en España y el mundo"] and to promote "any initiatives that may support the production, sale and exportation of books" ["cuantas iniciativas tiendan a favorecer la producción, el comercio y la exportación del libro"] (Decreto de 6 abril).[4] One of these initiatives (which I discuss in greater detail when I revist Latin American publishing in the epilogue) was the overhauling of Spain's paper industry. As shown in official reports as early as 1958, shortages in the paper industry were seen as a hindrance to the expansionary plans for Spanish publishing (Subcomisión del papel). And the new policies laid out in the *decreto* also required immediate changes in the approval process for the printing and distribution of books. These changes in turn were to result in the regime's abandonment of a significant part of its own political agenda of the 1940s and 1950s: "during the Franco period, the censorship bodies underwent a series of restructurings that betray the regime's ideological tension and shifts" (Labanyi 207).

1. THE NEW RULES OF CENSORSHIP

The new printing and publishing law is a perfect example of the government's reformist attitude in the 1960s. The law removed the *consulta obligatoria* [compulsory submission] imposed on all printed works in Spain up to 1966, which often required publishers to delete sections and alter manuscripts; they replaced it with the *consulta voluntaria* [voluntary submission] and the *depósito* [deposit]. Joan Mari Torrealdai mentions that, under the regime of compulsory submission, publishers often faced a costly and lengthy approval process. They were required to submit complete books or galley proofs, and no deadlines were set for the government officials to respond (11). The costly production delays that resulted were a severe hindrance to the success of publishers in the booming and fiercely competitive book market of the 1960s and 1970s. For years they had begged for leniency when it came to the censorship rules; the 1966 law was the regime's response to their demands. Fraga's public statements about the new law, however, made it clear that he was still in charge: it was for him to administer the law and set its rules. The State continued to have the right to prohibit any material it deemed inappropriate; however, the new rules allowed for direct negotiation with the censorship authorities.

For example, under the 1966 law, publishers (in theory) did not have to seek an explicit authorization to print books. Instead they could either "deposit" or "voluntarily submit" the complete text or galley proofs of the book for "final verification" by government officials, at which point it was now possible for negotiations to take place. Of the two options, voluntary submission was the safer way to gain approval from the censors, and became the preferred alternative for publishers like Carlos Barral (*Almanaque* 12–3), whose overt opposition to the regime's censorship practices (which is clearly documented in the *Archivo*'s files), together with his astuteness and willingness to negotiate with the relevant authorities, make his case exemplary of the beneficial results these new practices brought to the Spanish publishing industry. By contrast, under the regulations for *depósito*, publishers could bypass the submission of a work for review merely by depositing six copies of the printed book at the Ministry and receiving official clearance for distribution. (Barral often used this option with the Boom writers.) By law, this process could not take longer than "one day per each 50 pages or fraction thereof" ["un día por cada cincuenta páginas o fracción"] (*Prensa e Imprenta* 85). However, this option carried considerable risk, since the law also included the possibility of *secuestro* [sequestration] as a measure to avoid the circulation of undesirable printed material: "el Ministerio Fiscal podrá ordenar el secuestro a disposición judicial del impreso o publicación delectivos donde quiere que éstos se hallaren, así como de sus moldes para evitar la difusión" ["The General Attorney's Office may order the legal sequestration of any delinquent printed document or publication wherever they may be, together with the typesetter's forms in order to avoid their distribution"] (*Prensa e Imprenta* 64)

For this reason the *depósito* option, while "allowing" book production to go ahead without the regime's direct supervision, could backfire and result in significant economic loss. Some publishers nevertheless favored it because it offered the bureaucracy a finished product, a book ready to be marketed, with the expectation of a sort of up-or-down vote on the censors' part. This made it an appropriate channel for publishers to test the government's reaction to certain books they deemed "not censurable" (mostly foreign ones that they were considering for import or for potential Spanish editions). At the same time, it became a filtering device for the government to keep track of trends in the Spanish-language publishing industry.

As a result of these new options, the law promoted an apparatus of censorship that both implicitly and explicitly favored behind-the-scenes negotiations among censors, publishers, and writers. Manuel Abellán claims that the new law "forced publishers to take precautions with manuscripts—but, above all, to expurgate them—even more than before, given that they became subsidiary accomplices of any infringement of the law" ["obligó a los editores a vigilar—pero, sobre todo, a expurgar—mucho más que antes los manuscritos, ya que en el caso...[de haber] infringido de algún modo la ley, el editor era subsidiariamente cómplice del delito cometido"] (*Censura* 118). Carlos Barral, though, took the view that "it is easier to exchange ideas" ["existen más facilidades para el intercambio de ideas"] with the censorship authorities since, before the new law, publishers had no room to negotiate, in view of the absence of standardized regulations (*Almanaque* 12). Tactical maneuvering, of course, was to become the standard practice in the negotiations Barral would engage with the regime's authorities, as I will detail in chapters 2 through 5.

While the *consulta voluntaria* and the *depósito* were designed to expedite the distribution of books, the most significant change in the law was its redefinition of *silencio administrativo* [official silence]. This was a legal formula used by many censors when they had certain objections to the content of a work, but foresaw benefits in authorizing its publication. By officially declaring silence, the authorities did not explicitly approve of a given book or endorse its moral content; they simply refrained from blocking its commercial distribution (they "remained silent," as it were). From a legal standpoint, official silence has been described as a "fictional act" (Guillén Pérez 81) and as a "legal fiction" (García-Trevijano 67–8) in the Spanish judicial system. Under the Franco regime official silence had both negative and positive implications. Whereas the legislation of 1956 had defined it as a negative outcome of a petitioner's request, the printing law of 1966 interpreted official silence in a more positive fashion: "la respuesta aprobatoria o el silencio de la Administración eximirán de responsabilidad ante la misma por la difusión del impreso sometido a consulta" ["Approval or silence on the Administration's part shall exempt the publisher from any responsibility before the said Administration for the printed text submitted for consultation"] (*Prensa e Imprenta* 6).[5]

Close examination of these legal terms—*consulta obligatoria, consulta voluntaria, depósito, secuestro, silencio*—reveals how the new vocabulary of censorship responded to the interests of those involved in overhauling the Spanish book industry in the *apertura*. While the old rules of *consulta obligatoria* reinforced the concept of censorship as an entity of power that watched over each and every creative process and in effect censored it both before and after its completion, the *consulta voluntaria* redefined censorship officially as a practice that intervened only following completion of any piece of creative writing but in fact positioned it to become part of the production process. It became "a rule-embedded phenomenon" capable of being modified, through changes in conventions and regulations, in such a way as to make it possible for the censor to participate in the creative process itself (Jansen 8).[6] The government's new policies were designed in this way to displace censorship from the censors' desks to the publishers'. Thus, the red pencils would not be completely put away; rather, the authorities handed them down to publishers, and they in turn, to writers. Censorship did not disappear, then, under the *consulta voluntaria*.

Rather, the law implied a shift of the censorial subject, in accordance with an underlying assumption that book production came first and that approval for circulation *followed* the intervention of censorship in that process. Thus, publishers and government censors tacitly agreed that censorship did not have primacy over book production. This repositioning of censorship as part of the production process was disclosed by the introduction of the new terms *depósito* and *secuestro*, which corresponded to the former practices of postproduction censorship. But the upshot of all these new regulations was to favor competition in the book market among publishing houses and to empower the government's plan to expand the Spanish book trade. That said, the promotion of Latin American literature in Spain that resulted from these new arrangements did not please everybody. Rather it fueled discussions in journals and intellectual circles and triggered a reexamination of the literary and cultural relations between Spain and Latin America. In *Foreigners in the Homeland*, Mario Santana argues that the Spanish publishing and literary scene of the 1960s is encapsulated in the metaphor of the wheat and the chaff, which describes how the commercial success of the Boom in Spain provoked sibling rivalries between Spanish and Latin American writers. Santana examines the reaction of certain Spanish intellectuals who saw the 1960s Latin American novel as "foreign chaff" (*la cizaña extranjera*) in contrast with the Peninsular novelists who represent "the national wheat" (*la mies nacional*).[7] Many Spanish writers seemed to be afraid of the so-called invading chaff. Angel María de Lera, the 1967 Planeta Prize winner, refused to accept the criticized notoriety gained by Latin Americans in Spain, stating that "we don't believe any Colombian or Cuban is going to teach Spanish to Delibes...Enough is enough" (Santana 131). But linguistic issues were not all that was thought to be at stake. As Santana points out, "idiomatic baroqueness," "inventiveness," and "multi-leveled constructions" were among the complaints leveled by José María Gironella, who cried foul at the double standard to which Peninsular and Latin American writers were held: "much of the praise given to Asturias, Carpentier, Cortázar, Vargas Llosa...refers to narrative elements that—if they were to be used by those of us writing in Spain—would surely bring us a string of insults" (133). It is striking that these censorious statements replicated many of the comments made by the real censors in their evaluation of the Boom novels. I see these echoes as an example of the trickle-down effect the new censorship rules began to have on publishers and writers, just as the regime had intended. At the same time, they are a symptomatic response to the unexpected liberalization of literary culture that was a presumably unintended consequence of Spain's new economic ambitions.

2. THE NEW SEIX BARRAL

Seix Barral offered a more congenial contribution to the wheat and chaff debate in its 1969 *Catálogo General de Publicaciones*. This unusual two hundred page catalogue contained a detailed account of Seix Barral's collections and current publishing policies, together with a section on projects for future expansion. If the *Catálogo* reflected the government's interest in expanding the book trade, its prime function was to further the publishing house's interests by presenting the Boom writers in three different collections: *Biblioteca Breve*, *Biblioteca Nueva Narrativa Hispánica*, and *Biblioteca Formentor*. These three collections, designed to suggest market-based diversification and even competition within Seix Barral, were the vehicle of the firm's new international identity. From them we can gain insight also into how Latin American novels were first promoted in Spain. The *Biblioteca Breve* collection supposedly presented "a collection devoted to the publication of avant-garde works from various literary traditions" ["una colección dedicada a la publicación de obras de vanguardia de las distintas literaturas modernas"]; the *Nueva Narrativa* collection provided "a general overview of Spanish and Latin American writers" ["una visión general de todos los escritores españoles y latinoamericanos"]; and the *Formentor* offered "a general panorama of contemporary narrative of various literary traditions" ["un panorama general de la narrativa contemporánea en las distintas literaturas"] (Catálogo 22). Obviously, there is no clear-cut distinction among the three collections, and, in reality, Boom novels appeared in all three without regard to the supposed rationale behind each collection as formulated in the catalogue. The collections, in other words, were a marketing device intended to give the firm the appearance of having a wider and larger backlist and broader distribution than was actually the case. Another ploy was the numbering in the collections. As Pere Gimferrer confessed to me in a personal interview, Barral decided that the first number in the *Biblioteca Breve* collection would be 101 as a way of making it look larger (and possibly more significant) than it actually was in the early 1960s.[8]

Tactics such as these were inspired, as Carlos Barral recalls in *Los años sin excusa* [*Years without Excuse*], by the impressive scope of French literary journals and publishers—such as *NRF, Les Temps Modernes* and *Minuit*—and in particular the numbers of international authors whose writing they published. These new editorial policies of Seix Barral were a significant departure from the origins of the firm. Founded in 1911 by Victoriano Seix (1885-1933)—a professional lithographer trained in France who decided to make his fortune printing calendars, maps, circus posters, and pedagogical material—and Lluis and Carles Barral, owners of the printing press "Gráficas Barral Hermanos," the joint publishing venture had been a family affair from the outset, and as such it was to experience feuds and family rivalries in the years to come. After the Civil War, following the deaths of the founders—and, what's more, at a time when the school book market was meager—the families decided to split the two sides of the firm and in 1942 they founded "Editorial Seix Barral," which they conceived as a separate entity that would be able to carry out a new editorial line while enjoying the technical support of the printing house "Gráficas Seix i Barral" (Breu Història). In 1958, this firm created a publicity department and began its Latin American venture, following the initiative of its manager, Víctor Seix, the "money man," who traveled to America the same year and established distribution networks in Mexico, Peru, Chile, and Colombia. Carlos Barral, the "literary expert," simultaneously began to make contacts among young Latin American writers and international publishers, laying the groundwork for Seix Barral's future expansion. In the early 1960s, the firm took center stage and began to pursue the promotion of Latin American authors in deadly earnest. The death of Víctor Seix in 1967 was the signal for a major crisis, when the two families began a feud for control, the outcome of which was the launching of Carlos Barral's new publishing venture, Barral Editores, in 1969.

So the Boom years coincided nicely with Víctor's and Carlos' new plans for their old firm. The "new" Seix Barral had two clear strategies with which to reposition itself: on the one hand, a new market identity, and on the other international visibility. It was Carlos Barral who realized that expanding into the Latin America market, which had been a major source of income for the firm in the 1930s, was a way to achieve both goals. In *Los años sin excusa*, he explains that this move was a two-step enterprise: first, "it was a matter of building up a backlist with recent and important authors or else those who were exotic to the French and Italian channels of Argentinean publishers" ["se trataba de construir una *backlist* con autores importantes muy recientes, o exóticos a los canales italo-franceses de los editores argentinos"]; and second, "of imposing the content of this literary phase on the Spanish-language markets" ["imponer el contenido de esa etapa literaria a los mercados de lengua española"] (139).

In his essay on Editorial Joaquín Mortiz, Seix Barral's publishing partner in Mexico, Danny Anderson proposes that a study of the role of publishing houses as "cultural institutions" can provide "a broader basis for understanding why and how texts become important works of literature" (34). "Rather than following changes in narrative trends," he adds, "one can establish histories of publishing houses that promoted certain kinds of literature, and at various moments achieved qualified and temporary degrees of cultural hegemony" (35). The implication in the present context is that by examining the marketing strategies employed by the firms that distributed the Boom one may well be able to decipher a corresponding literary and aesthetic program. Tracing Seix Barral's role as the Boom's publisher is a way to achieve understanding of how the Boom came into being as a literary field.

A literary field, like any other social formation, is part of a hierarchical structure which consists of a set of fields (the economic field, the educational field, the political field, the cultural field, etc.), each of them with its own functioning and its own relations (Bourdieu, *Field* 6). Whereas in the economic field agents battle over the acquisition of economic capital, in the cultural field—one component of which is the literary field—competition centers on the acquisition of symbolic capital, defined as the accumulation of recognition, consecration, and prestige. Bourdieu proposes that the field of cultural production is "an economic world reversed," one in which economic success (i.e., writing a best seller) can preclude consecration and symbolic power in the literary field. This distinction between economic and symbolic capital is paramount for an understanding of how the publishing industry operates within and as a part of the literary field. Books have both economic and symbolic value ("cultural value," the Franco regime would argue). They are priced not only according to their printing costs, but also with regard to other factors that cannot be measured in economic terms, such as the author's reputation, the book's critical reception, or the publisher's fame: "symbolic goods are a two-faced reality, a commodity and a symbolic object," although their cultural and commercial value "remain relatively independent" (Bourdieu, *Field* 113).

Seix Barral's symbolic capital was based in part on the construction of Barcelona itself as a production site of the avant-garde; its marketing depended heavily on the annual literary prize that it sponsored, the *Premio Biblioteca Breve*. In his post as literary director of the firm, Carlos Barral functioned as an agent whose "symbolic investment" consisted of attracting Latin American writers by channeling a more international distribution of their works, which simultaneously increased the firm's profits. Thus, the Boom writers and Seix Barral (and arguably the regime's authorities) all became agents occupying the available positions in the field, as they engaged in competition for control of their interests (Bourdieu, *Field* 6–7). The Latin American writers compete for the production and distribution of their works and the fame attaching to their names. Seix Barral stands to derive financial benefits and cultural prominence from marketing them.

But the literary field is itself contained within the field of power, and Seix Barral's new market identity had to "fit" within the political structure of the time. Barral's new project for an avant-garde readership had to go forward within (and despite) the framework of the censorship of all printed material under the Franco regime. In fact, and as we have seen, the recent changes in the political-economic configuration of the "field of cultural production" were not at all at odds with Barral's attempt to create a new and more international reputation for his firm. The field of power had been altered by the government's new international liberalism, so that it was only apparently a contradiction for Franco's government to allow, and even to sponsor, the distribution of left-leaning Latin American writers. While Barral's new market identity was geared toward gaining more symbolic capital for his firm, it meshed seamlessly with the intentions underlying the new printing law and the regime's *desarrollismo*.

In such circumstances symbolic capital can be understood in theory as economic or political capital that is disavowed, or at least misrecognized—misrecognized and thereby recognized, hence legitimated, as a "credit," which under certain conditions, and always in the long run, guarantees "economic" profits (Bourdieu, *Field* 75). But symbolic capital's economic worth is not really disclaimed or repudiated by those involved in the promotion of Latin American literature in the 1960s and 1970s. Indeed, it is often considered more of an investment than a "credit," notably when we read the regime's own internal reporting: "Es preciso que el libro español no se encarezca en América como consecuencia de los dilatados plazos de pago que hay que conceder a los importadores de aquellos países... el libro es un artículo de consumo; pero el pago de compras de libros, [se halla] extraordinariamente diferido" ["it is imperative that Spanish books do not become more expensive in the Americas as a consequence of the deferred payment plan that we grant importers in those countries... books are consumer goods, but the payment for a shipment of books is extraordinarily deferred"] (Créditos a la Exportación).

This nexus of aesthetic and economic value seems particularly cogent to the market policies of the *apertura*, since government officials, publishers, literary critics, and even censors often raised questions of economic value and literary worth in the same breath. The value of publishing the Boom is constantly defined in terms either of economics (by the detractors of the marketing ploys of the Boom), or of aesthetics (by the defenders of the Latin American *nueva novela*). The critical debate on the Boom has mostly focused in similarly either-or fashion on its being, on the one hand, a merely commercial phenomenon (an economic boom), and, on the other, an innovative aesthetic transformation of Latin American narrative.[9] Seix Barral's new positioning of the Boom in the literary field—through the strategies of an enhanced market identity and international visibility—meant that contemporary Latin American novels were now widely distributed in Europe. Although Seix Barral at first aimed toward a restricted and more elitist production in line with the aesthetic renovation implied by the term *nueva novela*, it was soon able, therefore, to combine its symbolic investments with a relatively large-scale distribution of Latin American fiction geared toward the general public: "These two fields of production [restricted and large-scale], opposed as they are, coexist" (Bourdieu, *Field* 128). The two terms, Boom and *nueva novela*, are not opposed as much as they are complementary.[10]

The selling of *nueva novela* within the market parameters of the Boom was the point of departure, then, for Seix Barral's new image and international visibility as an avant-garde publisher. While the strategy of a new market identity relies heavily on "markers of prestige"—quality, openness to innovation, interest in international high culture, cosmopolitanism, and so forth (Anderson 13)—, Barral's project to acquire international visibility was based on a much wider distribution of his firm's backlist, thanks in particular to the publicity generated by the literary prizes the firm sponsored. By combining these two strategies, Seix Barral was to become an "agent of consecration," competing in the field of restricted production for "the power to grant cultural consecration" on the strength of its position in the large-scale field (Bourdieu, *Field* 121). It was an agent of consecration for the Boom writers. Its success also consecrated Barcelona's avant-garde status within the field of Hispanic cultural production.

I would argue that Barral's involvement in literary awards—the *Premio Biblioteca Breve*, then the *Prix Formentor* and the *Prix International de Littérature*—was a crucial part of this consecration function.[11] The idea behind these prizes had as much to do with the internationalization of the firm's range and the reinforcement of its avant-garde readership as with the consecration of individual authors and their texts. Barral brought his experience as a promoter of the *Biblioteca Breve* prize to the Formentor group, which offered an international audience. It was he who convinced the Formentor group to award the 1961 *Prix International* to Jorge Luis Borges, undoubtedly the precursor of the Boom writers; and it was the consequent success of Borges's work in the international market that launched Seix Barral in its new direction.

This process of reinventing a publishing house's trajectory "consists of the systematic use of a network of social relationships," which, in Seix Barral's case, included members of the Barcelona intelligentsia as well as published writers and well-established intellectuals who had already achieved prestige of their own (Bourdieu, *Field* 10). Barral looked in particular for the validation of international editors and writers, capable of endowing Seix Barral with the cachet it needed to accumulate symbolic capital—mainly in the form of literary success and prestige—which in turn would bring economic gains through large-scale sales not only of prizewinners, but also of some of the items in Seix Barral's backlist.

But the first step was the creation of an annual literary prize that would prove to be a springboard for the international success of the Latin American Boom writers, the *Premio Biblioteca Breve*.[12] In his memoirs, Barral himself is clear about his strategy, describing the prize as a "transatlantic literary bridge," and as "a publishing device [that] ended up becoming a wonderful cultural toy... it began to gain prestige, especially all over the Americas... and became the cornerstone of a possible literary policy that was a true discovery of Spanish American literature" ["instrumento de maniobra editorial [que] terminó en un maravilloso juguete de la cultura... se fue cargando de prestigio, sobre todo a lo ancho de las Américas... se fue convirtiendo... en el eje de una política literaria posible, una política de verdadero descubrimiento de la literatura americana"] (*Memorias* 572). The "true discovery" of America distances his personal enterprise from the regime's oft-renewed vows to "conquer" the Latin American book market.

So it is somewhat ironic that this "conquest" began with the economic success that the 1962 *Premio Biblioteca Breve* turned out to be. That year the winner was *La ciudad y los perros*, written by an unknown young Peruvian writer, Mario Vargas Llosa. The book rapidly sold out, and by 1971 there had been sixteen editions of the text and more than one hundred thirty-five thousand copies sold worldwide. This was quite an accomplishment for an avant-garde publishing house; at the time most new titles in Spain sold an average of three thousand copies. The award launched Vargas Llosa internationally as well as Seix Barral; their names were linked from that moment on and became inseparable from the success of the Latin American novel in the 1960s. Seix Barral marketed the books brilliantly. While most volumes from Spanish publishers had something (as Donoso puts it) "suspiciously old" about them, this firm made the Boom novels appealing to the general public with "cutting-edge, brilliant, and up-to-date contemporary covers" (Figs. 1.1, 1.2). According to Donoso,

Seix Barral's *Biblioteca Breve* books became the envy of all Latin American writers, who were displeased with the total lack of style and the defective presentation of their novels published in Latin America (Donoso, *Historia* 85).

One problem was that unfortunately the new promotional ploys concocted by Carlos Barral seemed too close to the government's own plans for the Latin American market. The contradiction his firm faced was something of a mirror-image of the government's dilemma: How could an avant-garde publishing house (*editorial cultural*) massively promote the writing of pro-democracy Latin American writers without becoming an active participant in the Franco regime's neocolonial plans for the Spanish book trade? Confronted with what was an inverted version of the same contradictions the government was faced with, Seix Barral also found a "magic formula" to resolve the paradox. The same formula responded to the "chaff" and "wheat" debate. In contradistinction to the regime's faith in the purity of Castilian Spanish Seix Barral's *Catálogo* proposed an all-inclusive *pan-Hispanic literature*, one not defined by geographical borders, but rather by the shared use of a common language with its many linguistic registers:

> En nuestra política de publicación de autores de lengua española tiene especial relieve nuestra voluntad de incorporación de los valores de la narrativa hispanoamericana a nuestra cultural nacional.... Entendemos que es literatura castellana toda aquella que se escribe en las distintas formas del castellano actual; que la lengua literaria castellana moderna es un mosaico de lenguas equidistantes de la lengua del barroco, del mismo modo que la lengua castellana actual es un mosaico de dialectos equidistantes de la lengua y de los dialectos de la época de la conquista. Entendemos que nuestra literatura contemporánea es una sola aunque se sitúe en puntos tan distantes como Santiago de Compostela, Santiago de Cuba, Santiago de Chile o Santiago del Estero.

> Of particular importance in our editorial policies for Spanish-language authors is our will to incorporate the values of Latin American narrative into our national culture.... We understand that Spanish literature is any literature that is written in today's varied forms of Spanish; that the modern Spanish literary language is a mosaic of languages that are equidistant from the Castilian of the Baroque, just as contempory Spanish is a mosaic of dialects that are equidistant from the Castilian language and the dialects of the time of the conquest. We

understand that our contemporary literature is one literature and one only, even though the actual linguistic experience may be sited in places as distant as Santiago de Compostela (Spain), Santiago in Cuba, Santiago in Chile, and Santiago del Estero (Argentina). (*Catálogo General de Publicaciones* 13)

Incorporating "the values of Latin American narrative into our national culture," Seix Barral's policies reconfigured the value of the alleged chaff as a constitutive and integral element of what I would call a "whole-wheat literature": one that retains the healthy components— the dietary fibers—of the chaff in the pursuit of a heartier pan-Hispanism, or if you will, a Hispanism free of chaff and full of bran. Despite some references that would seem to come directly from government reports—"the language of the Baroque," "the time of the conquest," or the use of Spain's patron saint Santiago to unify the diverse linguistic registers of the Spanish language—, the Seix Barral theory of "a mosaic of equidistant languages," unlike the official view, saw Spain not as the origin or point of departure for the promotion of Hispanism, but as one link in the chain of "equidistant" nations that shared certain literary and cultural traditions. Ancient notions of literary prestige and canon formation were radically redefined in the interest of expanding the market for books.

Nevertheless, and despite such efforts, the case of Seix Barral's *Catálogo* is also a good example of the way the government's plans and those of this avant-garde publishing house became closely intermeshed under the new economic policies, and thanks to the new rules of censorship. The *Catálogo*—which lists the works of major Latin American writers such as Alejo Carpentier, Guillermo Cabrera Infante, Carlos Fuentes, Mario Vargas Llosa, and José Donoso—was itself submitted to the Spanish censorship authorities in June 1969 and, after a thorough review, was officially "silenced" by two censors who saw it as an instrument of left-wing propaganda: "no reseña precios por lo que más que comercial es de propaganda" ["it does not indicate prices and therefore it is not commercial, but rather propagandistic"] (Expediente de *Catálogo*). Remaining silent seemed to one of the censors the most appropriate response to the political ideas of Carlos Barral, whom he viewed as a vocal member of the left-leaning intelligentsia against Franco's regime. Yet the censor recognized in someone he thought of as a known enemy policies so compatible with those of the regime itself that he perceived Barral as arrogating the official mission to himself: "conocidas las ideas políticas de Barral, no extraña que intente defenderlas con argumentos capciosos y que se arrogue la misión de liberar a

España del aislamiento cultural en que la tiene el Régimen (?)" ["Knowing Carlos Barral's political ideas, it is no surprise that he should try to defend them with twisted arguments and arrogate to himself the mission of liberating Spain from the cultural isolation the Regime is keeping it in (?)"] (Expediente de *Catálogo*).

Similarly, when Barral later submitted his memoirs *Años de penitencia* [*Years of Penitence*] to the censorship authorities, the censor saw the author as an "anti-regime, anti-falangist, anti-militarist, anti-clerical sex maniac" (Expediente de *Años de penitencia*). It was only through the intervention of Ricardo de la Cierva, the highest ranking official in the Censorship Division (who held the title of General Director for Popular Culture) that its publication was permitted. The regime had no illusions, then, concerning Barral's political views. But he had proven to be a successful publisher and to represent so well the economic interests of the regime that he could not be touched. On this occasion, as always, it was through behind-the-scenes negotiations that the ideological tensions between the production and marketing of books and the prevailing political agendas were resolved. In a letter to de la Cierva dated July 3, 1974, Barral thanks the General Director for "having personally read his memoirs" and "for his influence over the official readers," which had resulted in a substantial reduction of the number of corrections Barral was asked to make to his text: "Acepto las diecisiete sugerencias como condición de la publicación" ["I accept the seventeen suggestions [you made] as the condition of publication"] (Carta a Ricardo de la Cierva).

In the case of the catalogue, the censor's report I have quoted ended with a parenthetical question mark, indicating his disagreement with Seix Barral's supposed political position, combined perhaps with ambivalence about whether to censor the catalogue of a highly successful publishing enterprise. In the end, this censor opted for the legal device of *silencio* in order not to interfere with the promotion of Seix Barral's collections: "Así se escribe la Historia. De todos modos, más vale dejarlo pasar" ["Thus History is written. At any rate, we'd better let it pass"] (Expediente del *Catálogo*). Indeed, "let it pass" means "let them publish it," despite our reservations. The censor is unhappy; but he recognizes economic priorities. Generally speaking, the economic and legal considerations, recommendations and requirements I have found in censors' reports in the 1960s go along with Seix Barral's publishing program in this way. The need to overhaul the economy and the new internationalism it entailed prevailed over merely political or ideological positions. Another good example is the second censor's reaction to the *Catálogo*'s pro-Cuba stance, which he found inoffensive or at least tolerable: "en la página 158 y 160 clama por el socialismo liberador y aspira a la justicia social, modelo Cuba... por no aludir directamente a España estimo podría tolerarse" ["on pages 158 and 160 it pledges allegiance to the Cuban model of liberating socialism and social justice... since it does not refer to Spain directly I find that it may be authorized"] (Expediente de *Catálogo*).

3. BITCHING ABOUT THE BOOM

The Boom and its riches appeared to be in trouble as early as 1970. At that time the gathering crisis at Seix Barral finally came to a head: Víctor Seix's death in 1967 and the ensuing family feuds, Barral's political activism (in particular, the regime saw his meetings with the Formentor group as part of the Communist propaganda machine), and uncertainty about the economic prosperity of the publishing house produced a schism within the firm. The Barrals sold their stock to the Seix family, and Carlos Barral went on to launch Barral Editores, with the understanding that Seix Barral's backlist was not to be split, and that contracts with Boom authors could be transferred to the new firm if agreed upon by the parties involved (Letter from Balcells to Vargas Llosa, April 21, 1970). Barral's exit signaled the beginning of the Boom's end: "dio al traste con el órgano más influyente en la internacionalización de la novela latinoamericana" ["it broke up the most influential agent for the internationalization of the Spanish American novel"] (Donoso, *Historia* 126). And this breakup in Barcelona was followed by the dissension generated among Latin American intellectuals regarding the Padilla affair in Cuba in 1971. From that point on, the "bitching" began.

José Donoso is a case in point. A well-regarded Boom writer (albeit not an international celebrity), he is an agent (in Bourdieu's sense of the word) as well as a reporter. Donoso's active involvement in the Barcelona intelligentsia made him a key player in and observer of the Boom game, but he minimizes the importance of marketing strategies like those of Seix Barral—and other publishing houses of the time, Joaquín Mortiz in Mexico, or Losada, Emecé, Jorge Álvarez and Sudamericana in Argentina—arguing that publicity was not responsible for the popularity of the contemporary Spanish American novel.[13] It was rather, he suggests, that "the Spanish American novel began to speak an international language" ["la novela hispanoamericana comenzó a hablar un idioma internacional"] in a clear departure from the regional taste and aesthetic values that were dominant before 1960

(*Historia* 19–20). (He cites Sudamericana's modest launching of *One Hundred Years of Solitude* as an example of a novel that became a worldwide best seller on its own merit.)

His reservations about the Boom (his bitching, if you will) are the subject of his 1981 novel *El jardín de al lado* [*The Garden Next Door*].[14] I see this novel as the late-Boom literary manifestation that gives the most substantial account of how a Latin American author viewed this cultural and publishing phenomenon. It is particularly helpful to read *El jardín de al lado* in conjunction with Donoso's autobiographical account of the Boom years, *Historia personal*. But before we do so, it is worth drawing attention to the fact that, unlike his fellow Latin American writers, Donoso's experience with the Spanish censors was relatively inconsequential. Censorship never played a significant role in his career in Spain, and therefore he did not "benefit" from the "prestige" of having been banned by the Franco regime.

The censors saw "great literary value" in Donoso's work, and often commented that his novels were excellent, well written, and displayed great technical skills. Such was the case of *Coronación* [*Coronation*], which the censors approved in 1967 without a hitch in view of its "great tenderness and technical skill" ["gran ternura y habilidad técnica"] and its Baroja-like style (Expediente de *Coronación*). His *Historia personal* passed the censorship barrier without any trouble as a "personal testimony" of the Boom, and one that presumably fostered potentially profitable interest in the novels (Expediente de *Historia personal*). (By contrast the censors rejected Carlos Fuentes's essay *La nueva novela hispanoamericana* [*The Latin American New Novel*] due to its defense of the "revolutionary explosion" in Latin America and its "diatribe against Spain" [Expediente de *La nueva novela*]; an indication that the Spanish authorities favored the "economic boom" attached to the *nueva novela* and were not so much enamored of its "revolutionary" aesthetics.) The censors did have minor reservations concerning the eroticism in Donoso's *Este Domingo* [*This Sunday*], and what they saw as the "pornographic content" of *El lugar sin límites* [*Hell Has no Limits*], which was not cleared for importation in 1967 and was therefore not published in Spain until after Franco's death (Expediente de *Este Domingo*).[15] Likewise, the publication of his most important novel *El obsceno pájaro de la noche* [*The Obscene Bird of the Night*] was delayed for about a year by the censors' objections. Before his departure from Seix Barral, Barral had "selected" it to receive the *Biblioteca Breve* award in 1969, but the prize was not given that year on account of the schism at the firm. Barral himself demanded that no prize be awarded until the two parties could come to an agreement, since he felt that the

Premio Biblioteca Breve was "his." A written agreement dated March 3, 1970 confirms that: "el Premio en su origen, historia y continuidad está vinculado a la persona de Carlos Barral" ["In its origin, history and continuity, the Prize is tied to the person of Carlos Barral"] (Letter to Donoso, March 24, 1970, containing a copy of the *Biblioteca Breve* jury-member's agreement, on March 3, 1970).

Despite this setback, Seix Barral persisted in planning to publish *El obsceno*, pressuring the censors to accept it as the "potential" winner of the *Biblioteca Breve*. The censors in turn demanded extensive corrections, which the author and the publisher partially complied with in order to gain the approval for publication that was finally granted on July 7, 1971: "Comprobados el exp. 8979–70 y el presente depósito se aprecia que PARTE de las tachaduras han sido respetadas" ["Upon verification of file number 8979–70 and the current deposit, it is clear that SOME of the corrections have been incorporated"] (Expediente de *El obsceno*; emphasis in original). Similarly, *Tres novelitas burguesas* [*Three Bourgeois Novelettes*] (first submitted for approval in January 1973) met some resistance on the part of the censors, and Donoso was asked to revise and resubmit it to include the corrections the censors had demanded: "Comprobadas y conforme las tachaduras. 11 de mayo de 1973" ["Corrections checked and confirmed. May 11, 1973"]. But Donoso's "personal testimony" on the Boom makes no mention of any of these negotiations with the censors, as if they never took place.

The same is true of the narrative of *El jardín de al lado*, in which Spanish censorship is not an issue. The novel is a first person account whose narrator is an exiled Chilean author, Julio Méndez, seeking literary success among the consecrated Boom writers in Spain. After moving with his wife Gloria, a translator and reviewer, to Sitges—an enclave, forty kilometers south of Barcelona, for Latin Americans as well as other international expatriates—Julio tries to publish his book manuscript, a fiction based on his six-day imprisonment in Chile immediately after the 1973 coup d'état against Salvador Allende.[16] At the outset of *El jardín de al lado,* we learn that Julio's novel—written sometime between 1973 and 1980, as the Boom is waning and the censorship practices of the regime disappearing—has been rejected by his Catalan literary agent, Núria Monclús, who is at the center of a powerful network that includes all major publishing houses in Spain, as well as many writers associated with the Boom.

Julio's fixation on the literary success to which Barcelona's publishing industry is the "open sesame" fuels his desire to rewrite the manuscript into what he calls "a chef-d'oeuvre superior to the consumer literature that is so fashionable today and has raised up false gods like

García Márquez, Marcelo Chiriboga, and Carlos Fuentes" ["una obra maestra superior a esa literatura de consumo, hoy tan de moda, que ha encumbrado a falsos dioses como García Márquez, Marcelo Chiriboga, and Carlos Fuentes"] (13). To help him in the process of rewriting, a friend of the Méndezes, Chilean artist Pancho Salvatierra invites them to housesit in Madrid for the summer so that Julio can work undistracted on his novel while Gloria devotes her time to her translations and articles. In Madrid, Julio will complete his revisions of the manuscript, partly inspired by his constant peeping into the neighbor's garden, which resembles his mother's garden in Chile. Despite the inspiration of "the garden next door," Julio's revised manuscript is again rejected by the Barcelona publishing machine in the person of Núria Monclús. Confused and frustrated by his lack of literary success, Julio sells one of Pancho's paintings and goes off to Morocco with his wife Gloria. Their experience in Tangier becomes a turning point, both for the story of the couple and for the novel: while Julio decides to relocate to Morocco permanently in search of new sources of literary success, Gloria prefers to go back to their Barcelona milieu. Julio's first-person narration stops at this point, the end of the penultimate chapter, and gives way to Gloria's perspective on the story in the sixth and last chapter of the novel. Gloria's takeover as first-person narrator relocates the novel back in Barcelona, and more specifically at a luncheon with Núria Monclús, where the two women discuss the publication of Gloria's—and not Julio's—first novel. *El jardín de al lado* concludes with Núria's intriguing question: "—¿Bueno no es éste el capítulo que falta, el que no has escrito...?" ["—Well, isn't this the missing chapter, the one you haven't written...?"] (264). In the end, then, the novel ends inconclusively. The reader is faced with a dilemma: Who is writing this "missing chapter"? Exactly which or whose manuscript does it come from, Julio's or Gloria's, or some composite text? Has Gloria been the narrator all along? Is there also a missing chapter in Donoso's text?

The Méndezes come to Barcelona in 1973, but the work on "their" novel takes place in and around 1980, at a time when women writers are beginning to enjoy success in the Boom (and, for some, in the "post-Boom"). Within *this* literary field, Julio constantly belittles the success of the exclusively male authors whom he envies, like García Márquez, Fuentes, Vargas Llosa, and Cortázar. Most of his bitchery is directed toward the fictional Marcelo Chiriboga, who alongside these notable Boom authors, stands as the incarnation of "the unbearable tinsel of commercial fakery" ["el insoportable oropel de falsedades comerciales"] (118) that has become part and parcel of the Barcelona publishing industry. Julio is not wrong to bitch in this way about the Boom, which has moved Latin American narrative from restricted (or elite) production into the "falsedades" inherent in large-scale commercial publishing. The authors themselves have acquired star-like status and in turn have started writing for the public at large. While Julio resents their prominence and success, he feels painfully excluded from the group, and would like one day to achieve the stardom he thinks *he* deserves. His observations give point to Bourdieu's understanding that in the literary field "the writer...writes not only for a public, but for a public of equals who are also competitors" because "few people depend as much as artists do for their self-image upon the image of others, and particularly other writers and artists" (Bourdieu, *Field* 116). Julio is obsessively aware of this type of competition and constantly measuring his own image against that of the Boom writers, real and fictional: "¿Vería yo mi nombre allá arriba—pese a la contraria superagente mafiosa—entre los de Vargas Llosa, Roa Bastos, Marcelo Chiriboga, Carlos Fuentes y Ernesto Sábato?" ["Would I see my own name up there—despite the mafia super agent's opposition—alongside Vargas Llosa, Roa Bastos, Marcelo Chiriboga, Carlos Fuentes, and Ernesto Sábato?"] (35).

His rhetorical question shows that he understands Bourdieu's point well. In order to achieve literary success in the Barcelona milieu, he would need to occupy an available position from which to engage in competition for control of the resources specific to that particular field (Bourdieu, *Field* 6). His exclusion from the in-group thus translates into failure, and stands in the way of his return to Chile: "No puedo volver. ¿Cómo? ¿Sin un libro publicado en España, con la cola entre las piernas...?" ["I can't go back. How could I? Without having published a book in Spain, with my tail between my legs...?"] (165). His choice of words also betrays the masculinist impulse underlying both *his* sense of competition and Donoso's creation of an "androgynous" or double-gendered narrator who is ultimately identified with "the image of the literary agent, Núria Monclús, as a castrating female" (González 105). Without a single book published, Julio has no option but to hide his tail.

It is worth dwelling a while on Núria's reputation in the text as "the legendary mafia boss of the celebrated Latin American novelists" ["la legendaria *capomafia* del grupo de célebres novelistas latinoamericanos"] (44). In Donoso's text much of the literary success of the Boom is shown to revolve around her power. Núria has the power to grant cultural consecration within the literary field of the Boom. Moreover, she is often identified as the generator of economic capital, "a mercenary Catalan who was simply a merchant of literature" ["una catalana mercenaria que no era más que un mercader de literatura"] (29). It is precisely Núria's success as producer of symbolic as well as economic capital that makes her an object of envy and desire for Julio, and perhaps also for Gloria. Their competitiveness in pursuit of symbolic capital, namely, the literary success endowed by the Barcelona publishing industry, is wholly dependent on Núria's say-so.

In Donoso's novel, Julio's vision of Núria, who not only dictates literary trends in the publishing industry in Barcelona, but also has gained control of the economic capital upon which it is based, is that of an all-powerful divinity: "se murmuraba que esta diosa tiránica era capaz de hacer y deshacer reputaciones, de fundir y fundar editoriales y colecciones, de levantar fortunas y hacer quebrar empresas" ["it was rumored that this tyrannical goddess was capable of doing and undoing reputations, of founding and destroying publishing houses and collections, and of making fortunes and bankrupting firms"] (44). His exaggeration of Núria's powers does not give a fair picture, of course, of the actual parameters of Seix Barral's distribution of Latin American literature, or of Joaquín Mortiz's and Sudamericana's for that matter. But his critique of the commercial-mindedness and business practices that most publishers adhere to in the novel—a critique encapsulated in the portrayal of Núria—does find its target. In *Historia personal*, Donoso had described in equivalent terms the real literary agent of the Boom writers in Barcelona, Carmen Balcells, as a power figure who "seemed to have in her hands the strings that made us all dance like marionettes" ["parecía tener en sus manos las cuerdas que nos hacían bailar a todos como a marionetas"] (124).

In sum, what the Núria-Balcells goddess figure stands for, and what Donoso-Julio is unhappy about, is the fact that, with the Boom, elite literature has moved from the field of restricted into the field of large-scale production. Similarly, for Ricardo Gutiérrez Mouat, "the emergence of a culture industry in Latin America coincided with the modernization of the Latin American novel, a revival that culminated in the boom of the 1960s" (67). In "Narrador, autor, superestrella" Jean Franco points out that the expansion of Latin American narrative into the world market—one of Julio's major beefs—resulted in *autores superestrella* [superstar authors] typical of the age of mass culture. It is one of Núria's main interests to promote the star status of Latin American writers, and the deficiency of Julio's writing in her eyes is its lack of star quality. His revised manuscript, Núria says, is "mere rhetoric, imitation of what is fashionable among Latin American writers today" ["pura retórica, imitación de lo que está de moda entre los escritores latinoamericanos de hoy"] (224). He is an imitator, an epigone, not an innovator.

By contrast, Núria's favors go to the writing of a fictional Ecuadorian writer who has become an *autor superestrella* of the Barcelona milieu, Marcelo Chiriboga. This superstar of the Latin American Boom—a figure as symbolic in his way as Núria in hers—is simultaneously Julio's rival and bugbear, and his role model. The literary success of Chiriboga's best-selling masterpiece *La caja sin secreto* [*The Box Without Secret*] is the model for Julio's own conception of the success he would like to achieve. At first, he despises Marcelo for being "the most insolently famous of all the members of the dubious Boom" ["el más insolentemente célebre de todos los integrantes del dudoso boom"] (132). But before long he has to face facts. In the closing section of chapter 5, Julio admits:

> Mi novela es una mierda. La prosa de Chiriboga, en cambio, tiene una simplicidad deceptiva que se disuelve bajo la lengua, embargando los pulmones y el ser entero con un aroma que la corteza de su lenguaje no hacía esperar.... Quisiera escribir como Chiriboga. Pero no puedo.

> My novel is shit. Chiriboga's prose, on the other hand, has a deceptive simplicity that dissolves under your tongue, intoxicating your lungs and your whole being with an aroma that the outer crust of its language did not lead you to expect.... I would like to write like Chiriboga. But I can't. (242)

In measuring the quality of his own prose against Chiriboga's, as Julio constantly does, he is referencing two different models of writing. Both these models represent recognizable trends in the commercial and aesthetic renovation attached to the Boom and/or the *nueva novela*. Whereas Julio insists on the documentary nature of his own novel, he criticizes the excessive formalism and linguistic experimentation that are on display in the works of Cortázar, Fuentes, or Vargas Llosa. He considers their works excessively cosmopolitan, and lacking the kind of political commitment he brings to his own novel, with its account of his ordeal in a Chilean prison (46). So too, Chiriboga's masterpiece is an empty box, "a box without any secrets," without any—let's say—political, testimonial, or historical content; yet it displays great mastery of language. This formalism of Chiriboga's work, according to Julio, is the key to its success on the literary market: "La obra de Chiriboga es una obra inerte, en el fondo una invención de esa bruja de las finanzas que es Núria Monclús" ["Chiriboga's work is inert, deep down an invention of that financial witch, Núria Monclús"] (139). Chiriboga, whose literary persona has reappeared as a "real novelist" in Carlos Fuentes's *El naranjo* (1993) [*The Orange Tree*], and as the subject of university research in José Donoso's 1993 novel *Donde van a morir los elefantes* [*Where Elephants Go to Die*], is the only fictional author of the Boom in *El jardín de al lado*. One may read his presence, then, in conjuction with that of Núria, as a digest or epitome of the overall phenomenon that was the marketing of Latin American fiction. The playfulness of his literary persona, which is also highlighted by the fact that his name is phonetically close to *chirigota* (Spanish for joke, laughingstock), situates him by contrast with the alternative Julio-like literary persona of the "strong, male, politically committed figure," as a representative of the "new public role of the Latin American writer" (González 109), that is, the *autor superestrella*.

In the end, then, all the writers in Donoso's novel appear to lack the literary qualities Julio claims to have: Chiriboga is more of a "laughingstock" and a puppet in Núria's marketing plots than a genuinely accomplished writer, Gloria—despite her success, or her "glory"—is scarcely a convincing professional since she does not have a second novel and her first one appears to be incomplete, while the many real Boom writers mentioned in the text—Fuentes, Vargas Llosa, Roa Bastos, Sábato, Cortázar, and so forth—fail to meet the test because "they didn't have first hand experience as participants in a collective tragedy" ["desconocían la experiencia de primera mano como participantes en una tragedia colectiva"] (46).

Donoso's 1981 novel thus situates itself as a playfully censorious exercise in which the Boom is viewed through the lens of an excluded player. While Donoso himself was not as unsuccessful a writer as Julio Méndez, it does seem that, much like his fictional creation, he, too, has had to battle constantly in order not to be excluded from the group of the Boom notables. Carlos Barral's own fictional narrative about the waning years of the Boom, *Penúltimos castigos* (1983) [*Penultimate Punishments*], confirms this idea: "A Donoso le conocía poco" ["I didn't know Donoso very well"] (220), says Barral's in-group narrator.

Barral's novel starts off as detective fiction (Sam's body has been discovered, and we will later learn he was involved in drug trafficking), but it quickly deviates from the genre. Following the first chapter, it turns into a narrative that is self-deprecatingly centered, considering its author's identity, on an alcoholic, depressive, and physically diminished character named Barral. The novel's narrator is an unnamed artist who happens to be Barral's friend. Not surprisingly Barral happens to know all the major players of the Boom. Along with the defunct Sam and the unnamed artist, he resides in an also unnamed coastal town in

Catalonia, presumably Calafell. In the novel, the publisher's deteriorating mental health contrasts with his lucid although repetitive conversations with his neighbor (the artist) about aesthetics, literary creation, and the notables of the Boom (Jorge Edwards [34, 62], Carmen Balcells [211], José Donoso [220–221, 223], to name a few). The fictional Barral is much given to self-important statements about his "thirty years of avant-garde experimentation" (26), or the importance of finding "an all-encompassing aesthetic enterprise" (123).

But his visionary quest for "brilliant aesthetics" is what has landed the firm of Barral Editores, "his second publishing house" ["su segunda editorial"], in deep financial trouble to the point of near-bankruptcy (90–91). In real life, Barral Editores struggled to survive from day one. As early as December 1970, Barral himself wrote to Donoso (and so presumably to other Boom writers as well), reassuring him that the new firm was to take over Seix Barral's "guiding function" ["función rectora"] in the Spanish and Latin American book markets. In order for that to occur, however, Barral needed a larger cash flow, which he did not have—which is why he was inviting the Boom authors to join his lofty enterprise by acquiring small stock options of five thousand pesetas or more in the firm: "Caso de interesarte el proyecto pondría en tus manos una memoria que explica la naturaleza y el programa de las distintas colecciones.... Dicha memoria da igualmente cuenta del planteamiento económico del negocio y de sus previsiones de rentabilidad" ["In case you're interested in this project, I will send you a report that explains the nature and program of the various collections.... The report also gives an account of the firm's economic planning and estimated returns"] (Letter from Barral to Donoso, December 1970).

In *Penúltimos castigos*, we learn that ploys such as this to attract the Boom authors he had helped promote at Seix Barral did not work out as planned. This is one of the reasons why in the novel Barral is so depressed, and has "retired" to this small fishing town where in due course he will die in a drowning accident. But meanwhile, we learn that the rival publishing house Arbor (run by the former censor García, "the hyena" [146]) has been bought by a multinational firm; a move that signals the demise of "artisanal publishing houses" ["editoriales artesanales"]. Barral the author presumably sees the take over of Arbor as a premonition of what is in store in the real world for him: the "annihilation" of firms (such as his own Barral Editores) whose publishing policies have the character of a "cultural combat" ["combate cultural"] (146–152). The defunct "Barrals"—both the publisher who drowns and his "second" firm that goes broke—illustrate the misgivings the historical Barral presumably had about publishing trends in the post-Seix Barral years, which coincided with the Boom's end.

These fictions of Julio Méndez and the declining Barral can be read as tongue-in-cheek versions of their authors' respective nonfictional memoirs about the Barcelona publishing industry, and in Donoso's case as a roman à clef of the Boom (Julio and Gloria as José and María Pilar Donoso, Núria Monclús as Carmen Balcells, and so on). But while Barral equates the Boom's declining years with the end of his own career (which means the end of his idealized aesthetic enterprise, and thus the end of "cultural combat" as we know it), Donoso associates the Boom's end with the arrival of a new generation of Latin American writers, women in particular, who are supposedly taking over the literary market. This is the new marketing model that Núria Monclús is looking for. "We need more novelists like you" ["Se necesitan más novelistas como tú"] (248), she says to Gloria in the final chapter.

So one may read the implications of the novel's surprise ending as constructing a particular gender-based theory of textual authority, as suggested by Lucille Kerr (*Reclaiming*) and Priscilla Meléndez. This interpretation would open up a possible discussion of the Boom in terms of male vs. female fame. It is certainly true that the time frame of Donoso's novel coincides with the years, in the late 1970s and early 1980s, when the marketing of Latin American women writers was already underway. Gloria's takeover underscores the literary success of writers like Isabel Allende, Luisa Valenzuela, Rosario Ferré, Elena Poniatowska or Cristina Peri Rossi, whose success in the book market followed that of male authors in the 1960s and early 1970s by ten or fifteen years. As Oscar Montero points out, José Donoso's *El jardín* fictionalizes "a different model of the literary task" (451), one in which the position of male authors has been altered by changes in the literary field. These are none other than the changes anticipated by Núria's estimate of Gloria's future career: "This novel is extraordinary, but the real test is the second one" ["Esta novela es extraordinaria, pero la prueba de fuego es la segunda"] (248).

So the closing chapter of *El jardín de al lado* invites a discussion of the role women writers played during the Boom years. Gloria Méndez takes over Julio's novel (and Donoso's) in an allegory of women's publishing in the male-dominated market. They had never been an integral part of Seix Barral's publishing program, a fact that can be read as a form of market-driven censorship, and also as a blessing in disguise for many Latin American women writers who thereby escaped the regime's censors, although not the censorial practices of the market. (Incidentally, in the records I have examined at the *Archivo* there are no women censors of the Boom writers. Manuel Abellán lists two female censors in his 1954 list. Neither one appears to have examined the writers I study in this book.) But it turned out that the boys' club of the Boom was to have a sequel, the "female" Boom of the 1980s, when authors like Isabel Allende, Rosario Ferré, and Luisa Valenzuela took center stage.

In her essayistic fiction *El coloquio de las perras* [*The Colloquy of the Bitches*], Ferré herself reflects in tongue-in-cheek fashion on these publishing matters.[17] Emulating Cervantes's male dogs Berganza and Cipión in *El casamiento engañoso* [*The Deceitful Marriage*] (*Novelas ejemplares*), Ferré's bitches spend one afternoon loitering about the fortress by the sea in San Juan, Puerto Rico. Fina and Franca begin their colloquy with a critique of the way male Latin American authors (*perros*) and female ones (*perras*) have portrayed *féminas* (female characters, also referred to as *perras*) in their respective works. From the start, Franca comes across as the sensible critic, less interested in *murmuración* (like Cipión in Cervantes' colloquy) than in being the "voice of reason" that tries to tone down Fina's scathing attacks. When Fina bitches about Borges the "mummy," calling him an author who shows no real interest in female characters, Franca (censoriously) responds: "haces muy mal en llamar momia al mejor escritor que se ha dado en lengua española" ["you are very wrong to call the best writer the Spanish language has ever had a mummy"] (15). And soon thereafter Fina is reminded not to behave like Cervantes' Berganza : "—Cuídate de la murmuración, Fina. Recuerda las enseñanzas de Cipión" ["Beware of muttering. Remember the teachings of Cipión"] (18).

Of course, like her role model Cipión, Franca is not above a little bitching of her own, especially when it comes to admonishing Fina. But for the most part it is Fina who "mutters" rebelliously about the stereotypes *perros* have perpetuated in their fictions: Donoso's *féminas* are always "viejas chismosas y andrajosas" ["gossipy old bags"] (23), Onetti's and Fuentes's are virgins turned whores (18–20), and Cortázar's are often mistreated (27–8). Latin American bitches, she adds, do not do any better when they portray males in their own fictions: for instance, Isabel Allende's dogs are mostly dictatorial *caciques* and *putos* [fags, queers] (40).

When, after enduring Fina's bitching, it is Franca's turn to denigrate the Boom, she directs the colloquy toward a discussion of the exclusion of Latin American *perras* from the literary canon. According to Franca's *pesquisas* (her inquiries), well-known literary anthologies by male scholars like Anderson Imbert, Emir Rodríguez Monegal, Jorge Lafforge (whom Fina mistakenly calls "Jules Laforgue" [45]), and John

S. Brushwood are foremost among the guilty: "Los parámetros ejercidos por la crítica hasta el presente no han concordado con los criterios femeninos y existe un rechazo a nuestra escritura.... Los perros escritores, por otro lado, han dominado siempre el panorama crítico latinoamericano...." ["The established trends in criticism up to now have not measured up to female criteria, and there's a real rejection of our writing.... Meanwhile the male-dog writers have always dominated Latin American scholarship..."] (46). Franca's inventory of the scholarship confirms how few *perras* are actually included in anthologies, and, by extension, in the academy. But this criticism of males seems not to be to Fina's taste. *She* wants to bitch about the women critics. Why have so many renowned scholarly *perras* devoted so little attention to their fellow *perras*, and written instead on the works of male authors? She cites Sylvia Molloy's studies of Borges, Josefina Ludmer's of García Márquez, and Sara Castro-Klarén of Vargas Llosa (48) to reinforce the idea that the Boom excluded not only novels written by women, but also critical essays by women on women's fiction.

Seix Barral's 1969 *Catálogo* certainly confirms the exclusionary character of the male Boom. For instance, only two women writers (and not household names, precisely) were listed in its "Latin American Novelists" section—Mexican Ana Mairena and Argentine Marta Traba (43–51). Furthermore, it was not until 1971 that the *Biblioteca Breve* Prize was awarded to a woman, Cuban Nivaria Tejera for her *Sonámbulo del sol*. (Likewise, the short-lived Barral Editores Prize [1971–1974] did not have any female winners.[18]) But Ferré's bitches do not pay any attention to the publishing programs of firms like Seix Barral and Barral Editores (or Joaquín Mortiz and Sudamericana for that matter). Such programs and their leading figures (Barral, Balcells, etc) escape Fina's and Franca's scathing remarks; it is as if the promotional ploys and marketing strategies that defined the Boom were not at least partly to blame for the exclusion Ferré seems to complain about.

In hiding behind the critical voices of her bitches in order to present her own criticism of the Boom's "exclusive" male canon, Ferré is appropriating Cervantes's position of carefully calculated ambiguity. Like him, she can be both a critic, and a mere observer of "dog talk." (After all, she may have wished to publish, or better, still likes to publish with Seix Barral.) But in so doing she shows some of the censorial tensions and ambivalences that, in my view, inform all of the publishing narratives that were inspired by the Boom, as players in the game castigated the game as it had been, and as it continued to be played. In a similarly ambiguous fashion, Donoso hides behind Julio and Carlos Barral behind "Barral" as they criticize the publishing trends they perceive as having hindered their respective careers. The tension in Donoso's and Barral's treatment of the Boom years derives from the intrication of aesthetic innovation with the political and economic motives at play. But the dynamics of exclusion and inclusion that result, under such conditions, from the formation of a field and its canon, and the gendering of that dynamics in the case of the Boom, are what ultimately accounts for the surprisingly censorious (an oddly bitchy) tone that seems inseparable, it seems, from all these literary accounts of the Boom and its players.

CHRONOLOGY OF *PREMIO BIBLIOTECA BREVE*

(Under Carlos Barral's Supervision)

Award: 2,000 USD (approx.) and publication of the manuscript
1958. Luis Goytisolo (Spain), *Las afueras*
1959. Juan García Hortelano (Spain), *Nuevas amistades*
1960. No award
1961. José Manuel Caballero Bonald (Spain), *Dos días de setiembre*
1962. Mario Vargas Llosa (Peru), *La ciudad y los perros* [*The Time of the Hero*]
1963. Vicente Leñero (Mexico), *Los albañiles* [*The Bricklayers*]
1964. Guillermo Cabrera Infante (Cuba), *Tres tristes tigres* [*Three Trapped Tigers*]
1965. Juan Marsé (Spain), *Últimas tardes con Teresa*
    Finalist: Manuel Puig (Argentina), *La traición de Rita Hayworth* [*Betrayed by Rita Hayworth*]
1966. No award
1967. Carlos Fuentes (Mexico), *Cambio de piel* [*A Change of Skin*]
1968. Adriano González León (Venezuela), *País portátil* [*A Portable Country*]
1969. Juan Benet (Spain), *Una meditación*
1970. No award given due to the crisis at the publishing house.
    José Donoso (Chile), *El obsceno pájaro de la noche* [*The Obscene Bird of Night*] is selected for the prize.
    Carlos Barral leaves the publishing team of Seix Barral to found Barral Editores.

Fig. 1.1: Book cover. Adriano González León's *País portátil*. 1st ed. (Barcelona: Seix Barral, 1968).

Fig. 1.2: Book cover. Nivaria Tejera's *Sonámbulo del sol*. 1st ed. (Barcelona: Seix Barral, 1972).

Chapter 2

The Writer in the Barracks

Mario Vargas Llosa Facing Censorship

A 1973 photograph of Mario Vargas Llosa's book signing at Barcelona's *El Corte Inglés*, Spain's largest chain of department stores, can serve to epitomize his literary career in Spain under the Franco regime. In the photograph, the writer sits pensively at a desk next to a sign showing the triangular emblem of *El Corte Inglés* and announcing that "Mario Vargas Llosa will sign copies of his latest novel *Pantaleón y las visitadoras* [*Captain Pantoja and the Special Service*] from 11:00 a.m. to 2:00 p.m., and 4:00 p.m. to 8:00 p.m." (Setti 66). From being an unknown Peruvian writer the decade before, Vargas Llosa now faced long hours amidst a crowd of shoppers in this major book signing event. *Pantaleón y las visitadoras* came to these shoppers as a book of "great literary quality" that was being sold as yet another product endorsed by *El Corte Inglés*'s slogan of "guaranteed quality," which had made this multilevel department store a popular shopping center and a symbol of Spain's economic prosperity in the *apertura* years.

The photograph also illustrates how Vargas Llosa "made it" in the Spanish literary market, and how this market presented acclaimed or recognized authors. The image of Vargas Llosa at *El Corte Inglés*' bookshop also suggests that the Spanish literary market was to be "made" thanks to authors like him who were willing not only to endure promotional events at crowded and unpleasant department stores, but also arduous negotiations with the Spanish censorship authorities and publishing houses like Seix Barral.[1] Perhaps that was a small sacrifice for Vargas Llosa whose novels, despite the censors' misgivings and objections, were published and aggressively promoted in Franco's Spain. Vargas Llosa's successful career under the regime coincided with the government's overhaul of the publishing industry and with the new publishing and marketing trends of Seix Barral, which in 1963 was about to become a sort of a launching pad for many Latin American authors. As we have seen (chapter 1), these new trends were launched by the savvy Carlos Barral, Vargas Llosa's most fervent defender in his dealings with the Spanish censorship authorities as well as on the editorial board of Seix Barral.

An important factor in the authorities' decision to allow Seix Barral to publish Vargas Llosa's "obscene" and "immoral" novels, as the censorship files describe them, was their commercial success. That was indeed one of the most convincing arguments used by Barral, and certainly one that the censors also kept in mind in their evaluations. Vargas Llosa's commercial success was due not only to Seix Barral's efforts, but also, in part, to the Barcelona-based book club *Círculo de Lectores* [The Readers' Circle]. *Círculo* reached its popularity in Spain in the mid-1960s and 1970s, and has remained a successful book club ever since, thanks nowadays to its web site (www.circulo.es). Club members paid a small annual subscription fee to purchase books at a discount rate. Vargas Llosa's works and those of his fellow Latin American writers became top best sellers in the 1970s. *Círculo* often reprinted Seix Barral's editions in larger runs for its club members. Such was the case with *Círculo* reprints of Vargas Llosa's *La ciudad y los perros* (1969, 1972, and two editions in 1973), *La casa verde* (1969) [*The Green House*], *Conversación en la catedral* (1973), and *Pantaleón y las visitadoras* (1974, 1977). Through *Círculo* many Spanish households, mine being no exception, saw for the first time Latin American novels delivered to their homes. *Círculo* was inspired by foreign clubs like the U.S. Book-of-the-Month Club of the 1950s, which Janice Radway sees as responsible for the dissemination of middlebrow books and for the ensuing "sentimental education" such books offer (1–17).

But before Vargas Llosa's novels reached *Círculo*, Barral had aggressively launched Vargas Llosa on the worldwide book market with the publication of the 1962 *Biblioteca Breve* Prize winner *La ciudad y los perros*.[2] The novel came out in 1963 and rapidly became an international success. By the early 1970s, there had been sixteen editions in Spanish and translations into twenty different languages. For Carlos Barral the success of *La ciudad y los perros* was quite a milestone since in the Spanish literary market of the 1960s "books of that nature usually sold about 3,000 copies," and selling more than one hundred thousand copies "granted any book the status of 'bestseller'" (*Almanaque* 128). Unlike the first editions of *La ciudad y los perros*, *La casa verde* and *Conversación en la catedral*, Seix Barral launched *Pantaleón y las visitadoras* on a much larger scale with an initial run of one hundred thousand copies, something quite unusual for a first edition of a Latin American novel, or for a book by Vargas Llosa.

The censorship files show that previous first editions of Vargas Llosa's works had rather modest runs: 1,300 copies of *Los jefes* [*The Chiefs*] (Editorial Roca), 4,000 copies of *La ciudad y los perros* and *La casa verde*, 3,000 copies of *Los cachorros* [*The Cubs*] (Editorial Lumen), and 10,000 copies of *Conversación en la catedral* (Expedientes de *Los jefes*, *La ciudad*, *La casa*, *Los cachorros*, and *Conversación*). Many of these works would be reprinted several times and eventually reached the best seller status Barral had set at 100,000 copies. The sales prices, however, for the Seix Barral editions remained around two hundred pesetas per copy (or approximately $1.50) over a ten-year span. This "price fixing" was possible thanks to government subsidies (and tax breaks) that allowed the publishing house to produce paperback editions on a large scale and at reduced cost, and to successfully compete in the overseas book market. The large-scale production of Vargas Llosa's novels is perfectly consistent with the sales volume of *El Corte Inglés* and Seix Barral, and with the government's expansionist plans in the book trade.

In this respect, Vargas Llosa's arrival on the scene could not have been more timely. It coincided with the first years of the *apertura* when the Franco regime's austerity and rigidity loosened. During these years, while the military presence of the regime was still visible, civilian career politicians began to take center stage. One of the most notable figures of the *apertura*, Manuel Fraga Iribarne, a professor of law and former Undersecretary of Education, was appointed Minister of Information and Tourism in 1962. After Fraga's arrival at the Ministry, censorship practices changed radically, as discussed in chapter 1; and, I would argue, they became sort of a family affair. For one thing, the Director of Censorship Services, Carlos Robles Piquer, happened to be Fraga Iribarne's brother-in-law; and for another, the new procedures that allowed for direct negotiations between the censorship authorities, publishers, and writers were designed to produce quasi-familial relations among those involved in publishing. Now, the censored writers and their publishers would be face-to-face with the censorship authorities in both a literal and a figurative sense. But such direct negotiations did come at a price, since many authors, Vargas Llosa included, were often obliged, sometimes grudgingly, to alter their manuscripts. This new spirit of cooperation was, of course, unspoken. Barral and Vargas Llosa were often overtly critical of the regime's censorship practices, making their opposition perfectly clear. So much so that in order to understand the successful trajectory of Vargas Llosa one has to pay attention to the economic factors that conditioned his (and Barral's) outspoken opposition to censorship.

For instance, Vargas Llosa expressed his outright rejection of any form of censorship. But he himself admitted that censorship was inextricably a part of the literary market in which he chose to pursue the publication of his works. As a young writer in the late 1950s, Vargas Llosa saw no viable market for his works in his native Peru or in most Latin American countries: "How can literature exist in countries where there are no publishing houses, where there are no literary publications, where if you want to publish a book you must finance it yourself?", he pondered (Theiner 168). While, at that time, publishers in Mexico and Argentina did not face official censorship similar to the Franco regime's, he and other Boom writers found in Spain's prestigious publishing houses an outlet for their publications that their own continent did not offer. Vargas Llosa complained that in most of Latin America "the political authorities" had "established rigid censorship in the press, in the media and in the universities," making it impossible to "find encouragement" for literary creation or for "an audience" (Theiner 168). It must therefore have been his concerns with "rigid censorship" and the lack of viable publishing houses in Latin America that made him consider publishing in Spain, where censorship was becoming less "rigid" than in the 1950s and publishing houses had government support.

Barral also saw censorship as an obstacle to his firm's expansion plans, but his dealings with the censorship authorities show that he was adept at negotiating favorable decisions for many of the books he published. He would, of course, have denied that the new censorship procedures altered the outcome of his petitions in any significant manner. He was later to claim that more than 65 percent of the books he presented to the authorities were rejected for publication (*Almanaque* 31–2), but by 1969 his collections *Biblioteca Breve* and *Biblioteca Formentor* had almost four hundred titles (Expediente de *Catálogo*). In contrast with Barral's bleak estimate, the annual increase of new titles published in Spain in the 1960s jumped from two thousand to eight thousand new titles by the decade's end, and Seix Barral's collections likewise grew significantly during that decade.

These numbers clearly compromise Barral's claim to have been an outright opponent of censorship, signaling that in practice there was indeed a spirit of cooperation between publishers, writers, and censors. Similarly, the promotion of Varga Llosa in this literary market—where he collected many literary awards despite his outspoken criticisms of the military and of censorship—was indicative of his tacit cooperation with some of the cultural institutions of the regime. From his earliest incursions into the Spanish book market in 1959, he was awarded the *Leopoldo Alas* Prize for *Los jefes*, the 1962 *Biblioteca Breve* (arguably, an award for writers opposing the regime), and the 1963 *Premio de la Crítica* for *La ciudad y los perros*, and again the *Crítica* in 1966 for *La casa verde*.[3] Backed as it was by these awards, Vargas Llosa's "literary value" seemed unquestionable in the eyes of the Spanish censors, as Barral would often remind them when pleading for authorization to publish his works. It is important to remember that, while often appreciating the prize-winning literary qualities of Vargas Llosa, the censors were also quick to object to the "foul language" and "pornographic portrayals" in his novels. But this did not prevent them from endorsing publication of his works. For instance, the censor of *La casa verde* argued that, despite "its scabrous theme" ["su tema escabroso"], the novel balanced out "the pornographic with a strong literary quality and traditionalism" ["la obra salva lo pornográfico a fuerza de calidad literaria y tipismo"] (Expediente de *La casa*); and the censor of *Conversación en la catedral* pointed out that it was "a very well-written novel, as is usually the case with Vargas Llosa" ["está muy bien escrita, como es habitual en Vargas Llosa"] (Expediente de *Conversación*).

The censors frequently mentioned Vargas Llosa's mastery and literary qualities, then, as a justification for disregarding the political and sexual overtones in his novels or what they perceived to be linguistic improprieties. By the mid- and late 1960s this kind of "balanced" reaction to Latin American novels was not new, and actually appeared quite frequently in the censors' reports. They objected regularly to any work that was politically or sexually charged, a characteristic of most Latin American Boom novels; but they were nevertheless willing to overlook their initial objections when they saw certain values or qualities in these novels. Often the perception of literary quality (or concern for the preservation of the Spanish language) overrode the censors' moral, political, or linguistic concerns, and led them to open negotiations with authors and publishers.

This flexibility on the part of the censors, together with Vargas Llosa's own willingness to cooperate with them, was key to the publication of his works. In 1959, for instance, the censors demanded several corrections for *Los jefes*, which Vargas Llosa agreed to: "deben tacharse las palabras malsonantes de los folios 6 y 78" ["offensive words on pages 6 and 78 must be deleted"] (Expediente de *Los jefes*). Vargas Llosa implemented these changes, as he pointed out in a handwritten petition submitted to the Director of Censorship Services, in which he also acknowledged having made additional corrections to the final manuscript:

> A V.I. (Vuestra Ilustrísima) suplica se digne a autorizar definitivamente la edición de la expresada obra a cuyo fin adjunto las galeradas correspondientes a las páginas 1, 2, y 44 debidamente corregidas. Gracia que espera pueda alcanzar del recto proceder de V.I. cuya vida guarde Dios muchos años.
>
> I plead for Your Grace's final authorization to publish the abovementioned work, to which end I enclose the galleys corresponding to pages 1, 2, and 44 duly corrected. I await the approval of Your Grace whose life may God protect for many years. (Carta al Ilustrísimo 1959)

Likewise, Vargas Llosa agreed, as this example illustrates, to conform to the baroque formalities that governed official petitions in Franco's Spain. While he presumably found these formalities excessive, he followed them to the letter, and thus earned a certain recognition on the part of the censors who not only liked his style and literary qualities, but also would have been gratified by his disposition to conform to the rules of the bureaucracy.[4] Consequently, his pleas to the Spanish censorship authorities were always successful. With varying degrees of correction on Vargas Llosa's part, all of his works submitted by Seix Barral gained approval from the authorities. The censors also suggested changes to Vargas Llosa's essays published in 1971, *García Márquez: Historia de un deicidio* (Barral Editores), and *Historia secreta de una novela* [*Secret History of a Novel*] (Tusquets Editor). For *Historia de un deicidio*, the censor who signed the report as Gómez Niza, concluded that Vargas Llosa's "prolix and detailed analysis" ["un prolijo desmenuzamiento"] of the works of García Márquez, a "Peruvian author" ["autor peruano"], was acceptable for publication. He suggested "FYI" ["a título informativo"] corrections on "pages 149, 165, 166, 173, 507, 508, 583 and 604" ["págs. 149, 165, 166, 173, 507, 508, 583 y 604]," which the author did not implement. For *Historia secreta*, the censor, A. Vázquez objected only to the following phrases on page 8 of the typescript: "fascism in Peru" ["el fascismo en Perú"] and "adherence to fascist ideology" ["adhesión a la ideología fascista"]. His superior, the "Head of the Reading Department" ["el jefe de Negociado de

Lectorado"] authorized the essay as submitted, and it was published therefore with these two "objectionable" phrases (*Historia secreta* 18).

As he became more established in the Spanish literary market, the censors became even more lenient. For instance, they gave immediate approval to *Los cachorros* and declared "official silence" on *Conversación en la catedral* despite their reservations concerning both these novels. The censors expressed their concern with *Conversación en la catedral*'s obscenity, but concluded that it "seldom verges on the pornographic" ["la obscenidad pocas veces llega a la pornografía"] (Expediente de *Conversación*); so too with *Los cachorros*' depiction of young students "with a strong propensity for violence and moral indifference" ["con una marcada propensión a la violencia y a la despreocupación moral"] (Expediente de *Los cachorros*). But, they put aside their objections and as usual mentioned Vargas Llosa's "great literary quality" ["gran calidad literaria"] as justification for their approval of these novels (Expediente de *Conversación*).

This "great literary quality" continued to be recognized in Spanish cultural circles not only during the Franco regime, but also beyond. In 1993, twenty years after the publication of *Pantaleón y las visitadoras*, the Spanish cabinet led by the Socialist Prime Minister Felipe González granted the Peruvian writer Spanish citizenship, surely one of the most successful outcomes of Vargas Llosa's career of petitioning the Spanish authorities. While the Spanish media reported the event as the capstone to his literary career, almost no one noticed that the government had used a special procedure to approve Vargas Llosa's naturalization in record time, arguing that "exceptional circumstances" warranted its decision.[5] The "Hispano-Peruvian writer Mario Vargas Llosa," as the Spanish media now describe him, was inducted into the Royal Academy of the Spanish Language in 1996, having been awarded Spain's top literary prize, the *Premio Cervantes*, in 1994. These honors conferred upon him by Spanish institutions softened the effect of his unsuccessful bid for the Peruvian presidency in 1990, but, more significantly, served to show gratitude on the part of the Spanish government for his involvement in Spain's cultural scene since the early 1960s. From the government's standpoint, making Vargas Llosa a citizen of Spain seemed the logical recompense for his cooperative spirit in negotiating with the Spanish authorities, something that had been, much as for Barral, an affair that entailed both defiance and compliance.

While the Spanish cabinet argued that Vargas Llosa deserved to be recognized for his many contributions to Hispanic letters, the untold story was that his cooperative disposition toward the Francoist authorities had already made him a model citizen well before he became officially a Spanish citizen. In my view, the fact that it was a center-left government that granted him citizenship, thus seeming to reward Vargas Llosa's opposition to the Franco regime, had little real bearing on the decision. As Mario Santana has argued, Vargas Llosa was already a national figure in Franco's Spain, to the point that his case calls for a redefinition of the concept of "national literature" as something more like "naturalized literature": "A simple glimpse at literary journals and debates during the 1960s and 1970s in Spain will make clear that Vargas Llosa became a prominent presence and a model for young Spanish writers" (28). Likewise the Socialist government seemed to conclude that Vargas Llosa had been and would continue to be a permanent fixture on Spain's cultural scene, and that his novels had been "naturalized" into the Spanish literary market.

In order to show how this nationalization and naturalization took place, I propose in this chapter a close examination of the censorship history of Vargas Llosa's two most significant best sellers on the Spanish literary market of the 1960s and 1970s, *La ciudad y los perros* and *Pantaleón y las visitadoras*. These novels, written a decade apart, are illustrative respectively of Vargas Llosa's initial arrival on the scene as a critically acclaimed writer in the 1960s literary market, and of the consecration of his popularity in the 1970s. It is precisely this peak in Vargas Llosa's literary popularity in Franco's Spain that can be seen in the 1973 photograph of the book signing at *El Corte Inglés*. Such a phenomenon is best understood in relation to the changes in censorship practices during the *apertura* as well as Barral's maneuverings on the Spanish book market.

Following the argument of Ross Chambers's *Room for Maneuver*, I would argue that Barral and Vargas Llosa engaged with the censors in practices of oppositionality as opposed to practices of resistance. Barral's and Vargas Llosa's oppositional practices (i.e., rejecting censorship outright, but negotiating with the censorship authorities) functioned "within the structure of power." While their interaction with the censorship apparatus implied a challange to "the legitimacy of a given-power structure," Barral and Vargas Llosa did not exactly "resist" the power-system, that is, they did not seek to "overturn [it] by a counter-force." Rather, they conformed to the structure of power and sought the "room for maneuver" that it offered, which Chambers sees as the "space of play" or "a leeway" between the "possibility of disturbance to the system" and the "system's power to recuperate that disturbance" (xi–xv). It was clearly the new censorship procedures that made available such "room for maneuver" among authors, their publishers, and the censors.

Oppositionality of this kind also helps us to understand the authorial figures who face censorship in Vargas Llosa's novels. These figures originate in Vargas Llosa's personal dealings with military rule, which first emerged in fictional form in *La ciudad y los perros*' protagonist, the young cadet Alberto Fernández, and then reappeared in a more mature and conformist version in Pantaleón Pantoja, the protagonist of *Pantaleón y las visitadoras*. Such figures epitomize Vargas Llosa's obsession with writers who, like himself, are faced with the necessity of writing under military rule and censorship. Indeed they express his own perception of himself as, like them, what I call a "writer in the barracks."

In the barracks, which I take in both a literal and metaphorical sense, writers are constrained by military authority, but their writing may often imply an act of opposition (not of resistance) to military rules or norms. This opposition to military authority goes hand in hand with willing or unwilling compliance with the rules of the military. As a result, and in a way that might be exemplified by Vargas Llosa's ambiguous dissension and cooperation with the Spanish censors, writers in the barracks can wind up cooperating with military rule and even supporting it. *La ciudad y los perros* and *Pantaleón y las visitadoras* describe ambiguities of this kind through their protagonists' barracks writing. Alberto's erotic novelettes are regarded as a "perversion" and a "depravation" that attacks the moral fabric of the military academy; nevertheless they are allowed to circulate. Pantaleón's detailed and methodical reporting, in full compliance with military authority, nevertheless clearly bothers his superiors, who perceive it as implying criticism of the carelessness typical of most military reports, an abuse of his assigned duties, or an excess. Vargas Llosa's barracks novels express his opposition to military authority and imply discontent with the kinds of restrictions the Spanish censors imposed on his writing. But in order to get them published and distributed, he went along with the censorship system while taking full advantage of the possibilities for maneuver that it offered him.

1. FACING THE CENSORS, FACING THE MARKET

There is no better example of Vargas Llosa's and Barral's opportunist oppositionality toward the Spanish censorship authorities than what took place during the approval process of *La ciudad y los perros*. The novel, Vargas Llosa's and Barral's first international best seller, was submitted to the censors in February 1963, and after arduous negotiations, was finally published in September of that year. As it happened, that year was a crucial one for the Spanish publishing industry. As summarized in a confidential report from Spain's National Book Institute (INLE) titled "Spain Losing Its Book Market" ["España pierde su mercado librero"], the government was fully aware of the losses Spain was undergoing in the overseas book market, mainly in Latin America. The anonymous government official who wrote the report outlined "a somber outlook" ["un panorama sombrío"] for the future of Spanish books worldwide (España pierde 1). Vargas Llosa's novels appeared on the Spanish market at precisely the moment when this dark future had been predicted.

Furthermore, Seix Barral's promotional ploys and its efforts to distribute them internationally clearly responded to the regime's expectations as laid out in the reports of the INLE. *La ciudad y los perros*, as it turns out, was a publishing experiment not only for Barral and his firm, but also for the Spanish authorities who were eager to provide the necessary conditions for the growth of Spain's book trade. *La ciudad y los perros*, in sum, was a prototype that predicted what the Spanish literary market would become in the 1960s and 1970s. Its international launching signaled the beginning of the Latin American Boom at the same time as its commercial success reinforced the "pan-Hispanic venture" proposed (albeit with different arguments) by Seix Barral and the INLE.

The publishing story that ended with Seix Barral's 1963 release of *La ciudad y los perros* began in early July that year, when Vargas Llosa (most likely at Barral's request) took the unusual step of writing personally to the Director of Censorship Services, Carlos Robles Piquer.[6] In his letter, the writer expressed his dissatisfaction with the Spanish censors' unfavorable evaluation of his novel. After the customary introduction: "I am very pleased to address these lines to you" ["me es muy grato dirigirle estas líneas"], Vargas Llosa thanked Robles Piquer "for his kind suggestions" ["sus amables sugerencias"] regarding the proposed changes. He also announced in his letter that he had modified "eight of the supposedly immoral or irreverent paragraphs" ["ocho de los párrafos sospechos de inmoralidad o irreverencia"] and several "objectionable terms" ["términos objetados"]; he had also "softened some episodes with euphemisms and elliptical phrases" ["suavizado algunos episodios (con) eufemismos y frases elípticas"] in order to satisfy the censors' recommendations (Carta a Robles Piquer). But despite this willingness to implement changes in his novel as the censors desired, Vargas Llosa concluded his letter with a spirited defense of his right to freedom of expression:

> finalmente me siento en la obligación moral de decirle que...quiero cumplir un deber de cortesía con usted por las

amabilidades que ha tenido conmigo, pero que esto en nada modifica mi oposición de principio a la censura, convencido como estoy de que la creación literaria deber ser un acto eminentemente libre, sin otras limitaciones que las que le dictan al escritor sus propias convicciones.

Finally I am compelled by my moral principles to tell you that...I wish to be courteous to you since you have been so kind to me, but that this fact does not alter one bit my stance in principle against censorship. I am convinced that literary creation must be an eminently free act without any limitations, except those that are dictated by the writer's own convictions. (Carta a Robles Piquer)

Two months later, in his response to Vargas Llosa, Robles Piquer justified the need for censorship of certain books like *La ciudad y los perros*. In his view, censorship had beneficial effects on writers, since "the products of the printing press may hide, and often do hide, pseudo-literary manifestations that may harm the community as well as true writers" ["bajo los productos de imprenta, pueden ocultarse, y de hecho se ocultan las manifestaciones pseudo-literarias que perjudican a la comunidad no menos que a los verdaderos escritores"] (Carta a Vargas Llosa). This condescending tone returned in Robles Piquer's concluding paragraph, in which he addressed Vargas Llosa's work more directly: "estoy igualmente seguro de que las modificaciones que Ud. ha introducido en nada perjudican a la obra" ["I am also certain that the changes you have made are in no way detrimental to your work"] (Carta a Vargas Llosa). For Robles Piquer, censorship had a prophylactic quality, then, and perhaps a purifying effect, since through censorship "good" and "bad literature" could be set apart. But, as was so often the case when censors made reference to "great literary quality," Piquer's "good" and "bad" literature also concealed the Spanish authorities' interest in the economic value of literature and the profits "good" literature may generate. I see the odd phrase used by Robles Piquer—"the products of the printing press"—as indicative of his concern with the economic value of books.

In order to understand the history of the publication of *La ciudad y los perros* one must keep in mind that censorship practices were inextricably tied in this way to economics. Economic interests were actually decisive for the authorization of Vargas Llosa's first best seller, which, one should remember, had originally been rejected by the censors. Robles Piquer was willing to reconsider only because behind-the-scenes negotiations had already taken place between Vargas Llosa, Barral, and himself.

Robles Piquer's intervention also meant that the original censor's report on *La ciudad y los perros* had to be removed from the file. The original report is no longer in the current file, which contains only the order for final approval of the novel. So the novel was in fact "doubly censored" by the Spanish authorities, who having first rejected the novel, then "censored" the report that had censored the novel. Barral had submitted the novel with the title *Los impostores* [*The Impostors*] on February 16, 1963. This is the submission that was denied. On March 25, 1963, Barral resubmitted the novel, presumably hoping for the direct intervention of Robles Piquer. This was the initiative that led to the final official approval of September 28, 1963. Following the meeting and the epistolary exchanges that took place in the summer months, the only apparently significant change was the title of the novel: "By Superior order, it is AUTHORIZED with the title LA CIUDAD Y LOS PERROS" ["De orden Superior, se AUTORIZA con el título LA CIUDAD Y LOS PERROS"] (Expediente de *La ciudad*). The title in the original petition, *Los impostores* had likely proven problematic for the censors, who presumably disapproved of its provocative assimilation of military officers to impostors. But the title had already undergone a first change prior to the novel's submission to the authorities, since it competed for the *Biblioteca Breve* prize as *La morada del héroe* [*The Hero's Dwelling*]. The English title, *The Time of the Hero*, records this first title.

Even though the original censor's report was removed from the file, so that we do not know exactly what the initial objections to the novel were, the censor who evaluated *Los cachorros* in 1967 provides evidence of what these objections must have been. This censor must have had access to the original report on *La ciudad y los perros*, since he used it to inform his report on *Los cachorros*:

> Como en *La ciudad y los perros*, presenta aquí Vargas Llosa... una historia, más insinuada que referida, de la juventud estudiantil latinoamericana.... Las situaciones atrevidas aparecen doblemente veladas por los americanismos y el estilo insinuante del autor, que deja así perfectamente paliado (mucho mejor que en *La ciudad y los perros*, más fiel a la tradición narrativa) lo que pudiera merecer reparo.
>
> As in *La ciudad y los perros*, Vargas Llosa here presents a story about Latin American student youth that relies more on insinuation than on direct reference.... The daring situations

appear doubly veiled by Americanisms and the author's insinuating style; he thus perfectly palliates (much better than in *La ciudad y los perros*, and more in line with traditional narrative) what might deserve objections. (Expediente de *Los cachorros*)

For this censor, *La ciudad y los perros*'s use of multiple narrative voices and narratorial dispersion was objectionable, since it did not sufficiently "veil" the "daring situations" narrated in the novel. He obviously felt that a more linear (or traditional) narrative was "easier to censor" and for that reason less problematic, preferring *Los cachorros* to *La ciudad y los perros* in that respect, and approving of its more successful tecniques of "veiling." Other censors were to express similar concern regarding Vargas Llosa's literary craft, which generated both admiration and suspicion on their part. This was the case with *Conversación en la catedral*. The censor admired its literary quality, but was reluctant to accept Vargas Llosa's use of multiple forms of narration, which "defy" what the censor of *Los cachorros* had called "traditional narrative": "junto a la gran calidad literaria, reflejada en la narración mixta, o sea, mezclando el diálogo con la narración indirecta y el monólogo interior...hay evidentemente una intención parcial" ["along with the great literary quality that is reflected in the mixed narration, that is, the combination of dialogues with indirect narration and interior monologues...there is obviously a partisan intention"] (Expediente de *Conversación*).

But the censors' reservations about endorsing Vargas Llosa's multilayered and polyphonic novels did not deter Barral from pursuing their publication. He realized that their objections to novels containing "daring situations" and showing "partisan intentions" could be easily overcome by their (almost always mentioned) "literary quality." This quality demonstrated that Vargas Llosa wrote the kind of "good literature" the Director of Censorship Services advocated in his defense of censorship, and it has the further advantage that complex narrative techniques could sometimes, if not always, help to veil scabrous situations and unwelcome opinions.

But the question remains, what did Barral and Vargas Llosa agree to do in order to satisfy the censors' concerns about *La ciudad y los perros*? Vargas Llosa, as his letter to Robles Piquer quoted above pointed out, agreed to correct several paragraphs, and Barral sided with Robles Piquer's assertion that the proposed changes were "in no way detrimental" to the novel. In *Los años sin excusa*, Barral describes the negotiations with Robles Piquer as a kind of triumph for his firm, claiming that the changes made in the final version of the novel were minor in comparison to what the censors had originally proposed. While this might be true—after all, Barral's negotiating skills with the censors did often prove productive—his compliance with the regime's new censorship guidelines also reveals that he had some "intenciones parciales" of his own with respect to the authorities:

> Para los libros de especial significación e importancia, se pudo negociar la intervención directa—y lectora—de los altos funcionarios. No olvidaré nunca... el almuerzo que el director general Robles Piquer... nos ofreció a Mario Vargas y a mí con el fin de discutir las tachaduras censorias en el original de *La ciudad y los perros*, tachaduras que el autor no estaba dispuesto a aceptar.
>
> For certain special books it was possible to negotiate direct intervention —including reading—on the part of high-ranking officials. I will never forget a luncheon to which Vargas Llosa and I were invited by the Director of Censorship Services, Robles Piquer, in order to discuss the corrections proposed by the censor in the original manuscript of *La ciudad y los perros*, which Vargas Llosa was not willing to accept. (*Los años* 149)

At this luncheon the publisher, the writer and the director negotiated the changes that would result in final approval of the novel. It was a perfect example of the *censura oficiosa* that was about to become a standard practice. Barral's recollection, however, contradicts his own statements elsewhere about the "insignificant" changes that took place with the arrival of Fraga Iribarne at the Ministry of Information (*Almanaque* 31–32). In fact, these changes were significant ones. By contrast with the old practice of mandatory submission, censorship was now negotiable, and the more informal type of evaluation called "una lectura oficiosa" offered even more leeway. Finally, and as Barral also recalled, the censors' objections could be quite capricious at times, a fact from which oppositional advantage could on occasion be derived by giving way gracefully on relatively trivial matters, in order to appear flexible and open to suggestion:

> Robles explicó finalmente que había una sola cosa que no podía conceder. El militar de más alta graduación... aparecía motejado de 'cetáceo'... lo cual en un país gobernado por el brazo militar podía parecer alusivo y era inadmisible. Cetáceo era algo insultante.... ¿Cómo reaccionaría un ciudadano al

que en las calles de Madrid se le interpelase "so cetáceo"? Si dijese ballena, sería tal vez diferente.

Robles Piquer finally explained that there was one thing he could not allow. The highest ranking official in the novel was nicknamed "cetacean," which was allusive and inadmissible in a country governed by military rule. "Cetacean" was truly insulting.... How would a citizen in the streets of Madrid react if called "you cetacean!"? Now, to say whale might be different. (*Los años* 149)

According to Barral, this whimsical suggestion was incorporated into the final version of the novel. For his part, Vargas Llosa had at first tried to convince Robles Piquer that one of the novel's most interesting features was the animalistic portrayals of most characters (dogs, jaguar, boa) and that "cetacean" was simply an allusion to the Colonel's belly. But the Director insisted that the change to "whale" be made. While Barral suggests that this was the only change Vargas Llosa accepted—"O.K., whale. The author gave up; it was his only concession" ["Bueno, ballena. El autor cedió, fue su única concesión"] (*Los años* 149)—, the writer's previous record with the censors suggests that it is very likely that he incorporated additional changes as a result of his conversation with Robles Piquer.[7] This is confirmed by his July letter to the Director which, most likely, was a follow-up to the luncheon.

For the Spanish authorities, the spirit of cooperation shown by Vargas Llosa and Barral, along with the not so insignificant detail of the novel's favorable commercial prospects, was enough for the censors to reconsider it in a positive light. Vargas Llosa's case was a persuasive one, given that he was an award-winning writer who had been internationally recognized. For such was precisely the argument Barral presented to Robles Piquer in a letter written on July 30, 1963. In it, Barral confidently claimed that an international pool of readers "eagerly" awaited the release of what he asserted was an assured best seller on the market. We may be sure that he emphasized the international visibility and the massive distribution he foresaw for Vargas Llosa's novel, the aspect most likely to please the officials at the INLE who were trying to overhaul the Spanish publishing industry.

Barral had convinced the censorship authorities to allow the publication of *La ciudad y los perros*. Now, he had to speed up the censors' official approval while simultaneously laying the groundwork for the book's release on the international market. To this latter end, Barral presented the novel as the work of an internationally acclaimed author, and decided to include in the first edition of *La ciudad y los perros* a "tiny preface" (*prologuillo*) by the prestigious Spanish literary critic José María Valverde. The so-called *prologuillo* disappeared in the subsequent editions of the novel and only a section of it remained on the back jacket. The censors approved the *prologuillo* as well as a number of commentaries by notables of the literary market such as Sebastián Salazar Bondy, Julio Cortázar, Uffe Harder, Roger Caillois, and Alastair Reid. These blurbs, which were intended to validate Vargas Llosa among literary figures not affiliated with the regime, are reproduced in part on the jacket of the early editions of *La ciudad*.[8] Valverde's preface was to be included along with a brief biographical note about Vargas Llosa, a reference to the members of the *Biblioteca Breve* prize's jury, and a foldout map of Lima. As suggested by Santana, one of the selling points of the Boom novels in Franco's Spain was precisely the new "social realism" they presented. The foldout map of Lima and the biographical note on Vargas Llosa were designed to emphasize that there was something "real" about this story (Santana 87–90), which presented the harsh realities of a military regime in a setting relatively unfamiliar to Spaniards.

With the help of Valverde, Barral presented *La ciudad y los perros*, then, as a widely recognized novel that had the endorsement of renowned critics and contemporary writers. In his negotiations with Robles Piquer, these endorsements guaranteed the commercial success of the novel and purported to make its release all the more urgent in the competitive market of the 1960s:

> Por las razones que le indiqué—*retraso inevitable* del lanzamiento del libro a título ganador del Biblioteca Breve, *desventaja* en la concurrencia con el ganador del Prix Formentor que ha aparecido ya en Francia, *impaciencia* de la crítica latinoamericana que ha hablado ya de él basándose en la lectura del manuscrito, *necesidad de suministrar* ejemplares a los traductores extranjeros, etc.—*resulta imprescindible* lanzar el libro a principios de la próxima temporada, por lo que me he atrevido a dar la orden de impresión sin esperar a tener la definitiva autorización de censura, autorización que considero implícita en nuestras últimas conversaciones.
>
> *It is imperative that the book be launched* at the beginning of next season given the reasons I mentioned to you—*the inevitable delay* in releasing the book as winner of the *Biblioteca Breve* Prize, the *disadvantage* of competing with the concurrent release in France of the winner of the Formentor Prize, the *impatience* of Latin American critics who have been

talking about it based on their reading of the manuscript, the *need* to distribute copies to foreign translators, etc. For these reasons I have taken it upon myself to give the order to print without waiting for final censorship approval, which I consider implicit in our most recent conversations. (Carta a Robles Piquer; emphasis mine)

Very skillfully, Barral insisted that any delay in publication was disadvantageous in view of the competition *La ciudad y los perros* faced in a book market that was clearly anxious to receive copies of the novel. He reiterated once more the best seller quality of Vargas Llosa's novel, and argued that any delays in the publication process should be avoided. Readers and critics were impatiently awaiting its release. This move made it almost impossible for Robles Piquer to deny final approval, which became effective almost two months after Barral had given orders to print the novel. Robles Piquer, in the end, did not seem to mind Seix Barral's involvement in what he had called, only months before, "the literature of the dregs of society" ["literatura de los bajos fondos"]. The Director accepted this "product of the printing press" that was bound to be so successful in the book market.

The story of the publication of *La ciudad y los perros* has an exemplary quality. Exchanges like those among Vargas Llosa, Barral and Robles Piquer (and, more generally, among writers, publishers, and the censorship authorities) became common for Latin American writers pursuing the publication of their works in Francoist Spain. So what I find extremely interesting about *La ciudad y los perros* is how exchanges of this kind are reproduced, to a degree, in the novel's own portrayal of literary production and censorship under military rule. My contention, as already foreshadowed, is that in Franco's Spain, and in the face of the regime's new rules for book production and censorship, Vargas Llosa was a writer in the barracks. In Franco's barracks (the cultural institutions of the regime, liberalized as they were by the desire to promote Latin American literature), he confronted these rules, ultimately conforming to them while nevertheless achieving the publication of a book initially viewed as dangerous.

His career, in this respect, resembles Alberto Fernández's at the Leoncio Prado military academy, center stage of *La ciudad y los perros*. The "poet" of the academy, as the cadets call him, is a barracks writer in a strictly literal sense. While the story of his coming of age as a writer in a military school obviously recreates Vargas Llosa's own military experience during his formative years in Lima, my interest in *La ciudad y los perros* has relatively little to do with a merely autobiographical reading of the novel and is directed more particularly toward Vargas Llosa's obsession with barracks writing. My aim is to read the vicissitudes surrounding the publication of *La ciudad y los perros* into the novel's narrative concerning literary production and the distribution of literature when these are controlled by military authority. It is as if the publication history of *La ciudad y los perros*—and other "Boom" novels—was anticipated, or at least foreshadowed in the novel itself, inasmuch as it centers on the story of Alberto's coming to writing in the barracks. This is not to say that Alberto and Vargas Llosa face exactly similar censorship regimes in their respective book markets. While Alberto's writing first circulates clandestinely, and undergoes censure at the end of the novel, Vargas Llosa submits his writing to censorship, complies with its requirements, and is finally legitimately published.

Alberto is a "writer for hire" and a "best-selling" author of erotic novelettes in a military academy. His novelettes ("novelitas," "stories" in the English version)—*Los vicios de la carne* [*The Sins of Flesh*], "Lula, la mujer loca" (also referred as "Lula, la chuchumeca incorregible" ["Lula, the Incorregible Flirt"]), "La mujer loca y el burro" ["The Mad Woman and the Burro"], and "La jijuna y el jijuno" ["The Whore and the Whoremaster"] (*La ciudad* 1987, 329) [*Time* 338]—circulate clandestinely among the young cadets like best sellers on the literary market, and are censored by the military authorities. Only a few sentences from some of these novelettes are actually reproduced in *La ciudad y los perros*, but it is clear that they are inspired by *Los placeres de Eleodora* [*Eleodora's Pleasures*], an erotic novel which one of the cadets, Vallano, brings to the academy. This novel's arrival in the barracks is the starting point for Alberto's literary career; the cadets quickly make it their favorite read: "Préstamelo... cinco, diez, quince lo asedian gritando" (*La ciudad* 141) ["Come on, lend it to me.... Five, ten, fifteen cadets besieged him, shouting" (*Time* 145)]. But immediately after the barracks have given an enthusiastic reception of Vallano's recitation of selected passages from *Eleodora's Pleasures*, a *suboficial*, or noncom, confiscates the offending book, tramples it underfoot and burns it. It is the destruction of the porn that gives Alberto the idea of a pastime that will make him a little money. Erotic fiction can be a profitable enterprise as well as an outlet for his literary talents: "Y entonces yo dije por media cajetilla de cigarrillos te escribo una historia mejor que *Los Placeres de Eleodora*" (*La ciudad* 143) ["And then I said I'll write you a better story than Eleodora for half a pack of cigarettes"] (*Time* 147). But the destruction of *Eleodora's Pleasures* also foreshadows the "sequestration" of Alberto's own trashy stories at the end of *La ciudad y los perros*.

Alberto, then, cashes in on the prohibition of—and high demand for—erotica at the military school. Given that most cadets want precisely what is prohibited by the authorities, it is no surprise that, soon after their release, Alberto's novelettes become common currency in the barracks' economic exchange system. As one more commodity in the barracks, they are swapped for cigarettes, liquor, and exams. They are appraised as merchandise and valued as a unit of monetary exchange. Alberto himself evaluates his writing in frankly economic terms, seeing his literary career as a source of income: "buena plata he ganado a pesar de los estafadores" (*La ciudad* 143) ["I've earned good money in spite all of the deadbeats" (*Time* 148)]. For he is, above all, a "professional" writer meeting the demand in the barracks for pleasure:

> Cuando termina la redacción—diez páginas de cuaderno, por ambas caras—Alberto, súbitamente inspirado, anuncia el título: *Los vicios de la carne* y lee su obra, con una voz entusiasta. La cuadra lo escucha respetuosamente; por instantes hay brotes de humor. Luego lo aplauden y lo abrazan. Alguien dice: "Fernández, eres un poeta." "Sí, dicen otros. Un poeta." (*La ciudad* 143)

> When he finished writing it—ten pages in a notebook, on both sides of the page—Alberto had a flash of inspiration and announced the title: *The Sins of the Flesh*. He read the story to them in an excited voice. The barracks listened to him with something like awe, and now and then they laughed appreciatively. When he finished, they applauded him and clapped him on the back. Someone said, "Fernández, you're a poet." "That's right," someone else said, "he's a real poet." (*Time* 147–148)

Thus, *The Sins of the Flesh* launches Alberto's literary career in the market of the academy. His immediate success with the audience of his fellow cadets is noted by Boa, a member of "The Circle," the underground organization led by Jaguar that controls all the barracks' clandestine operations (stealing exams, selling cigarettes and liquor, altering the night guard schedule, etc.). Boa's desire to acquire Alberto's pornographic stories is a sign that "The Circle" anticipates good profits: "Y ese mismo día se me acercó Boa...y me dijo hazme otra novelita como ésa y te la compro...gran pajero, fuiste mi primer cliente y siempre me acordaré de ti, protestaste cuando te dije cincuenta centavos por hoja" (*La ciudad* 143) ["And that same day the Boa came over to me...and told me write another story like that and I'll buy it from you....Boa, a great jack-off, you were my first customer and I'll always remember you, you got sore at first when I told you fifty centavos a page" (*Time* 148)]. And so it is arranged. Alberto creates his erotic novelettes, and "The Circle" oversees their marketing. Thus, a "circle of readers" who demand and purchase Alberto's novelettes is created, and Alberto's writing joins the other commodities controlled by "The Circle" in the oppositional culture of the barracks. (As a subversion of military discipline of which the authorities are seemingly unaware, this oppositional quality heightens the "literary" value of Alberto's risqué texts, and suggests a possible parallel with the success of Boom writing in general, and of Vargas Llosa's piquant novels in particular, in the barracks of Franco's Spain.)

The circle of readers that is thus created supports Alberto's relatively massive production of erotic literature. His novelettes, however, cannot be massively distributed, but must be passed clandestinely from one reader to another in the circle. While Alberto is quite a productive writer—"Alberto leafed through the pages he had written: four stories in less than two hours.... He had written his four-page stories with hardly a pause" (*Time* 144–145)]—, his career depends on both of these circles: "The Circle" that promotes it and the circle of readers who buy and/or exchange his novels. So circulation and circles—each having a certain covert dimension in the military context—are the key factor in his success as a writer in the barracks.

This becomes all the clearer when Alberto accuses Jaguar of Arana's death, thus defying "The Circle" and triggering the end of his success in the literary market of the barracks. His defiance is a defiance also of the military authorities, who officially claim that Arana's death is accidental. Up to this point, Alberto's novelettes have circulated, as it were, under the "official silence" of the military authorities who tacitly allow the clandestine economy of the barracks to operate. But, after Arana's death, they search the barracks, seize the novelettes, and remove them from circulation.

A face off between Alberto and his superiors follows. Facing the highest military authorities of the academy, Alberto must defend his accusation against Jaguar. Unable to satisfy the Colonel's demand for documentary evidence in support of his claim, he is forced to withdraw his petition to reopen the Arana case. And of course his dissent from the official version of Arana's death does not go unpunished. Standing before the review panel chaired by the Colonel, he is forced to read out passages from one of his racy stories. The Colonel's reaction to his literary efforts contrasts with the cadets' reception:

> Eso sí que es un escándalo, cadete. Hay que tener un espíritu extraviado, pervertido, para dedicarse a escribir semejantes

cosas. Hay que ser escoria. Estos papeles deshonran al colegio, nos deshonran a todos.... Estos papeles son su ruina, cadete. ¿Cree usted que algún colegio lo recibiría después de ser expulsado por vicioso, por taras espirituales?... Yo soy un hombre con sensibilidad.... Y estos papeles me avergüenzan. Son una afrenta sin nombre para el colegio. (*La ciudad* 329–330)

This is a scandalous affair, scandalous. Only a twisted mind, a diseased mind, could write this sort of filth. These papers are a disgrace to the Academy, a disgrace to all of us.... These papers have ruined you, Cadet. Do you think any school is going to admit you after you've been expelled from here as a delinquent with a perverted mind?... I'm a sensitive man.... And I find these documents extremely painful. They're a blatant insult to the Academy. (*Time* 339–340)

The Colonel censures Alberto as an "inventive" and "degenerate" individual whose writings are a threat to the moral fabric of the academy and a dangerous example for the young cadets. Alberto writes "filth," and this kind of writing, the Colonel predicts, spells the end of his military (as well as literary) career. Notice that for the authorities of the Leoncio Prado Academy, there is no censorship proper, but rather a system—much like the one referred to by Robles Piquer—that "separates good and bad literature." As was the case with the esteemed Director of Censorship Services, the Colonel does not see himself as a censor: rather he is a "sensitive man" who, like Robles Piquer, has a duty to keep "bad writing" out of the academy:

por esta gran familia que formamos los leonciopadrinos, voy a darle una última oportunidad. Guardaré estos papeles y lo tendré en observación. Si sus superiores me dicen, a fin de año, que usted ha respondido a mi confianza... quemaré estos papeles y olvidaré esta escandalosa historia.... Por supuesto, usted guardará la más absoluta reserva sobre lo que se ha hablado aquí. (*La ciudad* 330–31)

I like to think of the Leoncio Prado as one big family. Therefore, I'm going to give you a last chance. I'll keep these papers, these incriminating documents, and I'll also keep a sharp eye on you. If your superiors tell me at the end of the year that you've earned the trust I'm giving you now... I'll burn these papers and forget the whole sordid story.... Naturally, you'll keep absolutely quiet about what we've been saying. (*Time* 339–40)

While the face off between Alberto and the Colonel is not, strictly speaking, about publishing (it is rather about seeking the truth concerning Arana's death), the circulation of the young man's spicy writing is at the core of the discussion. Even though the Colonel argues that the novelettes are "extremely painful" and a "blatant insult," he is not really concerned about them. Rather, he uses Alberto's novelettes to discredit the claim that Jaguar assassinated Arana by insinuating that it is just another of Alberto's "many fictions" or "fantasies": "Las anécdotas son muy interesantes. Las hipótesis nos muestran que usted tiene un espíritu creador, una imaginación cautivante" (*La ciudad* 326) ["Your anecdotes are very interesting, and your theories show that you have a creative spirit, a captivating imagination" (*Time* 336)].

So the Colonel decrees the suppression of these "fantasies," and allows Alberto to remain in the barracks, but as a now silenced writer. While they do silence Alberto as a writer, the Colonel's censorial powers point to the fact that in the literary market of the Leoncio Prado there is some room for negotiation with the censorship authorities. It is in this sense that *La ciudad y los perros* offers a commentary on literary production, distribution, and censorship under military rule. As I have indicated, Alberto's novelettes are first read, exchanged, and integrated into the economy of the military school. It is only later, when, for reasons having nothing to do with literature per se, the author becomes a threat ("a disgrace," "a degenerate") to the military system that they are seized. In the novel censorship appears as a postproduction phenomenon; nevertheless, Alberto's experience of censorship is closely related to the new policies of the last years of the Franco regime, in which production and censorship go hand in hand. The private negotiations between Alberto and the military authorities read like an anticipation of the new censorship practices that, when Vargas Llosa was writing his novel, were ahead for him as well as for his fellow Latin American Boom writers in Franco's Spain, practices that were to be first exemplified in the behind-the-scenes negotiations between Vargas Llosa, Barral, and Robles Piquer that led to the final approval of *La ciudad y los perros*. The novel fictionalizes these practices and the oppositionality they permitted as it reflects on how writers in the barracks find themselves subdued and controlled by a kind of negotiated censorship that fosters production, to the point of positioning sometimes ideology and morals as secondary concerns.

2. THE MARKETING OF MILITARY LITERATURE

Ten years after the international release of *La ciudad y los perros*, *Pantaleón y las visitadoras* appeared on the Spanish book market and became yet another of Vargas Llosa's literary successes. Barral, and the censors for that matter, seemed fully aware that the novel's depiction of the military would make it an instant international best seller. Many readers were bound to find *Pantaleón y las visitadoras* irresistible, given that for years this kind of book had been banned from publication in Spain. The plot was certainly an enticing one: the Peruvian military, concerned with the number of rapes committed by its troops stationed in the jungle, organizes an undercover prostitution ring ("Servicio de Visitadoras," or in the English version "the Special Service") to satisfy the sexual needs of its soldiers. The secret mission is carried out almost to perfection by the military's most able and methodical captain, Pantaleón Pantoja, whose brilliant organizational skills lead him to run what turns out to be one of the most accomplished outfits in Peruvian military history. To see a novel so risqué (or at least, so sexually explicit) on display at *El Corte Inglés* probably surprised many shoppers and potential readers who had themselves been living under the conditions of military-style moral censorship for years.

Why did the Spanish censorship authorities allow its publication? Why didn't they object to the novel's sexual explicitness and its overt linking of the military to prostitution? The short answer to these questions is that while the censors did raise some of the objections one would expect, their superiors, more concerned with the profits to be derived from what appeared likely to be a best-selling novel, allowed its publication in record time. The long answer has to do with the publishing career of Vargas Llosa in Spain and can be found in the confidential reports on *Pantaleón y las visitadoras*.

The novel reached the Ministry of Information on May 10, 1973, and it took the two censors who examined it only one day to write their reports. The submission was done under the *depósito* option of the 1966 printing law. Since the volume had 309 pages, and the law allowed the censors at least one day for each "50 pages or fraction thereof," they could have taken up to a week to complete their review; instead, they opted to expedite Seix Barral's request. The censors of *Pantaleón y las visitadoras* were Mr. García Campos and Mr. Martos, as indicated in a summary of Vargas Llosa's previous record with the censorship authorities included in the novel's file (Nota informativa "Pantaleón"). Their expeditious reporting contrasts with the eight months it took to approve *La ciudad y los perros* and five months for *La casa verde*. Given that the 1966 law had taken effect and that Vargas Llosa was already a fairly well-established author in Spain (and one the authorities tended to like), *Los cachorros* and *Conversación en la catedral* had likewise been evaluated within a week of their submission to the censorship authorities. Such speed speaks volumes concerning the censors' familiarity with Vargas Llosa and Barral, and particularly the anticipated commercial success of the novel, something that by then was expected of all Vargas Llosa's works.

In this connection, the first censor wrote in his report: "this work is going to have a great success in sales and is going to be widely reviewed" ["esta obra vá (sic) a tener un gran éxito de venta y vá (sic) a ser muy comentada"] (Expediente de *Pantaleón*). But the anticipated economic success of the novel was, for this first censor, less a matter for congratulation than one of concern. While acknowledging that the novel was a "humorous satire" ["una sátira humorística"] and not to be taken completely seriously, he concluded that this potential best seller was dangerous. In his view, it could not be authorized for publication. Consequently, he recommended the intervention, oddly enough, of the "Special Service" of the judicial system. He thought the "Special Prosecutor for Printing Matters" ["El Fiscal Especial de Prensa"] should begin sequestration proceedings.

In the eyes of this first censor, there were "numerous reasons" that supported his recommendation. One of his main concerns was the pervasiveness of "the sexual theme" ["el tema sexual"] in the novel, which had made it impossible for him to censor specific passages: "no hemos podido hacer tachaduras.... Todo el libro es sexo, como se puede comprender" ["we have been unable to delete anything.... The entire book is sex, as one can imagine"] (Expediente de *Pantaleón*). Note that the censor uses the first person plural "we" to emphasize the fact that both censors were of the same opinion about the novel's sexual component. This is in sharp contrast with most censorship reports (including reports on Vargas Llosa's other novels), which are usually written in the first or the third person (e.g., "*the undersigned reader* proposes its rejection" ["*el lector que suscribe* propone su denegación"]), or else make use of passive constructions in which the personal subject is omitted (e.g., "this work *can be interpreted* in two ways" ["esta obra *se puede tomar* de dos maneras"] (Expediente de *Pantaleón*; emphasis mine).

This "we" is also misleading since the first censor's concern about "a book that is nothing but sex" was *not* shared by the second censor who, as a matter of fact, defended the novel's theme and approved its publication. The first censor seems to have been unwilling to take the responsibility of authorizing an immoral and/or antimilitaristic novel, which involved the problem of deciding how seriously it should be taken: "La decisión de tomarlo en serio o en broma, corresponde a la Superiodidad, y si luego la autoridad judicial levanta el secuestro, ella cargará con la responsibilidad" ["The decision to take it seriously or as a joke belongs to the Superior Authority, and should the judicial authorities lift the sequestration, they will bear the responsibility for it"] (Expediente de *Pantaleón*).

The "Superioridad" did not follow the first censor's recommendation, but certainly took notice of the anticipated commercial success he had predicted for the novel. The perpetual problem of the censors was that of balancing the solid sales figures that Vargas Llosa's writing regularly reported against their concern regarding the political implications and the "obscene character" displayed by so many of his works, especially the earlier ones.

Conversación en la catedral, for instance, was regarded as a "political, Marxist, anticlerical, antimilitaristic, and obscene novel"["una novela política, marxista, anticlerical, antimilitarista y obscena"], one that not only depicted "love scenes between lesbians" ["escenas de cama entre lesbianas"], but also reflected a critical view of the elite and of the political repression of leftist movements in Peru. The novel, said the censor, "will make the current Peruvian government angry, without a doubt" ["sin duda, molestarán al actual gobierno del Perú"], and simultaneously it will give Seix Barral an opportunity to "establish comparisons and correlations" between the Peruvian and the Spanish political systems (Expediente de *Conversación*).

In the case of *Pantaleón y las visitadoras* its projected profitability carried the day when it came to a final decision. Fortunately the evaluation of the second censor had argued, unlike his colleague, that the exaggerated portrayals in the novel should be understood from "a strictly literary standpoint" ["desde un punto de vista estrictamente literario"] that would recognize "once more the mastery of this author and his great command of the [Spanish] language" ["una vez más la maestría del autor y su dominio del idioma"] (Expediente de *Pantaleón*). The novel, he concluded, did not offend the "military in general terms," but perhaps did attack the Peruvian Army, which was of little concern for the Spanish authorities. There was no direct reference to the Spanish military in the novel, which, as was often the case with the fictionalization of Latin American military figures and political improprieties, left no room for doubt as to its immediate target:

> Debido al tema es lógico que existan algunas libertades de lenguaje.... Entiendo que tal y como está tratado el tema de la novela, con una cierta ironía, amén de la oposición manifestada por ciertos militares a la creación del Servicio, no existe ofensa al Ejército en general, otra cosa será quizás en relación con el Ejército peruano.

Given the theme it is logical that there are some licenses in the use of language.... I understand that the novel's theme is treated with a certain irony, except for the expressed opposition of certain military authorities to the creation of the (Special) Service. There is no offense to the Army in general terms, its relation to the Peruvian Army is perhaps another matter. (Expediente de *Pantaleón*)

The opposing views of the two censors in regard to the novel's seriousness or playfulness had been indirectly addressed in the jacket copy Seix Barral simultaneously submitted to the Spanish authorities. On the back jacket, the publisher defined the novel as "a farce and a fable" ["una farsa y un apólogo"], employing "raw material" ["material bruto"] such as letters, officials documents and reports, and went on to declare that it was "a splendid satire" providing "a moral reflection" ["una espléndida sátira y una reflexión moral"] on the protagonist's devotion and dedication to a secret military mission carried out to "its last consequences" ["sus últimas consecuencias"].

Apparently, however, the censors did not pay close attention to the book jacket and their reading was not guided by the publisher's blurb, even though they were exercised by similar concerns. It took the intervention of the "special prosecutor," Fiscal Sr. Herrera, to resolve the issue, by concluding expeditiously and definitively on May 14, 1973 (only three days after the censors' reports were written) that, although the book jacket—for reasons not connected to the text—was not admissible, the pornographic content of the novel was "softened" by the fact that it is set in Peru:

> La cubierta fuera. No es tolerable. Aunque la novela es bastante *pornográfica* podría autorizarse, pero no de mantenerse la cubierta. Existen páginas muy cargadas, pero teniéndose en cuenta, que la situa (sic) en Perú, ello suaviza el contenido novelado.
>
> The book jacket is out. It is not admissible. Even though the novel is quite *pornographic*, it could be authorized, but not if the book jacket were to remain. There are highly charged pages, but the novel's content is softened given the fact that it takes place in Peru. (Expediente de *Pantaleón*; emphasis in original).

And so the disagreement was settled. Peru was not Spain, and the military in these two countries were different. The prosecutor, in the end, was more concerned about the anticipated massive display of the novel's sexy cover illustration (for instance, at *El Corte Inglés*) than he was disturbed by the ambiguities of the novel's satirical or farcical take on the Peruvian military. His outright rejection of Carlos Mensa's painting *Mono desnudo* [*Naked Ape*] demonstrates that "pornography" or "obscenity" in images sometimes weighed more heavily in the estimation of the censorship authorities than words.[9]

For Barral, it was obviously just the opposite. The written text had priority over Mensa's painting, which he quickly agreed to remove from the cover. On May 18, 1973, only four days after the "special prosecutor" had banned the jacket, and in order to make sure that no further problems with the censors would arise, Barral ordered the withdrawal of the novel's official May 10 submission at the Ministry of Information. That same day, after learning that Seix Barral was willing to resubmit the novel with a new jacket, the authorities declared, in advance of the fact, that "the Publishing House will eliminate the book jacket, and, as per the instructions of Prosecutor Herrera, we will allow the edition to circulate under Official Silence. Madrid. May 18, 1973" ["la Editorial anulará la sobrecubierta, circulando la edición por Silencio, de conformidad todo ello con el Fiscal Sr. Herrera. Madrid, 18 de mayo de 1973"] (Expediente de *Pantaleón*).

A day later, on May 19, Seix Barral confirmed in a written note to the censorship office that it would resubmit the novel with a different book jacket (Fig. 2.1, 2.2). The new submission officially took place on May 23, but somehow the new cover was approved on May 22: "Leido (sic) el contenido de la sobre-cubierta adjunta, que anuncia la obra de Mario Vargas Llosa, titulada 'Pantaleón y las visitadoras,' no ofrece motivo alguno objetable. Madrid, 22 de mayo de 1973. Firmado: Ángel Aparicio. Lector n. 18" ["Having read the enclosed book jacket that announces the work of Mario Vargas Llosa entitled *Pantaleón y las visitadoras*, there is no reason to object to it. Madrid. May 22, 1973. Signed by Ángel Aparicio, Reader number 18."] (Expediente de *Pantaleón*).

The fact that the new book jacket was approved a day before it was officially submitted underscores one's impression that all concerned—the censors as much as Barral—were in a hurry to approve publication. Even if the date was mistakenly entered in the report, it is still apparent that final approval took no more than one day. Rather than requiring a new reading of the novel, the censors were content to focus, as the "special prosecutor" had directed, on the new jacket, which depicted in red and green tones the hydroplane *Dalila* and the river boat *Eva*, in reference to the "Special Service's" means of transportation.[10] The censors perhaps did not realize that, in the novel, red and green are the "Service's" emblematic colors:

"green for the lush and beautiful countryside of the Amazon Region" and "red for the virile ardor of our recruits and soldiers" (*Captain Pantoja* 42). Less innocent than it appeared, the new jacket made direct reference to Pantaleón's designs for the prostitution service's emblem, but relied on an actual reading of the novel to make that connection.

The censored cover, on the contrary, revealed its meaning at a glance. The ape's face caught in a woman's naked body figured the sexual "primitivism" of army recruits in remote areas of the jungle. Mensa's painting embraced these primitive desires by portraying the suggestive image of a woman who, like a "visitadora" preparing to perform "a service," seductively undresses and, in so doing, reveals the fierce face of an ape.[11] The painting was not only an offense to morals but also an "antimilitaristic provocation," which the authorities could not tolerate (Armas Marcelo 319).

For Barral, the jacket incident would have been only a minor setback to his plans. Other jackets, like the one for *La ciudad y los perros*, had been quite successful despite their tamer imagery (Fig. 2.3). He was certainly more interested in gaining fast approval so as to begin the massive distribution he had planned for Vargas Llosa's new novel. So he chose not to challenge the censors' decision. The authorities, for their part, obviously welcomed Barral's response.

They too were interested in moving the approval process forward and, despite their objections to the novel's major themes (prostitution, religious fanaticism, the military's ambiguous morality) had opted therefore for censoring the pictorial rather than the textual. For, as one of the censors had made clear, it was impossible to delete specific passages in a novel that was "all sex."

One specific section of the novel's text, however, did catch the attention of the second censor. This was Pantaleón's first-year report on the "Special Service" (officially known as "SSGFRI," Special Service for Garrisons, Frontier and Related Installations). In it, Pantaleón confirms the institutionalization of the "visitadoras" (who now have adopted a "Hymn of the Special Service"), and provides statistical data to show his accomplishments, detailing, for instance, the number of "services" performed by the "visitadoras"—"540 monthly per specialist," and a total of "62, 610" for the year (*Captain Pantoja* 116-120). But this is not what the censor objected to. Rather, he saw the sexual explicitness exemplified by the "Hymn," as a valid example of the "licenses in language use" ["libertades de lenguaje"] that the novel's theme required (Expediente de *Pantaleón*).

Fig. 2.1: Book cover. Mario Vargas Llosa's *Pantaleón y las visitadoras* (Seix Barral, 1973) [censored cover]. *Source: Ministerio de Cultura. Archivo General de la Administración.*

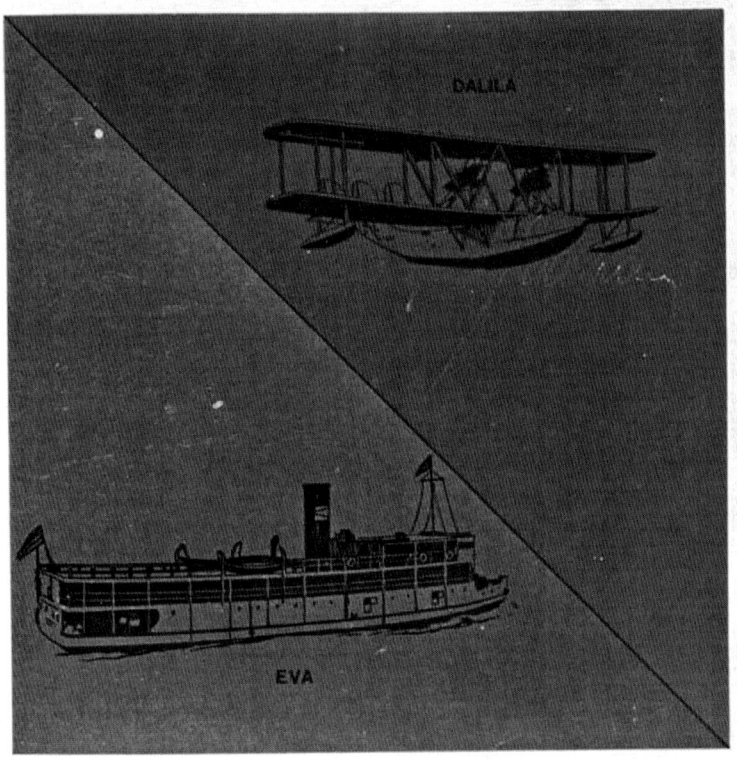

Fig. 2.2: Book cover. Mario Vargas Llosa's *Pantaleón y las visitadoras* (Seix Barral, 1973) [replacement cover]. *Source*: Ministerio de Cultura. Archivo General de la Administración.

Fig. 2.3: Book cover. Mario Vargas Llosa's *La ciudad y los perros*. 4th ed. (Barcelona: Seix Barral, 1974).

So it is ironic that, in the novel itself, the lyrics of the "Hymn" are censored by Pantaleón's superiors. He expeditiously agrees to the required changes, showing not only compliance with military authority, but also his personal agreement with the goals that underlie their demands. But Pantaleón's superiors are not concerned with language either; *their* demand is that the Hymn's refrain and first stanza be changed so as to include mention of navy personnel as well as infantry. Pantaleón sees that the requested corrections "improve" the "Hymn," and dutifully reports that they have been made: "Que se ha procedido a solventar las deficiencias del Himno, enriqueciéndolo con las siguientes modificaciones" (*Pantaleón* 1995, 170) ["Correction of the the shortcomings of the Hymn has gone forward by enriching it with the following changes" (*Captain Pantoja* 130; translation modified)].

Pantaleón's officialese and avoidance of the first person remind me, of course, of the cautious style of the Spanish censor's reports I have been reading. And so does his nervous subservience to authority and flattery of his superiors. Following the military's chain of command practices, he is obliged to praise his superiors' "recommendations" (which incidentally are quite capricious). These recommendations, he is careful to acknowledge, enrich and improve the "Hymn," arguably Pantaleón's only "literary creation," while he himself is guilty of an "unpardonable carelessness." By contrast, it is the very flawlessness of Pantaleón's own meticulously thorough reports that his superiors find unnerving, as General Scavino indicates: "Le ruego que en el futuro nos ahorre los detalles escabrosos de su trabajo" (*Pantaleón* 1995, 121) ["I request that in the future you spare us the scabrous details of your work" (*Captain Pantoja* 92)]. They detail his secret operation so extensively that they represent a threat to the secretive character of the mission.[12] And so, in the end, it turns out. Pantaleón's persistence as a report writer, and his determination to record every single aspect of his secret mission, results in the "Special Service"'s becoming an "open secret." Through his twenty-six reports meticulously recording the genesis, development, and dissolution of the "Special Service," Pantaleón inadvertly defies his superiors' order to keep a low profile, and the "cat"—if I may be forgiven a doubtful pun of my own—is out of the bag. As Pantaleón's reports filter through to the various factions of the military, internal opposition to his mission grows and the "Special Service" that is his pride and joy—has to be abandoned.

The novel reproduces only seven of Pantaleón's reports (dated between August 1956 and October 1957) along with another fourteen reports from his superiors. Pantaleón's first four reports offer a plethora of lubricious details about the preparations that led to the formation of the "Special Service"—contacts with the local brothel's madam, research on venereal disease, and "sexual aberrations," gathering "cheap manuals" on sexuality (Dispatch 1), evaluating costs and time schedules for "each service" (Dispatch 2), testing various oils and ointments for sexual potency (Dispatch 3), and setting up procedures for "utilization centers" (Dispatch 4) (*Captain Pantoja* 22–35, 39–43, 65–68, 112–115), all related in Pantaleón's brand of bureaucratic prose. Once the "Service" has been successfully established and the operation is in full gear, the novel feels able to omit Dispatches 5 through 14, skipping directly to 15, and then on to 18 and 26. These omissions of course produce an incomplete sequence, which leads the reader to wonder about Pantaleón's "missing reports," their content as well as whereabouts. Where are those reports? What do they say? Why are they not reproduced?

To me, it is surprising that the Spanish censors made no mention of the fact that more than 50 percent of the novel's text is in the form of these reports, or that the report sequence is so suggestively incomplete. The censors, themselves inexhaustible writers of official reports, were attentive to Vargas Llosa's mastery of "new" narrative techniques (e.g., Expediente de *Conversación*) but seemingly blind to this pastiche of prose closely related to their own. In this case, Vargas Llosa had conceived his novel as an example of "military literature," as a "literature composed of dispatches, passwords, proclamations, and long speeches" (Genesis 8). He felt he had "under-utilized a very rich component" of his experience in the military, and decided to appropriate the "jargon" of the military and to reproduce its "lifeless administrative jargon" (Genesis 12). But the censors either missed this point, together with its relevance to their own literary labors, or thought it inappropriate to draw attention to it.

Vargas Llosa's own experience, in this respect, relates to the dictatorial regime of General Odría (1948–56), to which his novels often refer. Ricardo Cano Gaviria calls Vargas Llosa "the vulture of Odría's eight-year term" ["el buitre del ochenio odriísta"], in that his writing appears to feed so frequently on "the carrion left over" from his personal experience of military life and life under a militaristic regime (Cano Gaviria 127). General Odría became Perú's president in October 1948, after carrying out a successful coup d'état against the duly elected president José Luis Bustamente y Rivero (1945–48). During his eight years as president, Odría cracked down on leftist groups and embraced both the dominant classes and the underclass through economic liberalism (Klarén 289–307). Vargas Llosa, who grew up during the so-called *ochenio odriísta*, drew heavily on his memories of the period in his early novels, namely, *La ciudad y los perros*, *La casa verde*, and *Conversación en la catedral*. The censors who read *Conversación en la catedral* agreed with this understanding of that novel: "es una diatriba contra el presidente Odría, y en menor medida, contra el presidente Bustamante" ["it is a diatribe against President Odría, an in a lesser degree, against President Bustamante"] (Expediente de *Conversación*). Joseph Sommers' argument that the language used by the military personnel portrayed in *Pantaleón y las visitadoras* departs quite significantly from that of the 1970's Peruvian Army, so that the novel therefore has "no historical relevance whatsoever" (108) fails to take account of the relevance of the Odría period to the novel. It is rather that, as argued by Efraín Kristal, Vargas Llosa's novels "can be read as a kind of amalgam of his own experiences" in "transmuted," "modified," and "self-contained" form (29–30). And, of course, it could also be argued, against Sommers, that the Franco regime offered Vargas Llosa a "modified" reminder of his previous exposure to the military in his native Peru. But Franco's censors, it seems, were oblivious to the very possibility of such a parallel.

Chapter 3

Cuban Nights Falling

The Revolutionary Silences of Guillermo Cabrera Infante

The publication history of Guillermo Cabrera Infante's masterwork *Tres tristes tigres* (1967) [*Three Trapped Tigers*] is, without a doubt, the most compelling case of productive censorship experienced by any Boom writer in Franco's Spain. Unlike many of his fellow Latin American writers, Cabrera Infante had tasted firsthand the censorship of authoritarian regimes before coming to Spain, having had to deal with it under both the Batista and the Castro regimes. But, odd as it may seem, it is precisely under authoritarian regimes that his writing thrives, and his literary career is effectively propelled by the very censorship he appears to fight against. As Michel Foucault and Judith Butler have suggested, writers under censorship (the Boom ones are no exception) internalize censorship as a form of exercized power and their attempts at circumventing it result precisely in the (re)production of such a discourse of power.[1] This is particularly true for Cabrera Infante, who always positions himself as a writer constrained by authoritarian forces, but, in the end, accommodates to them (and reproduces them) in his writing. Rather than limiting his creativity (as one might naively expect), his confrontation with authoritarian regimes and their censors is ultimately productive for his writing.

This becomes evident when one examines his early literary career in Cuba and his dealings with the Franco authorities in Spain. In the 1950s, Cabrera Infante was an innovative writer and film critic who opposed the Batista regime (his family included a number of Communist activists and had faced the *Batistato*'s oppressiveness as a consequence). In the early 1960s, he cashed in the political capital he had accrued from being persecuted by Batista forces and rapidly became a leading member of the Revolution's cultural elite. But by the mid-1960s he had abandoned the Castro doctrine and had agreed to publish an altered version of *Tres tristes tigres* that adhered to the Spanish censors' demands.

During the process that led to the publication of this novel in 1967, Cabrera Infante sought permanent residency status in Franco's Spain, astutely positioning himself as a "reformed revolutionary." Suspicious of the ambiguity of this emerging political shift, the Spanish authorities, however, denied his petition. Shortly thereafter (sometime in 1967) he settled in London, and by 1968 he had become a pariah of the Castro regime and one of the most visible Cuban exiled authors. That year *Primera Plana* published "La respuesta de Cabrera Infante" (translated as "Answers and Questions" and reprinted in *Mea Cuba*), a questionnaire about his views on revolutionary Cuba and about his reasons for leaving the island in 1965. In "La respuesta," Cabrera Infante mocks the leadership of Fidel Castro, refers to him as a "Krokodil soviético" [Soviet "Krokodile"] and lashes out savagely against revolutionary Cuba:

> Cuba ya no era Cuba. Era otra cosa—el doble del espejo, su *doppelgänger*, un robot al que un accidente del proceso había provocado una mutación, un cambio genético, un trueque de cromosomas. Nada estaba en su lugar.... El socialismo teóricamente nacionaliza las riquezas. En Cuba, por una extraña perversión de la práctica, se había socializado la miseria. (Cabrera Infante, *Mea Cuba* 32–34)

> Cuba now was not Cuba. It was another thing—the double in the mirror, its *doppelgänger*, a living robot in which some manufacturing slip-up had provoked a mutation, a genetic change, a chromosome switch. Nothing was in its place.... In theory, socialism nationalizes wealth. In Cuba, by a strange perversión of the practice, they had socialized poverty. (Cabrera Infante, *Mea Cuba* 14–15; translation modified)

These are the two Cubas, the Revolutionary one and its *doppelgänger*, that are at the center of Cabrera Infante's own literary career, as first a hard-core revolutionary and later a specular reflection of his revolutionary days. While this transformation helped his career in the Spanish book market, the inflammatory remarks against the Revolution in "La respuesta" got him blacklisted in Cuba and prompted the regime to expel him from the writer's union. The Cuban regime also blocked the circulation of his books on the island. For an upcoming Boom author who had parted company with the Revolution by 1965, Franco's Spain, where Seix Barral was promoting new Latin American writers, seemed the logical next step.

Carlos Barral, however, was himself a supporter of the Revolution and a participant in Cuban cultural institutions such as *Casa de las Américas*. Barral had first visited Havana in 1963 following an invitation from the poet Heberto Padilla, who later (in 1971) would become a symbol of anti-*Castrismo* in intellectual circles shortly after being accused by the Revolutionary authorities of subversive activities. In 1965, just as Cabrera Infante was planning his final exit from Cuba, Barral again visited the island to promote his firm and serve on the jury of the *Casa de las Américas* literary prize for best short story (Barral, *Almanaque* 15-20). Cabrera Infante's opposition to Castro, therefore, chilled his relationship with his new Spanish publisher. For the censors, on the other hand, Cabrera Infante's early involvement with the Revolution seemed more relevant than the oppositional stance against Castro he had adopted in the 1960s, and they would continue to evaluate his books with the greatest suspicion. This, however, ultimately turned out to be advantageous for Cabrera Infante. The difficulties he had with the Cuban and then the Spanish authorities placed him in the enviable position of being a censored writer who had suffered the "injustices" of two authoritarian regimes of opposing political ideologies. On the face of it, these censorial experiences in the 1960s must have seemed like a liability on the Spanish literary market; but during the 1970s, they in fact enhanced Cabrera Infante's literary cachet. Censorship, in a sense, becomes for him a commodity that matures and increases in value as he presents himself as an "always censored" writer, and this was especially the case after his exile from Cuba.

Having been censored "right and left" certainly helped him promote the subsequent reprints and translations of *Tres tristes tigres* as well as the novel's addenda (namely, "Metafinal" and "Epilogue for Late(nt) Readers").[2] But, as it turned out, his masterwork would become the sempiternal censored Boom novel, and I would argue that it remains a not fully uncensored text up to this day if we consider the radical transformation the novel underwent between 1965 and 1966 as a consequence of its passage through Spanish censorship. After Franco's death in 1975 and again in the late 1970s and 1980s, the author asked Seix Barral to remedy the censorial cuts in the 1967 edition by reprinting a more complete version of the novel, but the publishing house refused to do so. The reasons for Seix Barral's refusal are not clear. It seems quite likely, though, that the publisher, having banked his firm's reputation on a pro-revolutionary writer, felt somewhat betrayed by Cabrera Infante's public denunciation of the Castro regime as early as 1968. Likewise, it was not in Seix Barral's interest to publicly acknowledge that the novel released in 1967 was "less revolutionary" than the author had originally intended, or worse, that the publishing house had cooperated with the censorship authorities in an effort to negotiate a censored version of the novel. It was not until 1990 that Editorial Ayacucho published a "complete" version of *Tres tristes tigres* that included twenty censored sections not present in the 1967 edition. Seix Barral finally agreed to publish the *edición definitiva* in 1999—two years after Cabrera Infante was awarded the Cervantes Prize—in commemoration of the writer's seventieth birthday.

In preparation for that edition, Cabrera Infante sent a representative to Spain's National Archive to retrieve the novel's original galley proofs of 1965, which are currently held in the author's file. According to the story told to me by one of the employees of the Archive's photoduplication services, the author's agent said that Cabrera Infante had lost the original manuscript, which likewise could somehow not be located at Seix Barral. So it turned out that Cabrera Infante relied on the same Censorship Services that had altered his novel in 1965 and 1966 to revise and produce the definitive edition of 1999. This anecdote reveals a kind of post-mortem collaboration with Franco's censors, and underscores the fact that *Tres tristes tigres*'s relation to the censorship apparatus continued well beyond the novel's evaluation by the Spanish censors in the 1960s.

Cabrera Infante's autobiographical account, "Orígenes: cronología a la manera de Laurence Sterne" ["Origins: Chronology in the Style of Laurence Sterne"], confirms that censorship, in effect, shaped much of his writing and literary persona.[3] As early as 1952, in one of his first skirmishes with censorship in Cuba, Cabrera Infante was fined, detained, and forced to quit his studies at the School of Journalism because of the publication of a short story in *Bohemia* that contained "English profanities." The "cronología" goes on to indicate that, between 1954 and 1957 while Cabrera Infante worked for the film magazine *Carteles* under the penname of G. Caín, he began "a number of clandestine activities" that led to his interrogation before the "Bureau for Repression of Communist Activities" (Cabrera Infante, *Tres tristes tigres* 1999, 504). Given this anti-Batista pedigree, it is no surprise that, as already mentioned, when the Cuban revolution triumphed in 1959, he rapidly became a leading figure of the pro-Castro intelligentsia, heading the National Council for Culture and the newly created Film Institute. But, most visibly, he became the editor of *Lunes de Revolución*, the cultural and literary supplement of *Revolución*, the newspaper that was the voice of the regime. In his post as editor in chief, Cabrera Infante had the opportunity to publish in *Lunes* some of the short stories that the *Batistato* had censored. In 1960 Ediciones R ("R" for Revolution), another state-sponsored publishing venue, released a compilation of these short stories entitled *Así en la paz como en la guerra* [translated as *Writes of Passage*]. This edition included a preface explaining that the stories in the collection depicted "the nausea of living under Tyranny" (with a capital "T" in the original) in Batista's Cuba around 1958, a statement well in line with the mission of the Revolution's publishing house (Cabrera Infante, *Así en la paz* 1960, 9).[4]

In 1961 Cabrera Infante had his first confrontation with the regime when the Castro authorities blocked the release of his brother's documentary "P.M." ["Pasado Meridiano"]. The film authored by Sabá Cabrera Infante and Orlando Jiménez Leal portrayed Havana's night scene and luxuriated in the excitement and vivacity of Cuban nightlife and its devotees.[5] After a bitter confrontation between the cultural and political apparatuses of the regime, the film was characterized as reminiscent of the Batista years' exploitation of Cuban nightlife and of Havana's status as an anything-goes party spot. The "Comisión de Estudio y Clasificación de Películas" ["Commission for the Study and Classification of Films"] refused to issue the certificate needed for public viewing, claiming that the film "was poisonous to the interests of the Cuban people and their Revolution" in that it offered "a partial picture of Havana's nightlife that impoverishes, disfigures, and impairs the Cuban people's attitude in the face of the artful antirevolutionary attacks ordered by U.S. imperialism" ["una pintura parcial de la vida nocturna habanera, que empobrece, desfigura y desvirtúa la actitud que mantiene el pueblo cubano contra los ataques arteros de la contrarrevolución a las órdenes del imperialismo yanki"] (Acuerdo del ICAIC sobre la prohibición del film *P.M.*, Luis, *Lunes* 223–225). Because of Guillermo's involvement in the release of the film, the censorial experience of "P.M." turned out to be fatal for *Lunes*, which was shut down by the regime. The official justification was high production costs due to a shortage of paper. In other words, the Cuban government would not waste precious resources for a cultural enterprise that could turn against them.

By way of response to this censorial episode, Guillermo Cabrera Infante decided to create a novel about a nocturnal journey in prerevolutionary Cuba, one in which the devotees of Havana's nightlife (the "tigers") would be set against the emerging revolutionary forces in the background. This original idea was the driving force behind the creation of *Tres tristes tigres*, as the author has declared in several occasions. To set the scene, Cabrera Infante chose a huge black singer named *La Estrella*, loosely based on the deceased Puerto Rican singer Fredy. Just before the closing down of *Lunes,* Cabrera Infante had published a short story entitled "Ella cantaba boleros" ["She Sang Boleros"], which was a literary recreation of Fredy and the Cuban night scene that "P.M." so vividly portrayed. This short story would provide the main narrative line of *Tres tristes tigres*, and the censored film the inspiring force for Cabrera Infante's portrayal of Havana nightlife as seen through his "cinematic eye": "Entonces yo quise hacer P.M. por otros medios" ["so I wanted to remake P.M by other means"] ("Las Fuentes" 48).

This ultimately productive experience with censorship in Cuba anticipated the similarly productive experience that his dealings with the Spanish censors between 1965 and 1974 would turn out to be. While at first Cabrera Infante had been seen as a harsh critic of the Franco regime and an advocate of the Revolution, in Spain he now quickly repositioned himself as a reformed revolutionary. The publication history of *Tres tristes tigres* illustrates this repositioning. After two years of scrutiny by the censorship authorities and arduous negotiations with them led by his publisher Carlos Barral, the writer reworked his novel quite significantly in order to satisfy many of the censors' demands, and following the Director of Censorship's suggestions, he resubmitted it in 1966 under a different title. "Vista del amanecer en el trópico" ["View of Dawn in the Tropics"]—the original typescript that had won the 1964 *Biblioteca Breve* Prize—was thus presented to the Spanish censors in March of 1965 and resubmitted in October of 1966 as *Tres tristes tigres*.[6] As the outcome of a series of appeals and behind-the-scenes negotiations, the novel that finally appeared in 1967 was significantly different from the original typescript of 1964.

A decade later, in 1974, by which time Cabrera Infante had been recognized as a bonafide *anti-Castrista* (perhaps looking for his own redemption too, after having agreed to alter his novel as the censors had demanded), he published *Vista del amanecer en el trópico (Relatos)*, which was based on the censored leftovers or scraps from "Vista." In a sort of déjà vu episode, the Spanish censors at first thought that the 1974 *Vista del amanecer (Relatos)* was the same book they had previously censored in 1965. Despite this initial confusion, the collection was approved and published by Seix Barral. It included thirty-four passages describing guerrilla fighters and revolutionaries that had appeared as one of the main narrative lines in the 1964–65 typescript "Vista" but were not included in *Tres tristes tigres*. But Cabrera Infante transformed the content of these passages quite significantly since in *Vista del amanecer (Relatos)* they appear, not as a testimonial to the struggle against Batista (as they had in the original "Vista"), but rather as a critique of the Cuban Revolution itself, within the long-term historical context of needless violence in Cuba from colonial times to the present.

That censorship has had this kind of transformative effect on his writing is recognized by the author himself, who has been quite outspoken about it (albeit selective in his memory). In an explanatory preface entitled "Lo que este libro debe al censor" ["What this book owes to the censor"] published in the 1990 Ayacucho edition of *Tres tristes tigres*, Cabrera Infante acknowledges (perhaps in tongue-in-cheek fashion) that his dealings with the Spanish censors were far from being counterproductive for his novel. At the start he allows that censorship has been a prime force in his literary production from the outset —"Mi vida es la historia de la pelea de un escritor contra los censores" ["My life is the story of the squabble between a writer and the censors"] ("Lo que este libro" ix)—and by the end he is able to conclude with an ironic assertion that his novel resulted from teamwork between the censors and the writer: "¡Ah mi querido censor! Cuánto me habría gustado conocerlo, usted que es mi hermano, mi semejante, mi hipócrita lector. Después de todo, los dos hemos escrito el mismo libro" ["Oh my dear censor! I wish I had met you. You are my brother, my peer, my hypocritical reader. After all, we two have written the same book"] ("Lo que este libro" xiii).[7] It is this paradoxically cooperative spirit between the censors and the writer that turned out to be the determining factor in the final composition of *Tres tristes tigres*. When his American publisher asked him about the possibility of incorporating the censors' cuts into the English translation, Cabrera Infante declined to do so, arguing that his Spanish "censor had finally become a creator" and had produced the best "editorial work" he ever saw ("Lo que este libro" xiii).

But how much does his novel really owe to the censors? How are we to take the author's remarks? How to interpret their irony? As playful and self-deprecating, as they appear? Or as betraying a less obvious self-disculpatory motive? If we follow his version of events, it would seem that the effects of censorship on his work were in fact minimal and somehow inconsequential, whereas the evidence shows that they were actually considerably more significant than his tone suggests. To believe Cabrera Infante, the censors only altered passages that made slighting reference to the military and God or were too sexually explicit: "Cada vez que yo ponía tetas, palabra aceptada por la Academia y su diccionario...mi obseso censor la eliminaba y ponía senos...." ["Every time I used the word tits, a word that is accepted by the Academy's Dictionary...my obsessive censor crossed it out and replaced it by breasts...."] ("Lo que este libro" xii). But the available documentation at the *Archivo*, while it does show that some sexually explicit passages were deleted, contradicts the implication that the censors' alterations were minor. Moreover, the documents there show that Cabrera Infante's reworking of "Vista" into *Tres tristes tigres* following his departure from the Revolution after the "P.M" fiasco and the closure of *Lunes* came out of a compromise between his publisher and the censorship authorities that the author could not refuse, the only alternative being to have his novel published in Mexico: "La alternativa sería publicar el libro original en México y dejar que cayera en el olvido, ya que entre México y España se interpone, inmensa, la mar" ["The possibility would be to publish the original book in Mexico and let it be forgotten, since Spain and Mexico are separated by the boundless sea"] ("Lo que este libro" xii).

The truth of the matter, then, is that, over and beyond the "editorial work" the censors did for him, Spanish censorship was productive for Cabrera Infante in other ways as well. As the negotiations with Barral and the Director of Censorship Services were taking place in 1965, the writer was desperately seeking an exit permit from Cuba, to which he had had to return in order to attend his mother's funeral. This visit, according to the author's own confession, resulted in his desire to rewrite "Vista" extensively, given that by then he had moved away from the Revolution. Conveniently for him, the Spanish censors had blocked the release of "Vista" and were willing to give him the option of resubmitting it with extensive corrections. They would have had an interest of their own in doing so, since Cabrera Infante was obviously evolving in a direction they could only approve of, a direction that would also make it easier for them to approve a revised version of "Vista."

Having put the Cuban authorities on notice and fearing that he wouldn't be allowed to leave the island, Cabrera Infante capitalized on the opportunity given to him by the Spanish censors and used a letter from Carlos Barral in order to justify to the Cuban authorities the urgency of his departure:

> Para salir de Cuba, ahora al exilio, tuve que usar los proverbiales silencio y astucia de Joyce. Una de las argucias que empleé tenía la forma de una carta que me envió mi editor español Carlos Barral. Decía él que mi libro, que entonces se llamaba "Vista del amanecer en el trópico," requería mi pre-

sencia en Barcelona (que desde Cuba se veía como una ciudad menos franquista que Madrid, aunque franquismo y fidelismo compartían algo más que la intimidad de las efes) para corregir pruebas.

To leave Cuba, now an exile, I had to use Joyce's proverbial silence and astuteness. One of the smart moves I made was in the form of a letter that my Spanish publisher Carlos Barral sent me. He said that the correction of the proofs for my book, then called "Vista del amanecer en el trópico," required my presence in Barcelona (which from Cuba was seen as a less Francoist city than Madrid, even though "Fidelism" and "Francoism" shared something more than their F's)]. (Cabrera Infante, *Tres tristes tigres* 1990, xi)[8]

What is most interesting here is not whether the Cuban authorities bought his excuse to leave the island (why, one wonders, would they allow a de facto exile to go to Franco's Spain in order to publish a novel that was likely to be reactionary in some fashion?). Rather I find this episode telling in respect of the transatlantic forces that intervened in the publication of *Tres tristes tigres*. It is clear that the censors actively contributed to the novel's transformation from the original manuscript of "Vista." Furthermore, this transformation is unique in that censorship operates here as an equally productive force on both sides of the Atlantic.

The Cubans, in effect, released a dissident who had been censored in Cuba and was now seeking literary success in Spain, and the Spanish took in a reformed revolutionary who was a promising best-selling author willing to comply with the censors' requirements and to resubmit a revised version of his novel. Exposed as he was to censorial practices on both sides of the Atlantic, Cabrera Infante's case exemplifies the fluidly dovetailing interests of two authoritarian regimes. The Spanish saw in him a potential informant on anti-Franco activities in Spain and in Cuba. Meanwhile, through Carlos Barral's involvement with *Casa de las Américas* and conceivably through exchanges with the Spanish police, the Cubans could monitor Cabrera Infante's dissidence and keep a measure of control over his criticisms of the Castro regime.

1. THE CUBAN CONNECTION: SPAIN AND THE "INFANTES OF THE REVOLUTION"

Early in this story, Guillermo Cabrera Infante and his brother, the filmmaker Sabá Cabrera Infante, were pegged by the Franco authorities as promoters of revolutionary ideals. The Infantes had contacts among left-wing groups that opposed the dictatorial regime in Spain and their visibility in these circles was a serious concern for the censorship authorities who feared that approving Guillermo's manuscript "Vista" would encourage the promotion of left-wing ideals in Spain. But as had been the case with other Latin American recipients of the *Biblioteca Breve* Prize, the authorities, while feeling compelled to censor any ideology contrary to the regime, nevertheless weighed in the balance the significant revenues that a potential best seller like Guillermo's award-winning novel could bring on the book market. The censors were aware that both Infantes overtly disliked the Franco regime, but their main concern lay in the suspicion that through them (particularly through Guillermo who was in 1965 an appointed consular official) the Cuban government was sponsoring left-wing and pro-Republic groups seeking to unseat the Franco regime. Evidently, the Spanish authorities saw in Guillermo and Sabá two "heirs" of Cuba's revolutionary ideals. In a sense, they were viewed as "Infantes of the Revolution" (the label is mine and not the censors') whose mission was to proselytize on behalf of the Castro doctrine in 1960's Spain. The 1965 censor's report on "Vista" includes a memorandum from the "Oficina de Enlance" ["Liaison Office"] that is quite specific about the Infantes' role in promoting a left-wing agenda:

> Guillermo Cabrera Infante es un diplomático cubano acreditado en Bruselas, y cuyo hermano residente en España, y muy introducido en los círculos artísticos madrileños, desarrolla actividades pro-comunistas, ayudado financieramente por la representación diplomática cubana.
>
> Guillermo Cabrera Infante is a Cuban diplomat accredited in Brussels, and his brother who resides in Spain is very well known in artistic circles in Madrid where he engages in pro-communist activities that are financed by the Cuban diplomatic delegation. (Informe de Oficina de Enlace, "Vista" 1965)[9]

Aware as they were of Guillermo's involvement in the revolutionary intelligentsia and of his efforts to expose the Franco regime in *Lunes de Revolución*, but unaware, at this stage, of his growing disaffection from Castroism, the Spanish authorities at first refused to approve "Vista," then, on the grounds that not only was the novel politically charged but its author was an agent of the Cuban government. Under Guillermo's tenure *Lunes* had published several denunciatory essays against the Franco regime like "Una posición: veinte años de Franco" ["A Position: Twenty Years of Franco"] (30 March 1959), and most notably two special issues that must have seemed inflammatory in the eyes of the Franco regime.[10] The first of these, *La larga noche de España* [*Spain's Long Night*], appeared on July 18, 1960, and commemorated the twenty-fourth anniversary of the beginning of the Spanish Civil War with a dedication "to all those who fought, fight, and will fight for the Republic." The second issue on Spain, *La España rebelde* [*Rebellious Spain*] (February 20, 1961), included Guillermo's scathing assessment of the Franco regime in his article "Las vértebras de España" ["Spain's Vertebrae"]. This essay appeared along with a brief photographic report entitled "Lo que la censura no ve" ["What Censorship Does Not See"], which depicted the poverty in the city streets and shantytowns of Spain. The pictures show women lining up for food, a family with a baby living on the street, and a woman washing clothes in a shantytown. They are interspersed with drawings by Picasso (Fig. 3.1). These illustrations "are courtesy of the *Comité de Amnistía para presos politicos y emigrados politicos*" ["Amnesty Committee for Political Prisioners and Immigrants"] ("Las vértebras" 2).

While most of Cabrera Infante's political essays have been reprinted in anthologies like *Infantería* or *Mea Cuba*, these early essays have not circulated since they first appeared in the early 1960s. As Jacobo Machover has pointed out, *Mea Cuba* (an essay collection published in 1992) does not include any of Cabrera Infante's political essays prior to 1968 because they are "in stark contradiction with his posterior political stances" (165). Machover further asserts that Cabrera Infante "chose to take refuge in silence" ["prefirió refugiarse en el silencio"] after his departure from Cuba in 1965: "Toda su literatura tendrá como objetivo, inconfesado, de expiar la culpa. Eso explica en gran parte el silencio de su exilio definitivo y sus primeras declaraciones a la revista *Primera Plana*. Ese silencio oculta también un itinerario intelectual y político" ["All his literature will have the undeclared objective of expiating his guilt. This explains for the most part his silence in his final exile and his first statements in *Primera Plana*. This silence likewise covers up an intellectual and political itinerary"] (164–5).

"Las vértebras de España" is one of the "silenced" essays that has been, in effect, hidden from the public since it appeared in 1961.[11] This essay is particularly interesting, not just because it exposes Cabrera Infante's pro-revolutionary and anti-Franco political views, but also because it does so by using Madrid's nightlife to expose the regime's social inequalities. Emulating the nocturnal journey of his brother's documentary, "P.M.," "Las vértebras" presents seven vignettes (or

Figure 3.1: Photographs: "Lo que la censura no ve." *Source: Lunes de Revolución* (February 20, 1961).

scenes) in which three noctambulists—Cabrera Infante and two other "tigers," Ernesto Vera and Carlos Franqui (author of *Diario de la revolución cubana* [*Diary of the Cuban Revolution*])—wander the streets of Madrid "to meet its people in their habitat" ["para conocer a la gente en su habitación"] (7). Their first encounter is with an old man dressed in shabby clothes who seems appalled by the misery in the city, the poverty in the countryside, and the luxurious lives of rich landowners. The old man, a former émigré, who has lived in Argentina for ten years, confides to the three tigers that Spain also needs a revolution in order to end the injustices of an oppressive regime: "¡Aquí necesitamos un Barbas! (Se refería a Fidel)" ["We need a bearded guy! (He was referring to Fidel)"] (9). After a brief stop at a working-class pastry shop recommended by the old man, the night journey continues at "cabaret Casablanca," a well-known dance spot frequented by prostitutes, where the tigers are most struck by a shamefaced old woman who works in the establishment's bathroom distributing toilet paper and condoms, a job they describe as a "more painful form of prostitution" (10).

The tigers' exploration of Madrid nightlife's shabbier side is only the prelude to their more political encounters, which take place the following night when they meet an anarchist who fought against Franco during the Spanish Republic and, more importantly from the point of view of Cabrera Infante's future, two unnamed Spanish writers. The anarchist, "a thin man run down by years of misery" (12), is in the tigers' view the embodiment of "all that is good in Spain" and a noble example for men who fight against fascism and for the Cuban Revolution. The propagandistic tone of the essay peaks at the point when the anarchist is said to thank the Cubans for their conversation in this manner: "Cuando regresen a Cuba, dígale a ese Castro de vosotros qué (sic) en España también creen en él" ["When you return to Cuba, tell that Castro of yours that in Spain we also believe in him"] (13).

In the final vignette of "Las vértebras," the tigers receive firsthand information on the difficulties Spanish writers face under the Franco regime. As regards censorship, one of the two unnamed writers declares that writing in Spain is "a useless exercise," the other calls it an "absurd one" given that there are "three censorships and any page that manages to survive them comes out castrated in the process" (13–14). These two writers become Cabrera Infante's informants on the publishing conditions writers in Spain had to face. (In 1961—the time when the tigers wander in nocturnal Madrid—the new censorship regulations were not yet in effect and the censorial process was tight and not open to negotiation in contradistinction to what would occur in 1962 when Fraga Iribarne began to overhaul the censorship procedures.) Taking another jab at the Franco regime, the concluding paragraph of the last vignette offers a frank denunciation of the regime's censorial machinery together with criticism of the inaction of intellectuals in Spain who fail to fight it:

> En España todo lo que se escribe y que tiene alguna intención, hay que publicarlo en el extranjero. Las editoriales están dominadas por un capitalismo miserable y por la vigilancia sin sueño de los curas. Al ejército, como siempre, la cultura le pone cosquillas en el gatillo de la pistola. La Falange no ha incubado más que escritores resentidos, grandes aprovechados... y disidentes sin gran coraje.

> In Spain anything written in a certain spirit must be published overseas. The publishing houses are ruled by penny-pinching capitalism and relentlessly supervised by priests. As for the Army, as usual, culture gives them an itch in the triggers of their guns. The Falange has hatched only resentful writers, arrivistes... and dispirited dissidents. (13)

Only three years after the publication of these lines, Cabrera Infante was to join in the "penny-pinching capitalism" of the publishing industry in Spain. His nocturnal adventure in Madrid during the 1960s was not only an inspirational journey comparable to that of "P.M." and *Tres tristes tigres*, but also a fruitful one as well, if only because it reveals that he had already had occasion to test the waters and get a firsthand sense of the censorial machinery he would have to deal with in publishing his works in Spain. More importantly, it was an anticipation of the kind of denunciatory writing against Cuba that Cabrera Infante would undertake later in his career.

While essays like "Las vértebras" or the photographs in "Lo que la censura no ve" did not go unnoticed by the Spanish authorities, it is clear that they did not actually circulate in Spain, except perhaps in clandestine fashion. Given that to this day the Spanish National Library does not hold issues of *Lunes*, it is likely that the Spanish authorities received their information on Guillermo through diplomatic channels. Another possibility is that the Spanish censors were suspicious simply because he was a political appointee of the Cuban government and, even though communication between the Franco and Castro regimes had remained fluid and open since the early days of the Revolution, the ideological differences between the two regimes continued to be a major consideration in the censors' examination of novels.

But be that as it may, in *Mea Cuba* Guillermo Cabrera Infante offers a different view of how the Spanish authorities knew about his pro-revolutionary and anti-Franco writings. In an essay titled "Encuentro con la inteligencia de Franco" ["An Encounter with Franco's Intelligence"] Guillermo recalls that around 1966 the Spanish police rejected his application for permanent residency because he had refused to share with them detailed information about prominent militants in the Cuban Communist Party: "el policía me decía que la policía de Franco no le diría nada a la policía de Fidel Castro. Esos intercambios entre policías solían ocurrir." ["The policeman told me that the Franco police would not say anything to the Fidel Castro police. These exchanges between the police departments were frequent"] (*Mea Cuba* 138). This is an indication that exchanges between the two regimes did occur despite their opposing ideologies. But more importantly it suggests that it may have been the Cubans who volunteered the information on the Infantes to the Spanish police by way of making mischief for a turncoat. By 1966 Guillermo was no longer an active member of the Revolution's cultural apparatus and had become a de facto exile. This possibility is raised when Cabrera Infante mentions that the Spanish police enumerated some of the more incriminating essays he had written in Cuba expressing his opposition to the Franco regime:

> Me enumeró casi como un vendedor (un vencedor en mi caso) los números de *Lunes* dedicados a la República, a la guerra civil, a la literatura española del exilio. Lo que se llamó con patetismo político "la España que sufre".... Después de demostrarme mi interrogador, que era un índice, que la policía de Franco no tendría una mano larga pero sí una memoria prodigiosa, Proust posmoderno, pasó a solicitar mi colaboración. (Cabrera Infante, *Mea Cuba* 138)

> Almost like a newsvendor he listed for me the issues of *Lunes* devoted to the Republic, to the Civil War, to the Spanish literature of exile: what was called in a sloppy, tear-jerking way "long-suffering Spain."... My interrogator, an undercover cop, made it clear to me that Franco's police might not have a long arm but certainly had the longest memory, they were a postmodern Proust. Then he went on to solicit my collaboration. (Cabrera Infante, *Mea Cuba* 448; translation modified)

Even though the Infantes had been flagged in Cuba as critics of the Cuban regime after the "P.M." affair, for the Spanish authorities they were still under suspicion. Documents that the Foreign Affairs Ministry declassified in 2001 revealed that the Spanish government kept under surveillance second-rank Cuban diplomats who may have been cooperating with Communist groups in Spain. A classified memo on the activities of Spanish Republicans in Cuba dated December 4, 1959 details that Havana had become a major site for the activities of exiled activist groups like the "Unión de Combatientes Españoles" ["Union of Spanish Combatants"], the "Asociación Pro la Libertad de España" ["Association for the Liberty of Spain"] and the "Frente Unido Democrático Español" ["United Spanish Democratic Front"]. There was a rumor that these groups were projecting the unthinkable enterprise of launching an attack on Spain and Portugal from the Moroccan coast in an effort to unseat the dictatorial regimes on the Peninsula. While what the memo calls this "fantastic plan to organize landings from Morocco on the Portuguese coast" ["fantástico plan de organizar desembarcos en las costas portuguesas desde Marruecos"] lacked credibility, the Spanish authorities were nonetheless concerned with the significant following that the Havana-based groups had garnered among Spanish exiles in the Americas, notably in Mexico and Venezuela. (Another brilliant plan, the memo reveals, was to install a radio station in Morocco to broadcast to France, Portugal, Spain, and Latin America.) Although these exiles were seen as impractical dreamers and not a real threat, the Spanish authorities still suspected that the Cuban government was somehow behind them, and feared that with its support they might eventually manage to spread their "subversive propaganda" throughout Spain and Latin America. To forestall any Cuba-sponsored attempts to infiltrate Spain, the classified memorandum recommended the immediate surveillance of Cuban diplomats in Europe: "precisa vigilar nombramientos diplomáticos secundarios, más aún que los aparentemente más importantes" ["it is imperative to keep second-rank diplomats under surveillance, in particular those who are apparently less important"] (Nota informativa reservada sobre actividades de republicanos y comunistas españoles en Cuba 1–3).

This, then, was how Guillermo's consular position in Belgium came to arouse suspicion concerning the Infantes' activities in Spain, and, in becoming an impediment to the publication of "Vista," threw up an obstacle to his aspirations to conquer the Spanish literary market in the 1960s. More than any other Boom writer, Guillermo's dealings with the censors were caught between the polarized ideologies of two nations on each side of the Cold War. Such opposing ideologies, however, did not preclude an improvement in Hispano-Cuban relations during the Boom period when close relations between Spain and Cuba, which, in a sense, Cabrera Infante and Carlos Barral represented, continued to be the rule.

The Spanish Foreign Affairs Ministry file on Cuba also reveals that this mutual complicity between the Franco and Castro regimes was forged in the first days of the Revolution. As Cuba tried to define its new government following Batista's fall and the Revolution's triumph on January 1, 1959, Spain played a significant role in the negotiations between the Revolutionary leaders and various Latin American diplomatic missions. Spain insisted on maintaining "fraternal" exchanges with Cuba, the two nations having left behind the "maternal" (read "colonial") dependency of the past. This message of "fraternal cooperation" (which, of course, included political and economic cooperation) is laid out in a series of twenty telegrams between the Spanish ambassador, Juan Pablo de Lojendio (the Marquis of Vellisca) and Fernando María Castiella (Minister of Foreign Affairs) between January 1 and 10, 1959. The telegrams reveal that for Franco Cuba was a major economic and political interest, and that Castro sought Spain's support early on in an effort to bring other Hispanic nations to accept the Revolution. The goal, on Castro's part, was of course to legitimize the new Cuba through wide international recognition.

While securing its communication channels with the revolutionaries, Spain for its part worried about its investments on the island, particularly after the Iberia Airlines headquarters in Havana were vandalized. Right away Ambassador Lojendio publicly denied in the Cuban media that Spain had sold arms to Batista and emphasized that, in fact, many "persecuted revolutionaries" had received protection from the Spanish authorities; he followed up in an interview with Havana's *Diario de la Marina* dated January 8, 1959: "Mi Embajada no solamente no ha tramitado ninguna petición de armas, como tampoco lo hizo la Embajada de Cuba en Madrid" ["Neither my Embassy nor the Cuban Embassy in Madrid had filed any request for arms"] (*Diario de la Marina*, 8 January 1959; included in the Telegrams file). By denying involvement in arms sales and by procuring the safe repatriation of *Castrista* Cubans residing in Spain (Telegram from Castiella to Lojendio, 9 January 1959), Franco looked to ensure, and strengthen, his close ties with the revolutionary government. Had not his ambassador in Cuba described Castro, the son of a Galician immigrant (a *gallego* like Franco), as someone who "almost speaks with a Spanish accent"? (Telegram from Lojendio to Castiella, 8 January 1959).

However, the Franco regime also had less high-minded motives in its pursuit of a "fraternal cooperation" with the Cubans. Lojendio and Castiella expressed concern regarding the role the revolutionary regime would play with respect to anti-Franco groups on the island that were led mainly by Republican exiles. The day after the

Revolution's triumph the ambassador warned the Foreign Affairs Minister of the activities undertaken by Spanish exiles in Cuba: "elementos republicanos españoles tratan [de] aprovechar momento escitación (sic) revolucionaria y desorden en radio y televisión para propagar sus declaraciones" ["Spanish Republican elements are trying to take advantage of this time of revolutionary fervor and of the havoc at radio and TV stations to advance their own agenda"] (Telegram from Lojendio to Castiella, 3 January 1959). Two days later, Lojendio concludes that "leaders of the July 26 Movement have maintained contacts with Spanish Republicans" that could be detrimental to Spain's interests (Telegram from Lojendio to Castiella, 4 January 1959). According to one of the last telegrams in the series, these efforts to mute the opposition to Franco at the height of Cuba's revolutionary movement were successful: "the revolutionary regime has silenced the attempts by Spanish Republicans to spread disturbing propaganda" ["regimen (sic) revolucionario ha silenciado intentos propaganda perturbadora republicanos españoles"] (Telegram from Lojendio to Castiella, 8 January 1959).

Despite the Revolution's early willingness to "silence" the propaganda of Republican groups and to restrict their activities, Spain continued, of course, to monitor the comings and goings of people affiliated with the Revolution. When the Infantes appeared on the Madrid scene in the 1960s, they were thus almost inevitably seen as part of the "Cuban connection" the Franco regime thought was responsible for instigating Republican groups in Spain. The fact that Carlos Barral endorsed Guillermo as the winner of the *Biblioteca Breve* was another red flag for the authorities. They knew perfectly well about Barral's support of the Revolution and his trips to Cuba, where he was involved with intellectuals on the island. For instance, during his visit in 1965, he addressed a group of Republican exiles and other Spanish expatriates at an event sponsored by *SACE* (*Sociedad de Amistad Cubano-Española* [Society for the Friendship of Spain and Cuba]) and reported by the exiled community's newspaper *España Republicana* (Barral, *Almanaque* 21–29). But, in a way, both the Castro and the Franco regimes were willing to allow this kind of dissidence to operate since the Spanish wanted the Cubans to inform them of the whereabouts of the Republican dissidents in Spain while the Cubans had an interest in the surveillance of their nationals abroad. While the telegrams of the Foreign Affairs Ministry do not address the specific case of the Infantes or Barral's activities in Cuba, they do show that the early communications between the two regimes established the paradoxical relationship of cooperation between two ideologically adverse regimes that writers like Cabrera Infante came to epitomize, and, even more interestingly, ultimately benefited from in the Spanish literary market.

In this connection, it is important to note that Carlos Barral's visits to the island, while mainly seen by the Cubans as supportive of the Revolution's cultural apparatus, were promotional tours for his firm as well. Obviously, this is an aspect of his visits that would have pleased the Spanish authorities, who had been vigorously promoting the book industry as one of the regime's major exports and were concerned about competition from countries like Cuba. During Barral's first visit in 1963 not only did he promote the collections of Seix Barral (particularly his list of Latin American writers), but he also had an opportunity to become acquainted with the Cuban literary market and its publishing industry. In an interview with Mario Mainade, Barral explained to the Cubans his firm's pan-Hispanic approach to literature (a sure selling point in the Latin American book market) and announced the release of a new edition (published in 1965) of *El siglo de las luces*, by one of the island's most prolific writers and a major figure among the Revolution's cultural elite, Alejo Carpentier.[12] In the same interview, Barral offered a reflection on the Cuban publishing industry, which he saw as a future competitor but not an immediate one: "La industria editorial cubana, aún muy joven, progresa a una velocidad tremenda. Sus libros presentan portadas con un estilo a la altura de los más modernos del mundo... Además tienen portadas valientes que se destinan a un gran consumo" ["The Cuban publishing industry, though still young, is rapidly growing. Their books have highly modern and stylish jackets.... Moreover they offer daring jackets that are designed for wide consumption"] (Barral, *Almanaque* 17). This kind of information concerning marketing techniques was of interest both to Barral and to Spanish officialdom, each of whom (albeit with different agendas) were determined to conquer the Latin American book market of the 1960s.

2. "SILENCING" THE CUBAN REVOLUTION: FROM "VISTA DEL AMANECER EN EL TRÓPICO" TO *TRES TRISTES TIGRES*

When Seix Barral presented "Vista" to the Spanish censors in March 1965, the publisher could not predict that the approval process would be one of the most litigious and complex of all the Boom novels published in Franco's Spain. After all, the firm had managed to get approval for other Latin American novels that had won the *Biblioteca Breve* Prize (such as Vargas Llosa's *La ciudad y los perros* in 1962 and Leñero's *Los albañiles* in 1963), even though they too had seemed controversial to the censors from a political standpoint. But the Cuban Revolution and its possible ramifications among Spanish left-wing groups at home and in exile made Cabrera Infante's case particularly troubling for the Spanish authorities, who were asked to accept a novel about the revolutionary uprising in Cuba that simultaneously represented an erotic journey into Havana's cabarets and nightclubs. Carlos Barral, well known to the censorship authorities as an advocate for revolutionary Cuba, had to make use of all the legal means at his disposal (he filed two appeals before the censorship authorities) as well as his personal contacts with the Director of Censorship Services, Robles Piquer, in his effort to get "Vista" approved.

The history that led to the release of *Tres tristes tigres* in 1967 begins with the first censor's report on "Vista" in April 1965. Written by José Vila Selma (as identified in the documents of the appeal process) it lays out three major obstacles to the approval of "Vista": the novel's glorification of Castro's struggle against Batista, the "pornographic" and "irreverent" content of several narrative lines, and the author's "essential Marxist tendency," which for Vila Selma made his job as censor almost impossible: "Dada la manera como está concebida la narración no admite tachaduras y habida cuenta de la tendencia marxista esencial en la intención del autor" ["Given the way in which the narrative is conceived and the essential Marxist tendency in the author's intention (the novel) cannot be readily corrected"] (Expediente de "Vista" 1965). Two months after this report was filed, and before communicating the result of the evaluation to the publisher, the various censorship authorities concurred in an internal memorandum with the grounds laid out in the first censor's report for rejecting "Vista": the novel was "pornographic," espoused revolutionary ideals, and, equally disturbing, its author was "a Cuban diplomat accredited in Belgium" (Informe de Oficina de Enlace, "Vista" June 22, 1965). This internal memorandum was probably not sent to the publishing house as part of the notification process, but the animosity toward "Vista" in the first censor's report made it clear to Barral and Cabrera Infante that approval would not be gained without significant modifications to the text. Another indication of the censor's hostility to "Vista" that was similarly predictive of a contentious fight ahead lay in his remarks about the literary quality of the text, which he labeled "a bad imitation of the French school of the 'nouveau roman'" ["una mala imitación de la escuela francesa del 'nouveau roman'"] (Expediente de "Vista" 1965). This judgment added yet another stumbling block: in view of Spain's self-attributed role as guarantor of Hispanic culture, literary quality was one of the standards Spanish censors were most attached to.

Unwilling to accept the flat rejection of the novel, Barral responded, less than a month after receiving the first censor's scathing report, with an appeal or *recurso de revisión*, requesting on July 19 that a second censor examine the novel. This *recurso* was denied as this second censor, Ramón Álvarez Vignier, concurred with Vila Selma's evaluation of "Vista":

> Nos encontramos con una obra escrita en una imitación de la moderna novela francesa, que Sartre denomina la antinovela, ya que en la misma no se sigue ninguna de las reglas clásicas, en cuanto a tiempo, situación y desarrollo. Al faltarle al autor dominio sobre la materia, nos ha producido una obra entrecortada y sin hilación.... Por otra parte... quiere situar en la época de la lucha entre Castro y Batista... para expresar *su tendencia y simpatía marxista.*
>
> We are confronted with a novel that imitates the modern French novel, which Sartre calls the anti-novel since it does not follow any of the classical rules of time, situation, and plot. Unable to master his material, the author has produced a fragmented and incoherent work.... Also, the novel is situated at the time of the Batista-Castro conflict... in order to express its *Marxist sympathy and tendency.* (Expediente de "Vista" 1965; emphasis in original)

Echoing the first censor's reservations (the novel was flawed, had too many pornographic passages, and was a Marxist manifesto of sorts), Álvarez Vignier, as required by the *recurso*, presented a more detailed report on the novel's lack of merit. He went on to excoriate the publisher for not having "presented any convincing argument in defense of the book and for having failed to explain his reasons for requesting a new examination of the novel" ["no alega ningún argumento en defensa del libro y de las razones que mueven a solicitar esta nueva lectura en revisión"] (Expediente de "Vista" 1965). In short, he rejected "Vista" outright, and concluded that Barral's appeal had no legal merit.

But Barral's determination and insistence on this occasion was remarkable, and it represents a departure from his handling of certain other, similarly contentious, Boom writers (Manuel Puig comes to mind). He responded to this second report on September 16 by filing yet another appeal, this time a *recurso de alzada* (literally an elevated appeal or final appeal), which required the intervention of the highest censorship authority. The *recurso de alzada* was likewise denied, and, in October 1965, the publisher was notified that there were no other legal means at his disposal to pursue the publication of "Vista." The *recurso de alzada* presented four supporting statements (*alegaciones*); the first two were procedural and explained that the novel had been submitted according to the 1938 printing law, and a *recurso de revisión* filed after the initial rejection; the other two (numbers 3 and 4) addressed the legality of the censors' findings and the implications of their refusal to accept "Vista." In the third statement, Barral argued that there was no "factual basis" ["base facticia"] on which to prohibit the novel's "circulation in the Spanish national territory," a prohibition that, in his view, was "contrary to law" ["no se ajusta a derecho"]. He based this claim on a narrow reading of the censors' questionnaire that led him to conclude that the novel did not "contain offenses against Spain, its government, the Catholic Church and its institutions, nor disseminate ideas that could be regarded as dangerous" ["no se contienen ofensas a España, a su gobierno, a la Iglesia católica ni a sus instituciones, ni se difunden ideas que puedan considerarse peligrosas"].[13] In addition, Barral claimed that there were "no subversive ideas of any sort" in the novel despite the fact that it "takes place during the revolutionary conflict in Cuba" ["aunque el libro tenga lugar en Cuba durante la guerra revolucionaria en ningún lugar del libro se hace propaganda de ideas subversivas"] (Recurso de alzada, Expediente de "Vista" 1965).

Barral's claim that "Vista" contained nothing subversive flew in the face of the reputation his firm enjoyed in the censors' eyes as an avant-garde, left-leaning publishing house devoted precisely to the dissemination of "subversive ideas." But he was forced to defend the text within the terms of the 1938 law. As anticipated in the third justificatory statement, Barral's legal argumentation centered therefore on the question of whether the government could lawfully prohibit the novel's circulation, which was perhaps a discreet way of reminding the censors of the revenues he expected from Cabrera Infante's "Vista." The fourth statement further addressed the legal and economic implications of the censors' refusal to allow the publication of a novel destined for distribution, not only in Spain, but also in Latin America and Europe:

> Por primera vez no podrá publicarse uno de los grandes premios de novela de los que se otorgan en España. La inocultable prohibición repercutirá en todos los países de Hispanoamérica en los que el premio goza popularidad así como en los círculos literarios de todos los países europeos en detrimento del prestigio del Orden Jurídico español y de la juricidad de los actos de la Administración Española.

For the first time one of the greatest literary prizes of Spain will not be published. The unconcealable prohibition will have repercussions in all the Latin American countries where the prize enjoys great popular acclaim and in European literary circles, and will be detrimental to the prestige of Spain's Judicial Order and to the juridical acts of the Spanish Administration. (Recurso de alzada, Expediente de "Vista" 1965)

Barral's claims failed to move or please the censors. For their response to the *recurso de alzada* on September 26, 1965, a third censor was brought in to read the novel yet again and write a final report. This third reader, Manuel María Massa, was clearly irritated by the *recurso de alzada*'s claims, and, not surprisingly, rejected all of Barral's arguments. While Massa mentions in passing that the novel's political agenda was indeed an issue, his response to Barral's third statement focuses very largely on issues of moral grounds. He asserts that the novel's "descriptions cannot be characterized simply as crude or expressive of sexual customs" but are "clearly pornographic from a moral standpoint and depressing at a social level" ["descripciones que no se pueden caracterizar únicamente como crudas o expresivas de un costumbrismo sexual, sino claramente pornográficas desde un punto de vista moral y deprimentes desde el plano social"] (Expediente de "Vista" 1965). In other words, he did not object to the novel's setting in the midst of the Cuban Revolution so much as to a novel he thought morally indefensible.

Likewise, Massa was not very receptive to Barral's fourth supporting statement. Riled by the assertion that the censors were jeopardizing Spain's standing in international judicial circles, he labeled it a "self-interested opinion" without any legal force whatsoever. He likewise discarded Barral's claim that the novel should be cleared for publication because it was the recipient of an important literary prize: "tampoco hay motivos suficientes para autorizar escenas que no sólo van contra la moral, sino que repugnan el más elemental sentido de decencia y educación cívica" ["nor are there sufficient reasons to authorize scenes that not only go against morals, but also disgust the most fundamental sense of decency and civic education"] (Expediente de "Vista" 1965). For him, the prize "has no bearing whatsoever on the negative moral qualification of the work" ["para nada influye en la calificación moral negativa de la obra"] (Expediente de "Vista" 1965). As of September 26, 1965, then, Seix Barral had exhausted all his legal options, and it seemed the novel would have to appear elsewhere.

But Barral's series of appeals were only the first assault in his effort to gain approval for Cabrera Infante's novel. A second phase, more personal and less legalistic, followed. This phase took place behind the scenes between February 3 and November 2, 1966. During that time, as Barral and Cabrera Infante corresponded with the Director of Censorship Services, Carlos Robles Piquer, they both came to understand that for "Vista" to be approved the Revolution would have to go unmentioned and the sexually explicit language reworked in such a way as to satisfy the censors' objections. This formulation defines the compromise finally reached by the Spanish censors and Cabrera Infante, after a year and half of negotiations. And it was the reworking of Cabrera Infante's text in light of this agreement that resulted in the transformation of "Vista" into the best-selling novel *Tres tristes tigres*. The need to "silence" revolutionary ideals was the clear message Cabrera Infante had received from all three of the censors who scrutinized "Vista" between March 16 and September 28, 1965. But it was a message that in the end the author gladly accepted, given that by the time the censors had fully confirmed their rejection of the novel he had already begun his own (actual and ideological) parting company from the Castro regime.

Already during the appeal process Cabrera Infante had begun to rewrite his manuscript, and, in consultation with his editor (who in turn had consulted with the censorship authorities), he now agreed to resubmit his novel under the new title, *Tres tristes tigres*. Barral had indicated to Cabrera Infante that failing to submit to the Spanish censors' demands would result in "exiling" his book to Mexico, where it would most likely be published by Seix Barral's partner Editorial Joaquín Mortiz. Trapped in the kind of cultural elitism he had practiced in Cuba and now in Spain, the Cuban author, who despised Seix Barral's sister publishing house in Mexico, was reluctant to accede to this option: "Adonde iban a parar los cadáveres esquizoides de Seix Barral para ser enterrados al otro lado de la frontera: la muerte o la muerte" ["There Seix Barral's schizoid cadavers would go to their rest on the other side of the border: death or death"] ("Lo que este libro debe al censor" xii).[14] To avoid being forgotten in what seemed to him an obscure publishing venture in Mexico, Cabrera Infante followed Barral's advice, and on February 3, 1966 wrote a five-page personal letter to the Director of Censorship, Robles Piquer, explaining his rationale for the transformation of "Vista" into *Tres tristes tigres* and requesting a re-evaluation of the novel under the auspices of the new law governing the publication of books, which was due to take effect later in the year.

This letter is an acknowledgement of the positive effects censorship had had for "Vista," a frank (if perhaps also strategic) admission that the censors' concerns about the novel's stylistic flaws were right on target, and, above all, a plea to have his novel examined a fourth time by the censors. Cabrera Infante tried to persuade the authorities that *Tres tristes tigres* was a different book, and that as such it deserved (from a legal perspective) a new evaluation by the censors. To this end, he thanked Robles Piques for being "kind" and "attentive" to his request, and allowing his desperation to show, expressed a new willingness to cooperate. Publication of the novel was presented as of the utmost importance for his literary career: "ésta (sic) novela mía que desespero por ver impresa, publicada y exhibida y criticada en esta hospitalaria tierra de España" ["this novel of mine that I desperately seek to see in print, published and exhibited and criticized in this hospitable land of Spain"] (Carta a Robles Piquer).

Despite the fact that the same "hospitable land" had rejected his petition for a residency permit and blocked the release of "Vista" for over a year, Cabrera Infante now applauded both the delay and the outcome of the appeals—"puedo felicitarme [por] la interdicción y los períodos entre el rechazo y la negativa final" ["I can congratulate myself on the interdiction and the time that elapsed between the initial and final rejections"]—since, during that time, he had had the opportunity to "revisit the text to make its acceptance viable" ["frecuentar el texto para viabilizar su aceptación"]:

> Tal frecuentación no sólo me permitió ver graves errores de construcción novelística o meros gazapos gramaticales o las inevitables erratas de imprenta, sino reconstruir el libro mismo, al punto que puede considerarse *otra obra, bien diferente* de la que su señoría conoció en el pasado.
>
> Not only did this revisiting allow me to see grave errors in the novel's construction or simple grammatical mistakes and the inevitable typos, but it also allowed me to reconstruct the book itself, to the point that it can be considered *another work, a very distinct work* from the one your lordship knew in the past. (Carta a Robles Piquer, 3 February 1966; emphasis in original).

Addressing the concerns raised by the censors, Cabrera Infante highlights the "grave errors" of "Vista" (the censors had thought the novel a bad imitation of the French *nouveau roman*) and the significant changes he now proposes to make to the offending original. These, of course, he justifies as part of the normal process of revising a work that had been in publishing limbo since 1964. One of the more transparent pretexts he resorts to in the letter is his excuse for eliminating the revolutionary vignettes, which the censors had very largely marked down for deletion in the manuscript presented by Seix Barral. Cabrera Infante explains that he has opted to remove these vignettes in *Tres tristes tigres* because in 1966 his intentions have changed. What he really wants to offer now is "a lyrical solution not an epic one" to the historical events portrayed in the novel: "las viñetas intersticias y finales han desaparecido, dejando su lugar a una solución lírica en vez de épica, personal en lugar de colectiva, transcendente más que histórica" ["the interspersed vignettes and the final ones have disappeared, giving place to a lyrical solution not an epic one, personal instead of collective, transcendent rather than historical"] (Carta a Robles Piquer 1966).

The authorities found Cabrera Infante's explanations less than compelling. This is clear from a confidential note that was produced before determination of the official response, in which the letter is described as "utter nonsense" ["un galimatías"] (Nota sobre el libro "Amanecer en el trópico," undated). It is quite likely that Robles Piquer consulted with those who were familiar with the dossier, and with people in the legal department. There were indeed some real legal issues, such as the fact that the review process for "Vista" had ended with the *recurso de alzada*, so that, as the note spelled out, "the dossier ha[d] been finalized" ["el expediente ha sido concluso"]. But in the event, the note offered the possibility of another review if substantial revisions in all of the areas that the censors had objected to in "Vista" were to be effected in *Tres tristes tigres*, although it went on to warn that "if the work is not modified to a reasonable extent it will undergo the same fate," despite its new title ["la obra sino (sic) viene modificada razonablemente correrá la misma suerte"] (Nota sobre el libro "Amanecer").

While it is not clear whether Barral or Cabrera Infante ever saw this note, it is entirely possible that given the personal exchanges between Barral and Robles Piquer, its message got passed on to the writer. Robles Piquer's official response of March 3, 1966 simply thanked Cabrera Infante for his "ample and interesting explanations" (a carefully noncommittal remark given the content of "Nota") but warned him (much along the lines of the "Nota") that "despite the change in the title it would be difficult to argue" to the censors that the novel was a "radically different" text. At the end of his letter, Robles Piquer recommended that the publisher and the writer wait until the new printing law took effect later in the year, at which point they could expect a less stringent evaluation of the novel (Carta a Cabrera Infante, 3 March 1966).

Following this recommendation, *Tres tristes tigres* was submitted on October 8, 1966 and cleared for publication on November 2, 1966 on the condition that several "obscene, pornographic, irreverent, antimilitaristic, and political" passages be omitted.[15] Despite this conditional approval, the censor who examined the new version of "Vista" had been just as disgusted as his predecessors with the novel's "pornographic episodes," its overall vulgarity, and its lack of linear narrative structure ("la novela es realmente ilegible" ["the novel is really illegible"]). However, he did note the elimination of the episodes concerning Castro's revolutionary struggle (Expediente de *Tres tristes tigres* 1966).

Cabrera Infante describes his interaction with the censorship authorities quite differently from the story told by the files. In a letter addressed the following December to Mario Vargas Llosa, he denies receiving any response from the Spanish censors, and asserts, as if no negotiations with the censors had ever taken place, that the novel may have to be published elsewhere than in Spain:

> escribí a la censura y ni siquiera me contestaron la carta, así que el libro tendrá que publicarse fuera de la Madre Patria. Aproveché el tiempo para hacer cambios en el libro, quitar cosas (todas las injustificadas, injustificables viñetas revolucionarias, volví al plan primitivo, y reestructuré toda la parte final, añadiendo una porción de novela que tenía en un borrador y que iba a formar parte del libro y puse el título que yo quería antes, que quizá te guste. Ahora se llama *Tres tristes tigres*, que es el comienzo de un trabalenguas cubano, "Tres tristes tigres en un trigal. . .")

> I wrote to the censorship authorities and they did not even respond to my letter, so the book will have to come out outside of the Mother Land. I made good use of my time to make changes to the book, suppress things (all the unjustified ones, unjustifiable revolutionary vignettes, I went back to my original plan and restructured all of the last part adding a previously drafted section and incorporating it into the book, and I changed the title the way I wanted it before, hope you like it. Now it is called *Three Trapped Tigers*, which is the beginning of a Cuban tongue-twister, "Three trapped tigers in a wheat field. . . .") (Letter to Vargas Llosa, 29 December 1966)

The fact that this letter is dated December 29 is surprising since the records at the National Archive clearly indicate that *Tres tristes tigres* was cleared for publication on November 2 and the publishing house notified of the approval on November 11 (Expediente de *Tres tristes tigres* 1966). It is as if Cabrera Infante's letter to Vargas Llosa were purposely written to cover up the fact that these negotiations had taken place, stressing that he had written to the censors, but did not expect any further communication with them while, in fact, the communication channels had been quite active. The possibility of some kind of cover-up on Cabrera Infante's part is also supported by the fact that his letter to Vargas Llosa is open to the public at the Firestone Library's Rare Book Division at Princeton University, while his letter to Robles Piquer—a copy of which is also included in the author's personal collection at Princeton—is restricted until the year 2020 as per the writer's request (the author's recent death may soon lift some of these restrictions). Fortunately for researchers, a copy of the original letter is currently available at Spain's National Archive.

While the censors' reports, memoranda, and correspondence such as Robles Piquer's letter to Cabrera Infante all point clearly to the fact that the Cuban Revolution had to be suppressed if the novel was to gain approval in Spain, one can see from the materials at the Firestone Library how Cabrera Infante responded to this requirement. Since 1988 the Library has held the various drafts of *Tres tristes tigres* and *Vista del amanecer en el trópico (Relatos)*, as well as some of the cutouts from the "Vista" galley proofs that the author actually pasted onto the pages of the 1966 bound manuscript "Tres tristes tigres." This bound manuscript is the one the author submitted to the Spanish censors on October 8, 1966, after Barral's appeals failed to gain approval for "Vista." The materials in Spain and Princeton complement each other convincingly, and the available documentation makes it easy to identify which of the author's own cutouts of "Vista" made it (by a transatlantic transfer) into the Princeton manuscript. Among these bits there is the missing page 89 of the "Vista" galley proofs at the National Archive, which is pasted onto page 200 in the Princeton manuscript "Tres tristes tigres."

When one compares and contrasts the Princeton manuscript with the "Vista" galley proofs, it is evident that Cabrera Infante depoliticized his novel (while retaining references to Batista's ailing nation) and opted for a highly braided narrative structure that transformed the more linear narratives of "Vista." By 1966 the novel had become an apparently playful text that included, along with endless puns and departures from traditional page layout, blank pages (*Tres tristes tigres* 1967, 261–3), mirror pages (*Tres tristes tigres* 1967, 264–5), and graphic illustrations (*Tres tristes tigres* 1967, 211, 214, 217–8). The novel's new playfulness also generates a new tiger, Bustrófedon (the fourth tiger along with Silvestre, Cué, and Códac), a figure representative of Cabrera Infante's Joycean aspirations. Bustrófedon (whose name refers to writing one line from left to right and the next from right to left) emerges in the 1966 version as the tigers' inspirational leader, their linguistic ideologue, and, above all, a skillful master of puns, tongue twisters, and parodies. The figure of Bustrófedon, with his multitudinous linguistic games, signals a clear shift on Cabrera Infante's part from the political themes of "Vista" to the aesthetic exploration of *Tres tristes tigres*. At the same time, the "left to right" and "right to left" writing implied by his name alludes to the author's own political shifts in the period when "Vista" was being written, and then transformed into *Tres tristes tigres* and *Vista*. While politics is apparently denied by Bustrófedon's playfulness, his own (playful) name (playfully) brings politics back in again. The political message of the original "Vista" remains detectable even as it disappeared, in a typical case of Cabrera Infante's development of the proverbial Joycean "silence and astuteness." Thus, as a result of the evolution hinted at, we have a dispersed text that includes, in the newly added chapters, a number of digressive sections: "La Muerte de Trotsky," "Rompecabeza," "Algunas revelaciones," and "Bachata" (*Tres tristes tigres* 1967, 205–443), which deviate from the main narrative line (Cuban nightlife at the time of the revolutionary uprising) and divert attention from it so that it occupies a much less prominent place in the novel as a whole.

This move toward complexity and linguistic play clearly differentiates *Tres tristes tigres* from "Vista." Revolutionary vignettes and political messages are replaced by self-conscious exploration of a new novelistic form based on wit and puns that gestures toward the idea of *novela total* (the "all-encompassing novel"). An extreme view of the novel's new character is expressed by one of the tigers as they discuss the Bustrófedon-inspired proposal for "aleatory literature":

> La única literatura posible para mí, sería una literatura aleatoria.... O mejor una lista de palabras que no tuvieran orden alguno.... Se repartiría al lector, junto con el libro, un juego de letras para el título y un par de dados. No habría más que tirar los dados.
>
> The only possible literature for me would be aleatory literature.... Or better, a list of words in random order.... The reader would receive with the book a set of letters for the title and a pair of dice. All he would have to do is to throw the dice. (*Tres tristes tigres* 1967, 330–331)

Needless to say, *Tres tristes tigres* does not follow this proposal to the letter. But Cabrera Infante's method of composition is loosely based on the tiger's precepts. This is evident when the author cuts and pastes the original chapters of "Vista" haphazardly so as to produce the puzzle-like composition of the new text. A few examples of this technique will suffice. The 1966 version takes apart the therapy sessions that appear in one single narrative block "El último show" in "Vista" (1965, 76–79) and inserts them as eleven separate sections in *Tres tristes tigres* (1967, 71–4, 80–1, 127, 133, 157–9, 169, 204, 271, 279–80, 289, 446–7); the chapter "Nights in Havana" ("Vista," 1965, 46–50) is likewise cut and pasted randomly into the opening pages of the "Debutantes" section, whereas it was originally placed in the middle; and the epilogue of *Tres tristes tigres*, "Una desconocida en el parque" (which replaces the final vignette of a dying revolutionary hero in "Vista"), comes from an early episode in "Vista" titled "El último show" (86–87).[16]

Such changes, which show Cabrera Infante's interest in fragmenting and dispersing the more linear narratives of "Vista," are designed to make *Tres tristes tigres* a complex assemblage that puzzles the reader with its textual dispersion. Textual complexity of this kind was problematic for the 1966 censor, who complained that the novel was "illegible." His suspicion was aroused that something lay hidden in the multiplicity of voices and nonlinear narrative lines. And indeed, an argument could well be made at this point in which the transformation of "Vista" into *Tres tristes tigres* would be read as indicative of the author's pursuit of a complex narrative form capable of producing (in a self-censorial fashion) what, in "Censorship and the Imposition of Form," Pierre Bourdieu describes as a tantalizing effect of concealment: "specialized languages often produce the effect of concealment by excluding certain agents from communication" (*Language* 138). Certainly, the novel aims at "systematic alteration" of the common language (137), the upshot of which is to discourage nonspecialized readers from accessing the text. Even for more experienced readers, the displacement of focus toward disentangling formal intricacy and wordplay also effectively "screens" such political comment as remains from "Vista," in the sense that a screen simultaneously hides, and reveals the hiding of, what it conceals. Something that is not stated, and cannot be stated, is somehow being uttered in such a text, which functions in that way as an "indexical" sign, but of an unconventional kind in that it indicates an object whose identification is left entirely to the reader's own responsibility. Such is the "proverbial silence and astuteness" the author prizes.

Despite *Tres tristes tigres*'s formal virtuosity, though, it is fair to say that even without the censored vignettes the novel is not completely devoid of political commentary. The 1966 version incorporates a parodic section on Trotsky's death that obviously caught the censor's eye without seeming as problematic as the revolutionary vignettes in "Vista": "lo único que ha hecho es sustituir el capítulo de la acción castrista por otro dedicado a la muerte de Trotsky" ["the only thing he has done is to replace the chapter on Castro's activities by one devoted to Troksty's death"] (Expediente de *Tres tristes tigres* 1966). Furthermore, political commentary remains in the novel in the form of open criticism of Batista's regime. But in the absence of any glorification of the revolutionaries' struggle against this dictatorial regime, the attack on Batista seems not to have troubled the censors.

Their change of heart in this respect is not surprising if one examines their corrections on the "Vista" manuscript. These are quite extensive when it comes to passages that explicitly address the revolutionary cause. For instance, they disapproved of any phrase that was critical of authoritarian regimes. The following censored sentences are typical: "Trató de poner fin a una tiranía" ["He tried to put an end to tyranny"] ("Vista" 1965, 7) or "Nos persigue la Tiranía y no Nos persigue la policía o el ejército. No dijeron exactamente que les perseguía la Tiranía y eso fue lo que los convirtió en héroes" ["We are persecuted by Tyranny and not the police or the army. They didn't exactly say that Tyranny was persecuting them and this made them heroes"] ("Vista" 1965, 93). Similarly, the original manuscript's portrayal of state institutions was scrapped; in particular the scenes that show the brutality with which such institutions dealt with any form of insurgency: "la policía, el ejército, la secreta o lo que fuera descubrió el lugar y cercó la casa-vivienda y los hicieron salir, gritándoles con un megáfono que se rindieran. Los fueron matando mientras salían uno a uno" ["the police, the army, the secret police or whoever found out the place and surrounded the rooming house, and they made them come out, shouting at them with a bullhorn to surrender. They killed them one by one as they came out"] ("Vista" 1965, 44). Correspondingly disturbing for the censors was the description of the revolutionary guerrilla members as heroes issuing a final message of hope before their death with a view to encouraging those who would pursue the cause: "Entre la prisió (sic) y la muerte, escojo la muerte" ["Between prison and death, I chose death"] (1965, 100), or the closing sentence of "Vista," "la imagen del heroe (sic) muerto cuando vivo" ["the dead hero's image alive"] ("Vista" 1965, 105). This kind of outspoken exaltation of the revolutionary cause reflects Cabrera Infante's militancy in the early years of the Revolution, and its semi-propagandistic style (all the revolutionaries and insurgents are heroes who will go down in history while the police and the army are tyrants) as good as invited the Spanish authorities to require the deletion of such passages. The anti-Franco resonance was unmistakable.

But these are the passages that disappeared in *Tres tristes tigres*, leaving only some subtle references to the fighting in the Sierra and the jabs at Batista's regime, which were acceptable to the censors because the Franco regime had not supported the *Batistato* during its final phase. Most of the political commentary that remains in *Tres tristes tigres* depends on a metaphor: that of the ailing health of the cabaret singer Cuba Venegas, The Star [*La Estrella*] of Cuban nightlife and the female protagonist of "Ella cantaba boleros." Venegas epitomizes nocturnal Havana, and is often referred to by the tigers as Cuba, so that there is an implied equivalence between the starlet's physical condition and Batista's Cuba: "Cuba tenía que descansar, se sentía enferma, 'mala,' me dijo" ["Cuba had to rest, she felt sick, 'bad' she told me"] (*Tres tristes tigres* 1967, 112) or "y ví a Cuba, entera como está, más alta y más bella y más puta que nunca" ["and I saw Cuba, forthright as she is, taller, more beautiful, and more of a whore than ever"] (*Tres tristes tigres* 1967, 272). The parallel between the starlet's physical condition and the country's is kept up throughout the entire novel. It culminates in the artist's death, which signals both the death of Cuban nightlife and the death of Batista's regime. Cuba dies from indigestion while touring in Mexico and her death is seen by Códac, the tiger who narrates her story throughout the novel, as the end of an era that no one will remember: "lo que sí que es verdad es que ella está muerta y que dentro de poco nadie la recordará" ["what's really true is that she is dead and soon nobody will remember her"] (*Tres tristes tigres* 1967, 286).

The parallel between Cuba Venegas and Batista's Cuba was the core idea of "Vista," and it survives into *Tres tristes tigres*. Indeed, in deferring to the Spanish censors' demands, the 1967 version focuses even more strongly on Cuban nightlife, adding three new sections to "Ella cantaba boleros" (120–6, 128–32, 160–68) and making *La Estrella* the narrative center of the novel, as the author suppresses all direct reference to the revolutionary guerrillas and buries his allusions to the fighting in the Sierra Madre in the mix of voices, puns, and graphic illustrations that gives *Tres tristes tigres* its texture. In the end, then, Cabrera Infante appropriated Cuban nightlife as a quasi-nostalgic representation of a vanished Cuba for an exiled writer; and thus, ultimately, as a delayed response to the Revolution's censorship of "P.M's" depiction of nocturnal Havana.

The stark changes between "Vista" and *Tres tristes tigres*, which for the most part have gone unnoticed in previous scholarship, speak volumes concerning Cabrera Infante's chameleon-like series of personal and literary transformations, played out in his dealings with the authorities of Franco's Spain. In a relatively short period of time (fewer than three years, 1958–61), he had fought Batista, feverishly supported the Revolution, written and spoken against the Franco regime (1960–61); and now in 1964–65, he was willing to turn his back on Castro and amend the political content of his novel to satisfy the censors' demands, which themselves now corresponded substantially with his own new political orientation. Thanks to the encounter with Spanish censorship, "Vista" had been transformed and, arguably, improved if we accept the author's own characterization of the benefits of the censors' intervention. Indeed, it was transformed beyond recognition. The sexually explicit descriptions of Cuban nightlife had been softened as Cabrera Infante replaced the more "obscene and pornographic" passages with innuendo. The relatively linear narrative of "Vista" had been converted into a highly complex amalgam of voices and interspersed narrative lines. Last but not least, overt description of the guerrilla groups against Batista had disappeared, thus "silencing" the Cuban Revolution.

3. CENSORSHIP REMAINS: A REVOLUTIONARY'S CAREER

Despite the successful publication of *Tres tristes tigres* in 1967 and *Vista del amanecer en el trópico (Relatos)* in 1974, Cabrera Infante remained a censored writer in Spain (and therefore also in Latin America since Spain exported his books there) throughout the 1970s and 1980s. Seix Barral, the publishing house that had so obstinately defended his works in the 1960s, was partly to blame for this situation. In an article published in *El País* on the release of the 1999 Seix Barral edition of *Tres tristes tigres*, Ángel Harguindey mentions that the "literary discrepancies" between Seix Barral and Cabrera Infante continued after the appearance of the first edition of the novel, particularly after the Cuban author came out publicly against the Castro regime. After Cabrera Infante's defection, the publisher began to hold back the distribution of *Tres tristes tigres*, which led to its "first public disappearance" in 1968.

Why this happened is not fully clear. María Mudrovcic claims that Barral was "not pleased" with the author's "new condition as an exile" that had supervened as Cabrera Infante was reworking "Vista" for the censorship authorities (*Mundo nuevo: cultura y guerra* 100–101). But the firm had already invested quite significantly in the release of *Tres tristes tigres* and Barral himself had used a lot of his personal capital with the censors to ensure that the novel would appear in 1967. In the 1970s, Seix Barral was still interested in reprinting the existing galley proofs of the novel, but in no hurry to invest in the production costs for a new text, particularly when the Cuban revolutionary writer they thought they were promoting in 1964–65 had turned out to be such a disappointment. The publisher resumed "active distribution" of the novel in 1970, and in 1997, the year Cabrera Infante received the Cervantes Prize (after Gabriel García Márquez had publicly refused to accept the award), launched a massive distribution, capitalizing on Cabrera Infante's literary honors after having refused to back him when he defected from Cuba.

The records at the National Archive show that Seix Barral continued to submit requests for reprints of *Tres tristes tigres* after the 1967 release and by 1969 was seeking permission to reprint the novel's third edition. The censor (that would be censor number 5 for "Vista"/*Tres tristes tigres*), who examined this request, revisited some of the earlier concerns about the novel's vulgarity and explicit sexual content, describing it as a "continuous retailing of vulgarities and obscenities, and nonsensical and irreverent sentences" in which "the author seems to enjoy uncovering the anatomical features of prostitutes and their normal and abnormal sexual activities" ["continuada retahila (sic) de vulgaridades, obscenidades, frases descabelladas, irreligiosa...el autor parece gozar en descubrir los aspectos anatómicos de las prostitutas así como sus actividades sexuales normales o anormales"] (Expediente de *Tres tristes tigres* 1969). Despite this fifth censor's reservations, and in view of the prior approval of 1966, the reprint was allowed under the *depósito* option which cleared the way for its circulation. From that moment on, all subsequent requests to reprint the novel were rubberstamped by the censorship authorities, as was the case with the paperback editions of 1970 and 1971, and the 1974 and 1975 reprints (Expedientes de *Tres tristes tigres*, 1970–75). The fact that Seix Barral continued to submit requests to the censors is indicative of the wide circulation and profitable sales of the novel, but, since the publisher requested permission only for reprints and paperback editions, it is fair to assume that they continued to release the 1967 censored text, which financially made more sense to them than having to come up with the printing costs for a new uncensored edition. Encouraged by the international distribution of Cabrera Infante's works, the firm also reprinted *Así en la paz como en la guerra* in 1971, and in 1973 *Un oficio del siglo XX*, two early texts that had appeared in Cuba's Ediciones R while Cabrera Infante was an active member of the Revolution's cultural elite.

Despite these publishing successes in Spain, Cabrera Infante remained somewhat unhappy about the 1967 release of *Tres tristes tigres*, which was not only a censored text, but, I would argue, a doubly censored text that had been scrutinized by the Spanish authorities and self-censored by the writer himself. Vowing to have his book fully restored, or perhaps designing some kind of cover-up of his collaboration with the censors (such as he had previously attempted in his letter to Vargas Llosa), Cabrera Infante revived *Tres tristes tigres* in 1970 with the publication of an alternative ending titled "Metafinal," which first appeared in the inaugural (and only) issue of the Miami-based journal *Alacrán Azul*, and was later included in the 1996 edition of *Ella cantaba boleros*.[17] The author's insistence on revisiting and rewriting his masterwork not only signals a desire to correct the censorship he underwent in Franco's Spain, but also it is suggestive of the lasting productive influence censorship was to continue to have on his literary career. Nevertheless, and despite his repeated attempts to convince Seix Barral to issue a new text, the censored version of *Tres tristes tigres* continued to appear up to 1990. It was only then that Editorial Ayacucho published the so-called complete and uncensored version of the novel in a critical edition that included "twenty passages the Spanish censors found objectionable" (*Tres tristes tigres* 1990, 341–345). This edition reproduces, in an appendix, twenty censored passages that were suppressed in the novel's 1967 edition, but this appendix does not reproduce the cuts and modifications revealed by a close examination of the "Vista" galley proofs or the Princeton manuscript. It merely lists some minor censorial corrections that date from the 1966 submission to the censors and makes no mention of the omitted vignettes from "Vista."[18] (Most likely, the appendix was produced in consultation with the author, who failed to provide any information about the censored political vignettes.)

While the 1990 Ayacucho edition appeared to put to rest the author's obsession with having the novel published as an uncensored text, in 1996 Cabrera Infante revisited the novel once again by publishing *Ella cantaba boleros* as a separate book at Editorial Alfaguara. But censorship continued to haunt him, since *Ella cantaba boleros* reproduced in linear fashion the eight censored sections from the 1967 edition of *Tres tristes tigres*. By an oversight, *Ella* reveals its status as a censored book when the phrase "Aquí hay un corte de censura" ["There is a censors' cut here"] appears in the middle of page 268: "y sin transición me dice que se lo va a quitar para no estrujarlo, pero que no se quitará nada más, que se quedará en refajo, y se lo quita. *Aquí hay un corte de censura*" ["and without any transition she tells me that she will remove it without squeezing it, but that she won't remove anything else, that she will be in her undergarments, and she removes it. *There is a censors' cut here*"] (Cabrera Infante, *Ella cantaba* 1996; emphasis mine). This is not a literary device of any sort, but an actual indication that the censors had deleted a long paragraph of the section "Ella cantaba boleros" in *Tres tristes tigres* because of its sexual content. The deleted paragraph is published in the 1990 and 1999 editions of *Tres tristes tigres*, and details a scene in which *La Estrella* removes all her clothes and ends up in bed with one of the tigers; she refuses to have intercourse, and he "relieves himself with the help of his skillfull hands" ["aliviado por sus diestras manos"] (*Tres tristes tigres* 1999, 184).

In this way, then, censorship followed Cabrera Infante's career in Spain even as he desperately tried to set the record straight by attempting to "complete" and reedit what the censors had removed from his works. His writing rests heavily on the very censorial practices he appears to fight against, and the results of his interactions with the censorship authorities are always in an important sense productive. I mean that censorship actively contributes to his publishing career and does so not only by means of its "editorial" contributions (the changes it imposed), but also by providing an incentive to publish the "same" works over and over in an effort to erase the traces of censorship in them, so that these works evolve in interesting ways. Likewise, the Revolution (which the author often links to his censorial experiences in Cuba and in Spain) provided another incentive to similar effect, and "revolutionary writing" in varying senses of this phrase, is the backbone of his writing both in Spain and Cuba.[19] Cabrera Infante initially made use of the Cuban Revolution to promote his works in Cuba (including the ones that Batista had censored) and his cachet as a revolutionary writer to convince Barral and his firm to undertake the publication of "Vista." As he settled in Franco's Spain, he began to promote antirevolutionary attitudes (while still writing about the Revolution), and by the late 1960s he had repositioned himself as a defector who had suffered the injustices of Castro's rule, a key theme which was to govern both his literary production and his professional career as a writer in exile.

Perhaps the most blatant case of Cabrera Infante's use of censorship and the Revolution is the publication of the "censored leftovers" (or the "censorship remains") from "Vista" in the 1974 collection *Vista del amanecer en el trópico (Relatos)*. By using the same vignettes and the same title as had been censored in 1965, Cabrera Infante sought to settle an old score (much as he would again attempt to do in the 1990s).

When *Vista (Relatos)* reached the Spanish censors, they at first thought he had resubmitted the already censored and rejected "Vista" of 1965.[20] This is apparent from the censorship dossier, which includes a memorandum from the Director of Censorship stating that "it is not possible to authorize the work" ["no cabe autorización de la obra"] since "dossier number 2015/65"—corresponding to the 1965 "Vista"—had already been rejected (Expediente de *Vista del amanecer en el trópico* 1974). But soon the censors realized that the new *Vista* was not a revolutionary text in the least, given that the *added* vignettes in 1974 were critical of the Castro regime and of the violence and repression that have long dominated the history of Cuba. Several of the final vignettes focus either on *balseros* fleeing Cuba (vignettes 95 and 96), or on the discontent of those remaining on the island (vignettes 99 and 100) (*Vista* 1974, 215–231). While *Vista* incorporated some of the very sentences they had suppressed in "Vista," the censors could see that Cabrera Infante was no longer part of the "Cuban connection" of the 1960s. So they authorized the collection, but only under the *silencio* option (Expediente de *Vista del amanecer en el trópico* 1974). (There is a continuity—and one not without its ironies—between the author's self-silencing in relation to his early pro-revolutionary stances, and the censor's willingness to silently look the other way in 1974.)

Not unlike the censors, scholars have wondered too about the connections and continuities between the original manuscript "Vista" and the 1974 collection *Vista*. As pointed out by Gil López, Cabrera Infante confirmed the suspicions of many scholars in a 1982 interview with Álvarez Boland in which he acknowledged that the original "Vista" vignettes were used in *Vista* (*GCI: La Habana* 366).[21] The untold story here is that these vignettes had been censored outright by the Spanish authorities and that the author had to reframe them within a much different political context in order to gain approval of *Vista* in 1974. As explained in the prologue to the 1984 reprint of *Vista*, Cabrera Infante conceived this work as the "reverse of *Tres tristes tigres* and its counterpoint," and it is appropriate that the publisher, Plaza & Janés, had it included in a series entitled "Biblioteca Letras de Exilio" ["Library of Letters from Exile"] (*Vista* 1984, 8), underscoring the political shift away from the text's original conception.

When *Vista del amanecer en el trópico (Relatos)* appeared in Spain, the Franco regime was in its slow-but-sure decline, and Cabrera Infante had established himself as a renowned author and a bona fide political enemy of the Castro regime residing in London. It cannot be coincidental that his shifting political views between 1964 and 1975 ran parallel with key moments of his literary career in Spain: the toning down of his pro-revolutionary stances and his subsequent exit from the island coincided with the censor's first evaluation of "Vista" in 1965; similarly his compliance with the Spanish censor's demands in 1966 and the publication of *Tres tristes tigres* in 1967 coincided with the beginning of his exile in London and his subsequent denunciation of the regime. That these political shifts had productive outcomes for Cabrera Infante the writer is evidenced by the fact that by 1974 the original 105-page galley sheets of "Vista" in 1965 had become two distinct books:[22] *Tres tristes tigres*, the 451-page best-selling novel that consecrated him as the most notable Cuban author of the Boom generation, and *Vista del amanecer en el trópico (Relatos)*, a collection of 101 vignettes concerning Cuba's violent past that originated in the censored sections of "Vista."

Textual maneuverings of this kind (the cut and paste/add and borrow technique that is so pervasive in his works) show that omission and alteration (two censorial practices par excellence) are crucial to the generative history of Cabrera Infante's "Vista," *Tres tristes tigres*, and *Vista*. They reflect an undeniable continuity of practice between the external authority of a dictatorial regime (official censorship) and the internal process that resulted from it (self-censorship). It is censorship that conditioned his writing career in Spain, and it is to the interaction of official censorship and its creative personal twin that we owe *Tres tristes tigres* and *Vista del amanecer en el trópico*.

Chapter 4

From Melquíades to Vernet

How Gabriel García Márquez Escaped Spanish Censorship

On September 21, 2001, Barcelona's *Casa Batlló* on Passeig de Grácia, one of the most emblematic buildings of Catalan *modernisme*, became the setting for the auction of a unique manuscript: the author-corrected galley proofs of Gabriel García Márquez's *Cien años de soledad* (1967) [*One Hundred Years of Solitude*]. The auction house, Subastas Velázquez, justified its choice of location by underscoring García Márquez's ties with Barcelona. After years of precarious living conditions in Mexico City, where the author wrote *Cien años de soledad* between 1965 and 1966, Gabo (as he is best known in literary circles) decided to settle in Barcelona in October 1967; he resided there until 1975. There he would interact with an emerging colony of Latin American expatriates and fellow Boom writers as well as with notables of the Catalan intelligentsia such as Carlos Barral. Not only was this city the place "from where he maintained contact with the world and with Latin American literature," the auction house's catalogue announced, but it was also the residence of his agent Carmen Balcells, who symbolizes the more than thirty-year relationship between García Márquez and Barcelona: "ésta fue y es su ciudad y hasta Barcelona nos desplazamos para subastar el día 21 de setiembre de 2001 las dichas primeras pruebas de galeradas de *Cien años de soledad*" ["this was and is his city, and to Barcelona we go to auction the aforementioned galley proofs of *One Hundred Years of Solitude* on September 21, 2001"] (Subastas Velázquez 4).[1]

Subastas Velázquez launched this event as one of the most significant and unique auctions in their history, and the press followed suit with a barrage of articles about the novel, its author and the circumstances that led to the auctioning of the galley proofs, calling the event "un hecho doblemente inédito por tratarse de un autor vivo y porque es la primera vez que en España se realiza una subasta de estas características" ["a doubly unique event since an auction like this for a living author has never taken place in Spain before"] (Manrique "Instituciones públicas" 45). In view of all the media hype and the fact that García Márquez is a "sure thing" on the book market (it is widely rumored that he received ten million dollars for his 2002 memoirs *Vivir para contarla* [*Living to Tell the Tale*]), the auction firm saw very encouraging prospects for a successful sale. The opening price was no small change, 95 million pesetas (roughly half a million dollars). A price hard to match for private collectors, and even for government-funded collections and libraries or university archives. Such a high-end cost contributed to making the auction the widely publicized cultural event that it was. It was a stimulus, too, for critics, journalists, and García Márquez himself to revisit the publication history of the Boom generation's flagship novel; and for us it is an occasion to reflect on how literary manuscripts become commodities on the market at large.

What led the auction house to put such an exorbitant price tag on these proofs? After all, as galleys they are twice removed from the original handwritten notebooks; and they can be regarded as an autograph document only because of the dedication on the first page and the handwritten corrections made by García Márquez. These autograph markings, however, do not seem to justify the high price on their own. As Eligio García Márquez, the author's brother, has confirmed in *Tras las claves de Melquíades* [*In Search of Melquíades' Secrets*], the original notebooks were destroyed by García Márquez and the typescript of *Cien años de soledad* he sent to Editorial Sudamericana in 1966 was lost when the publishing house moved to the San Telmo neighborhood in Buenos Aires. It is because of the disappearance of these originals that the galley proofs are now considered, "according to UNESCO," the only autograph document of the novel (Marcos). The press incorrectly asserted that it was the "manuscript" of the novel, which only existed in the form of García Márquez's handwritten notebooks. Subastas Velázquez made a similar claim when they tried to sell the galleys as the "sole available autograph material" for *Cien años de soledad*, and the closest there is to an original manuscript: "desconocidas hasta ahora y único material obtenible como documento autógrafo de la novela más importante en lengua castellana del siglo XX" ["unknown until the present, and sole available autograph material for the most important Spanish-language novel of the twentieth century"] (Subastas Velázquez 13/19; translation modified).

The galleys were a gift from García Márquez to the Spanish filmmaker Luis Alcoriza and his wife Janet Riensenfeld, who were two of the author's closest friends in Mexico. García Márquez, as it turns out, had never returned these galleys to Sudamericana for fear they might get lost in the mail, and sent a list of corrections instead. At the time Sudamericana had given the author an advance of five hundred dollars for the novel's typescript. By 2001, the value of a García Márquez "original" had multiplied a thousand times, at least according to the auction house's estimation. Uninterested in the existing speculative market for García Márquez's originals such as the one they owned, Alcoriza and his wife kept these galleys as a personal gift and never tried to sell them. It was only after their death that their heir Héctor Delgado pursued the sale, without the consent of García Márquez who nevertheless declared the auction legitimate while distancing himself from it:

> Que no haya dudas de que es una operación legítima.... Lo único que me parece injusto de esta historia inverosímil y memorable es que Luis y Janet vivieran sus últimos años con cientos de miles de dólares guardados a salvo del tiempo y las polillas en el fondo del baúl, por la invencible dignidad ibérica de no vender el regalo del amigo que más los quiso en este mundo.
>
> Let there be no doubt that it is a legitimate operation.... In this incredible and memorable story the only thing that seems unjust to me is that Luis and Janet lived their last years with thousands of dollars safely stashed away from time and moths at the bottom of a chest. Nothing but invincible Iberian dignity prevented them from selling the gift from the friend who loved them the most in this world. (García Márquez, "La novela" 32)

García Márquez suggests here—writing before the actual outcome of the auction was known—that a forgotten original (such as the galley proofs) hidden at the bottom of a chest can accrue enormous value while in oblivion. When it is unearthed, its speculative value begins to rise. The novelty of a recently discovered original has great potential to generate considerable economic returns on the market. But there is more: this process of discovering "valuable manuscripts" parallels the enterprise undertaken by the Buendías in the novel, when the first generation forgets Melquíades's "papers" or "parchments," and the following generations beat their brains trying to interpret them. The parallel, though it may seem a bit strained, was evidently on García Márquez's mind. In the literary realm, he created a manuscript inside the novel that in the end becomes the novel, as Aureliano Babilonia deciphers the last verses of Melquíades' parchments. Similarly, in the literary market, he has constructed a playful narrative about the original manuscript of *Cien años de soledad*. This is the narrative that was laid out in "La novela detrás de la novela" ["The Novel Behind the Novel"], in which the author confesses his own speculation with manuscripts and original documents as part of the personal story that brought *Cien años de soledad* to light. "La novela" appeared in the Sunday edition of *El País* on July 15, 2001, three months before the auction, as a front-page leading story. The newspaper subtitled García Márquez's essay "La odisea literaria de un manuscrito" ["The Literary Odyssey of a Manuscript"], deliberately echoing in this way the speculation and intrigue regarding the various "originals" concerned—the handwritten notebooks, the typescript submitted to Editorial Sudamericana, and the corrected galley proofs based on the typescript that surrounded the forthcoming sale.

García Márquez begins his recollection by telling us about one Friday afternoon in early August 1966 when he and his wife went to the post office, in Mexico City, to send the typescript to Paco Porrúa, the literary director of Editorial Sudamericana. They were several pesos short and could only mail half the typescript to Buenos Aires, the consequence being that he and his wife spent the weekend trying to come up with the money to send the other half. They pawned a small heater and a blender, and with the cash from this transaction managed to mail the rest of the typescript the following Monday. Like the mailing, the composition of the novel, as García Márquez recalls it, had taken place under arduous financial conditions. They were broke, several months late on their rent, and struggling to acquire even enough paper for García Márquez to complete the novel: "Mercedes se gastaba medio presupuesto doméstico en pirámides de resmas de papel que no duraban una semana" ["Mercedes spent half of our home budget in pyramids of reams of paper that barely lasted a week"] (García Márquez, "La novela" 31).

Not unlike Melquíades in the novel, García Márquez enjoys playing with manuscripts and originals and the economics attached to them. Among his many references to the economic conditions endured while he was writing the novel, he often describes an economy of swapping (*trueque*) of the kind we have just seen: a small heater is traded to buy stamps and personal items are pawned to buy paper. But this is quite similar to the early economy described in the novel, where (well before the arrival of the United Fruit Company) Macondo's primitive economy is based on similar "swaps" or *trueques*. In this economy, the male Buendías, particularly the founder José Arcadio, are known for their "careless" investments in Melquíades' "inventions" (the magnet, the magnifying glass, etc), and it is their wives who are left to find a balance between their eccentricities and the domestic economy.

Manuscripts, for García Márquez, function in similar fashion and conform to this type of rudimentary economy. Their value is seen first as that of the raw material—that is, the reams of paper or (in the novel) the "parchments." In García Márquez's (nonfictional) world, what drives the household economy is a personal investment in seeing the conversion of this raw material into a manuscript, which is later manufactured as a book. Interestingly, in the novel, parchment and manuscript are often used interchangeably to describe the documents left behind by Melquíades. However, the choice of words also depends on which character is speaking about them. For instance, the matriarch Úrsula describes the parchments in their raw material condition as "papers" when she introduces them to Aureliano Segundo, the third-generation Buendía who begins deciphering Melquíades's "papers" (García Márquez, *Cien años* 1996, 294–6). At this point the narrator refers to Melquíades' "manuscripts," viewing them as the product of Melquíades' work as a writer.

A similar distinction between raw material and the conversion of such material into a literary document can be found in García Márquez's account of the novel's composition. In Mexico, the Márquezes struggled to make ends meet so as to invest in paper and in the utilization of this paper for García Márquez's manuscripts. By contrast the José Arcadios and Aurelianos devote their productive time not to writing but to deciphering the parchments or to making "gold fish" as amateur alchemists. In both these cases, they look for sources of future economic returns. But in the case of the parchments, the more they are transformed from raw material into a decoded (i.e., coherent) manuscript the Buendías can understand, the closer the family is to destruction. The difference between the Márquezes and the Buendías is that for the former work is productive and valuable while the latter don't recognize the value of what they have, so that their deciphering of Melquíades' parchments doesn't add to the value these "papers" already have.

Similarly, it is a search for something that might be considered the "original" manuscript of *Cien años de soledad* that drives the events leading to the auction. In a way that evokes the hidden secrets in Melquíades' parchments, García Márquez destroyed his manuscript "parchments" (his notebooks), which would have been a much-coveted commodity to be auctioned off and certainly an assured sale at *Casa Batlló*:

> Cuando recibimos el primer ejemplar del libro impreso, en junio de 1967, Mercedes y yo rompimos el original.... No se nos ocurrió pensar ni mucho menos que podía ser el más apreciable de todos.... Mi decisión no fue nada inocente ni modesta, sino que rompimos la copia para que nadie pudiera descubrir los trucos de mi carpintería secreta.
>
> When we received the first copy of the printed book in June 1967, Mercedes and I tore up the original.... It did not cross our minds that it might appreciate (in value) more than any other (manuscript).... My decision was not in the least innocent or modest. We tore up the copy so that no one could see the tricks behind my secret carpentry.] (García Márquez, "La novela" 32)[2]

By destroying his original García Márquez alters the economy of manuscripts, and drives speculation on a possible original, which the auction firm claims to have in the galley proofs. Since the original manuscript inside the novel ("los pergaminos de Melquíades") is the key to understanding the fortunes of the Buendía family (and since ultimately the novel and the parchments are metaphorically equivalent), it is no surprise that the press eagerly picked up on a possible correlation between the manuscript inside the novel and the autograph proofs being sold in Barcelona.

But these meaningful connections and the interest the surfacing of the corrected galleys aroused were not enough for the auction to be successful. In the end, private collectors, museums, libraries (as well as the Spanish and Colombian governments) failed to bid for the $500,000 galleys. In a statement released before the auction the Colombian government, one of the interested bidders, announced it had decided not to go ahead with purchase of the galleys, given the budget constraints its Ministry of Education was facing at the time. The government's refusal to bid at the auction sparked the criticism of several prominent literary critics, who argued that the galley proofs should remain in Colombia or at least in the Hispanic world, fearing that "they would end up in the depository of a U.S. university, or in the private hands of a collector"] (Manrique, "Colombia no participará").

The Spanish government, for its part, at first expressed interest in bidding for these unusual galleys, as did many private collectors and university archives. By law, the Spanish government (given that the auction was held in Spain) had "preferred rights of acquisition"; but in the end it decided not to exercise them. In fact, no one actually matched the starting price of ninety-five million pesetas, and the galley proofs did not sell (and haven't so far). The auction house identified the events of September 11, 2001 and the instability these events brought to the world economy as the key factor in the unsuccessful auction at *Casa Batlló*. While it is true that the markets suffered a significant blow after September 11, 2001, so that investors became cautious about making new purchases, I think the auction house simply miscalculated the market value of the galleys. (Obviously, they hadn't read "the manuscript" of *Cien años de soledad* closely enough.) In any case, García Márquez's assumption, in "La novela," that they could bring in a small fortune proved unfounded. The parallel with the fate of Melquíades's manuscripts was more predictive than he had thought.

From a purely scholarly viewpoint, the galleys are somewhat disappointing. They show only stylistic corrections and a few sentences that the author added to the final typescript.[3] However, Subastas Velázquez claimed that these galleys contained many surprises and revealing secrets concerning García Márquez's craftsmanship:

> Extraordinario documento, que contiene más de un millar (aproximadamente 1026) de correcciones por errores en la composición y descuidos de los cajistas, efectuadas por García Márquez...son el documento más feaciente del buen escribir de Gabo. Los cambios deparan *muchas sorpresas*. (emphasis mine)

> This extraordinary document contains more than a thousand (approximately 1026) corrections of errors of composition and typesetter's lapses, made by García Márquez...these are a very real demonstration of his literary craft. The changes offer *many surprises*] (Subastas Velázquez 13/19; translation modified).

From the pages of these galleys that are displayed in the catalogue it is very difficult to see the many surprises Subastas Velázquez announced. The annotations simply look like the kind of corrections of typographical errors that occur when a typescript is converted into printed galleys.[4] But to whet the appetite of hunters of García Márquez's originals a sales pitch—the "many surprises"—was essential.

The auction house's claim that the galleys amounted to an original was soon put into question when Dasso Saldívar, García Márquez's biographer, wrote a piece in which he mentions four copies of the novel's original typescript, (copies that can be presumed to be) identical to the one García Márquez submitted to Sudamericana. They are most likely carbon copies that the author distributed among his friends in Mexico and Colombia.[5] In "El rastro de las copias mecanografiadas" ["The Search for the Typewritten Copies"] Saldívar claims that two such copies still exist (Sudamericana misplaced two typewritten copies, the one García Márquez sent and the one personally delivered by fellow Colombian author Álvaro Mutis). These remaining carbons are located in Baranquilla and Mexico City. One is the property of Patricia Cepeda, and the second belongs to Emmanuel Carballo, the husband of Neus Espresarte, a Catalan expatriate and coowner of Ediciones Era, where García Márquez published *La mala hora* and *El coronel no tiene quien le escriba* [*No One Writes to the Colonel*]. Saldívar gives a physical description of one of these two surviving carbons that dispels any possibility of confusion with the auctioned galleys: "está sin título, y suman 590 páginas de tamaño carta, en papel *bond* de 60 gramos, de 28 líneas a 60 golpes cada una" ["it has no title, and there are 590 letter-size pages in bond-type paper of 60 grams, 60 strikes per each twenty-eight lines"] (Saldívar, "El rastro" 45). García Márquez for his part corroborates Saldívar's account but adds a twist by claiming that "there may be other copies somewhere in the world" ["en alguna parte del mundo puede haber otras copias"] ("La novela" 32), a suggestion that reinforces my earlier point about the author's obsession with unearthing forgotten originals.

Unlike the auctioned galleys, these copies do not have any of the autograph corrections that made Subastas Velázquez claim that the corrected galleys were truly original and unique. It is not clear whether these additional typescripts affected the sales value of the corrected galley proofs or not. What I find interesting, in the end, is that García Márquez bears a great responsibility for the speculation on his "originals," having not only destroyed the manuscript notebooks, but having also refused to send the corrected proofs back to Buenos Aires and distributed several copies of the typescript, thus creating an economy of manuscripts driven by the lack of "the original" and the existence of several texts that are close to the missing original. To make identification of an autograph manuscript even more complex, García Márquez handwrote two dedications on the corrected galley proofs, once in 1967 and a second time in 1986 at a dinner party held at the Alcoriza's house. For the auction house this "repeated dedication" was one of the unique features of the galley proofs: "Para Luis y Janet, una dedicatoria repetida, pero que es la única verdadera: del amigo que más los quiere en este mundo, GABO 1967. Confirmado, GABO 1985" ["For Luis and Janet, a repeated dedication, but the only true one: from the friend who most loves them in this world. GABO 1967. Confirmed, Gabo 1985"] (Subastas Velázquez 13/19). But the twice genuine dedication did not appeal to potential buyers as much as the auction house had hoped, and the dedication's cachet as autograph material, in the end, did not help the sale of the galley proofs.

Failing to find a buyer at the *Casa Battló*, the galleys finally traveled to London, where the prestigious firm Christie's organized a second auction in November 2002. The British auctioneer listed them at the reduced price of $320,000 but again no one met the opening bid. The bidding at Christie's reached $200,000, a price well short of the asking price of $500,000 in Barcelona. As a result, Christie's decided to pull the galleys out of the auction, and they were returned to their owner, Héctor Delgado. London-based antiques specialist James Tindley predicted that Delgado would have to wait a while before auctioning them again, since each time these galleys go on the market and fail to sell they lose their appeal for potential future buyers (Gómez, "Las galeradas" 37). In other words, the more the galleys are put on display, the further they fall from their largely unmerited status as an undeserved original, with the result that they decrease in value.

The unsuccessful sale of the galley proofs proved the point implicit in García Márquez's parallel with the Melquíades papers that while his "original" manuscripts accrue value through years of oblivion, this value does not necessarily translate into economic returns once they are unearthed. A recently discovered document's failure to generate economic returns seems to be a lesson his readers and his auctioneers have to learn. The economy of manuscripts and originals García Márquez designed for *Cien años de soledad* continues to expand beyond the pages of the novel, as the search for Melquíades'/García Márquez's parchments goes on.

1. WISE AND UNWISE CATALANS

Subastas Velázquez failed to mention in their catalogue one of the most obvious connections between *Cien años de soledad* and Barcelona, the wise Catalonian—"el hombre que había leído todos los libros" ["a man who had read all the books"] (García Márquez, *Cien años* 1996, 500/*One Hundred* 366).[6] This omission probably had no bearing on the auction. However, it does demonstrate the larger point that in the narratives about the autographs of *Cien años de soledad* that emerged in connection with the auction little attention is given to what the novel is really about, or to the manuscripts inside the novel. While both the cultural press and the auction house's catalogue explained the well-known connection between García Márquez and Barcelona (i.e., the fact that he settled in this city in 1967), no mention was made of the novel's crucial character, who is not only a native of Barcelona but also owns a peculiar bookstore that resembles an obscure depository of forgotten texts: "más que una librería parecía un basurero de libros usados" ["more than a bookstore, it looked like a dump for used books"] (*Cien años* 500/*One Hundred* 366). This is another example of García Márquez's obsession with hidden and mysterious texts that escaped the cultural commentators of the auction.

Perhaps Subastas Velázquez thought that the material manuscript and the literary manuscript (the one inside the novel) offered no particular connection out of which a profit could be made. Such, of course, was not the reaction of many interested parties in the auction, who sensed that talking about what the press called a "manuscript authored by García Márquez" was inevitably linked to the ones inside the novel. Interestingly, the auction house's catalogue reproduces the galley of a corrected section that happens to be about the wise Catalonian (corresponding to page 322 of the Sudamericana edition). Obviously, they failed to make the connection even as they displayed the corrected page in their catalogue (Subastas Velázquez 16).

In the novel, Aureliano Babilonia, following Melquíades's instructions, "unearths" in the midst of the wise Catalonian's messy shop "the five books" he will need in order to finally decode Melquíades' manuscripts. Despite the wise Catalonian's warning—"el último hombre que leyó esos libros debió ser Isaac el Ciego, así que piensa bien lo que haces" ["the last man who read these books must have been Isaac the Blindman, so consider well what you're doing"] (500/366)—, Aureliano purchases these books and continues his engagement with the manuscripts. Just before the end of the novel, as Aureliano and his aunt Amaranta Úrsula are about to become the parents of a baby with the tail of a pig, the wise Catalonian returns to Barcelona where he will die. While aunt and nephew succumb to forgetfulness of time and engage in their incestuous relationship, the wise Catalonian becomes their only source of guidance; he helps them hold on to reality and supplants the vanishing Melquíades, whose apparitions wane as Aureliano comes closer to deciphering the manuscript:

El último hilo que los vinculaba con el mundo se rompió en el sexto mes del embarazo, cuando recibieron una carta que evidentemente no era del sabio catalán. Había sido franqueada en Barcelona, pero la cubierta estaba escrita con tinta azul convencional por una caligrafía administrativa, y tenía el aspecto inocente e impersonal de los recados enemigos. (*Cien años* 1996, 551)

The last thread that joined them to the world was broken on the sixth month of pregnancy when they received a letter that obviously was not from the wise Catalonian. It had been mailed in Barcelona, but the envelope was addressed in conventional blue ink by an official hand and it had the innocent and impersonal look of hostile messages. (*One Hundred Years* 410)

Somewhat as in this literary homage to Barcelona and to García Márquez's Catalan friends, the publication history of his works is replete with wise and unwise Catalans in the book trade who at one point or another decided (or not) to try to attract him as an author. In this history, one of the most infamously unwise moves by a Catalan would be Carlos Barral's editorial gaffe when as early as 1966 he received a telegram from García Márquez offering him *Cien años de soledad*. At that point, a much wiser Catalan, the agent Carmen Balcells, had already been handling García Márquez's affairs, and given the familiarity she had with Barral and his firm, it seemed logical for García Márquez and Balcells to pursue publication at Seix Barral. Rumor has it that there was even a secret deal by which *Cien años de soledad* would "compete" for the *Biblioteca Breve* Prize, win it, and be launched massively in the international book market, as had been the case with previous winners such as *La ciudad y los perros* or *Tres tristes tigres*. However, the written history of the failed publication of *Cien años de soledad* in Spain tells a very different story.

In his memoirs, Carlos Barral denies that García Márquez was ever in line to be awarded the prize and recalls this episode as a misunderstanding that arose from his failure to answer García Márquez's telegram:

García Márquez *no concurrió nunca* [al premio], y debería saber que yo no publiqué *Cien años de soledad* a causa de un malentendido, a la falta de respuesta puntual a un telegrama, y no por un error editorial ni a consecuencia de una torpe lectura del manuscrito—que nunca vi—, como maliciosamente se ha pretendido. Otra cosa es que a mí no me parezca ésa la mejor novela de su tiempo. *García Márquez no concurrió nunca al premio ni propuso manuscritos a la editorial*, pero fue jurado del mismo y sus criterios y recomendaciones, mucho más sutiles y exigentes de lo que él quisiera aparentar, fueron muy tenidos en cuenta.

García Márquez never competed (for the prize), and it should be known that the reason I did not publish *Cien años de soledad* was a misunderstanding, my failure to respond promptly to a telegram, and not that I made an editorial error or because of an inept reading of the manuscript—which I never saw—as has been maliciously suggested. Another thing is that I don't think this is the best novel of its time. *García Márquez did not ever compete for the prize or propose manuscripts to the firm*, but he did act as member of the jury and his criteria and recommendations —a lot more subtle and demanding than he would care to admit—were given very serious consideration. (Barral, *Memorias* 576; emphasis mine).

It is interesting that in this short paragraph Barral twice asserts that García Márquez did not compete for the *Biblioteca Breve*, and defends his skills as publisher against those who are supposed to have accused him of having misread the "manuscript" of the most successful novel of the Boom generation. Barral could not have seen the manuscript of *Cien años* since the author never shared his handwritten notebooks with any prospective publisher. What he would have received was the same typescript García Márquez sent to Sudamericana and not the manuscript version. But this passage also shows that Barral was not willing to pursue the works of García Márquez with the same fervor he demonstrated for other Latin American Boom writers. In a similar account of this episode published in a 1982 interview with Dasso Saldívar, he confesses that he did not know García Márquez's oeuvre very well at the time he received the telegram, whereas his wife (who had also worked as a literary agent) was quite enthusiastic about it (Barral, *Almanaque* 190).

Saldívar's own account tends to agree with Barral that the Catalan publisher never actually saw the novel's typescript and simply received an invitation to look at it. This invitation, however, was an early one, as Saldívar places it sometime around July 1965, which seems to indicate that García Márquez was looking for a publisher for the novel well before the novel was completed. His brother Eligio situates its composition between July 1965 and August 1966 and dates the advance García

Márquez received from Sudamericana for his unfinished work on October 17, 1965. The actual contract with Sudamericana, which was obviously handled by Balcells, is dated September 10, 1966 (García Márquez, *Tras las claves* 64–70). Balcells negotiated wisely and brought to the table her more than ten years of experience and a good working relationship with fellow Catalan Antonio López Llausás, the director and major stockholder of Sudamericana. (López Llausás had arrived in Argentina in 1939, and soon thereafter Sudemericana reached an agreement with Victoria Ocampo's *Sur* "to use its imprint on one of its collections" [King 104].)

Taking these dates into account, Saldívar concludes that the "legend" of Barral's refusal to publish *Cien años de soledad* is false, but acknowledges that one of Seix Barral's readers, the Catalan poet Gabriel Ferrater, read the novel and immediately urged Balcells to convince García Márquez to submit it for the *Biblioteca Breve* Prize, for which he had been a member of the jury in the past. Apparently, Balcells talked to García Márquez about this option, since the visibility of the *Biblioteca Breve* would have assured instant exposure on the international markets. But García Márquez, known for his aversion to literary prizes and honors (he rejected the *Premio Cervantes* the year Cabrera Infante was given the award), refused to pursue the Seix Barral route. He was obviously bothered also by Barral's failure to respond to his telegram. This was a wise move on his part, since it was unclear at the time what kind of restrictions he would have had to face from the Spanish censors, and presumably also from Barral's own editorial interventions. Sudamericana, on the other hand, would have seemed an easier route and a more honorable one, since by then he had accepted the advance, even though the final contract had not been signed.

The behind-the-scenes maneuvering over the publication of *Cien años de soledad* is also reported by Eligio García Márquez who, thanks to the access granted by Gloria López Llovet de Rodrigué (the granddaughter of López Llausás) at Sudamericana, was able to examine the correspondence between García Márquez and Porrúa (García Márquez, *Tras las claves* 62). In one of the letters unearthed from the archives of Sudamericana, García Márquez talks about having a "verbal agreement" to place the novel with a publishing firm he does not identify but that Eligio believes to be Ediciones Era, García Márquez's publisher in Mexico (63). Yet another (wise) Catalan publisher Neus Espresate had founded Ediciones Era in 1962: it was a small but well-respected firm where García Márquez had been glad to publish his early writing when it was increasingly sinking into oblivion in Colombia. The main concern García Márquez had about Era was their policy of publishing small editions of no more than one thousand copies and the fact that their international distribution could not compete with firms like Seix Barral or Sudamericana.[7] Given that the author completed the novel in Mexico, it is safe to assume that Neus Espresate would have known that *Cien años de soledad* was approaching completion and that her press was one that García Márquez would have rated highly. Whatever verbal agreement García Márquez and Neus may have had, though, it was not enough to prevent him from pursuing other deals with Catalans in Barcelona (Barral, Balcells, and Ferrater) and in Argentina (López Llausás). The vague allusion in the letter uncovered by Eligio does not exclude the possibility that a secret deal with Seix Barral was in the works.

In my reading of the various accounts of this publishing narrative concerning *Cien años de soledad* I have found no reference to censorship and the important role it may well have played in García Márquez's final decision to go with Sudamericana. While Barral justifies his inaction in failing to respond to García Márquez's telegram as a mixture of laziness and lack of interest in the author's early works, it remains unclear to what extent he envisioned difficulties with the Spanish censors in the event of pursuing publication in Spain. He would certainly have been well aware that in order to publish García Márquez's work he would have to engage in arduous negotiations with the censors. After all, García Márquez's support of the Cuban Revolution and his friendship with Castro were well known. While this support for the Castro regime would not necessarily have been an impediment to publishing in Spain, Barral probably also anticipated problems with the censors when it came to the sexually explicit (or in the censor's parlance, pornographic, obscene, or immoral) passages of the novel. This in turn would probably not have been a huge handicap for Barral, who by then had become an expert negotiator with the Spanish censors. But once again (Puig's case comes to mind) Barral seems to have failed to attend to his own internalized censorship and as a result did not push for the publication of *Cien años de soledad* by Seix Barral.

Several further reasons seem to have informed his decision. By 1967, there had already been some tensions between the Seix and the Barral families as to what direction the firm should take. Barral's run-ins with the authorities (who had labeled him nothing short of a Communist activist) were of great concern, and members of both families probably feared that the government might shut down their enterprise. Under these circumstances, Barral probably felt that it was not worthwhile to engage in lengthy negotiations with the Spanish censors in order to get approval for yet another left-leaning Latin American Boom writer whose writing he did not know well enough or simply disliked. Another element that probably informed his decision was an assumption that he could rely on his network of international publishers and agents like Balcells to bring any new talents to his prestigious publishing enterprise. He may have thought that in this instance they had not presented a sufficiently convincing case for him to undertake complex and time-consuming negotiations involving the Spanish censors, García Márquez, and himself.

Soon, however, Barral would realize how unwise his decision truly had been. Not only did he miss out on the most important publication of the Boom, but he also failed to accumulate the kind of bargaining capital he would need a few years later in order to prevent the break up of Seix Barral. In 1970 he would launch Barral Editores (having filed papers for its creation as early as 1964). One of the first titles to appear in this new publishing venture did indeed represent a wise move. It was the critically acclaimed essay on García Márquez's publishing career that was for years the seminal work in the scholarship, Vargas Llosa's *García Márquez: Historia de un deicidio*.

Early signs that Barral had made a huge mistake in not pursuing García Márquez's telegram came as eighteen hundred copies of the novel were sold in the first week after its release. On June 5, 1967 *Cien años de soledad* appeared in Buenos Aires. By Eligio's account, this release became a huge cultural event and led to the rapid sale of the entire first run of eight thousand copies for the first edition. The successful launch came as a surprise to everybody including Sudamericana. The success was ultimately due to a *gallego* by the name of Paco Porrúa—the brains behind the publication of *Cien años de soledad* and *Rayuela* [*Hopscotch*]—who took a chance on García Márquez's works and pushed for a larger than usual run, which at the time was only about three thousand copies. García Márquez himself had seen this move as a most imprudent business decision and warned Sudamericana that by printing eight thousand copies for the first edition they risked going immediately bankrupt.[8]

Porrúa's daring move had the strong backing of López Llausás, whom his granddaughter Gloria described as "a good Catalan" ["un catalán de los buenos"] who achieved results and knew how to take risks with unknown authors (García Márquez, *Tras las claves* 22–23). The wise Catalan Llausás is the one who gets results and achieves rewards—that is, economic returns and international visibility—for his firm, while the unwise Barral has to live in disrepute for having missed an opportunity to produce such results.

But in reality it is the savvy *gallego* Porrúa—who was supervised by López Llausás—who deserves most of the credit for this wise move by Sudamericana. Porrúa—who had joined Sudamericana in 1958 (Saldívar, *viaje a la semilla* 446)—became acquainted with García Márquez's work when he read Luis Harss' collection of interviews with emerging Boom writers *Los Nuestros*, published by Sudamericana in 1966. He then contacted Harss to get copies of *La hojarasca*, *La mala hora*, and *El coronel no tiene quien le escriba*:

> La ventaja que tuve sobre Barral con este escritor es que yo pude leer todo lo que había publicado García Márquez antes de ponerme en contacto con él. Por eso yo ya me esperaba algo excepcional cuando me contestó que tenía comprometidos los derechos de esas obras, pero que podía entregrarme una novela que estaba escribiendo.
>
> The advantage I had over Barral with García Márquez is that I could read everything he had published before I established contact with him. That is why I expected something truly exceptional when he replied that all the rights for his works were tied up, but that he could send me the novel he was writing. (Jarque 36)

So Barral was unwise in that he did not foresee that Sudamericana could take an up-and-coming Boom writer and launch him internationally with great success, even if this writer was not one he would have recommended for his own firm. Sudamericana simply "one-upped" Barral, and they did so by pursuing García Márquez in an old-fashioned way (reading his early works and understanding his potential as a best-selling author as Porrúa did) and without resorting to the editorial maneuverings (agents, literary prizes, etc) that were standard practice in Barcelona and elsewhere.

So it is, then, that the publishing history of *Cien años de soledad* is linked to the moves of wise and unwise Catalans in the book trade. Unlike his fellow Boom writers who relied on the Catalan connections of the Barcelona publishing industry, García Márquez opted to pursue the Catalan exile and expatriate community in Mexico and Argentina, partly because of elements beyond his control (an unanswered telegram), and partly, doubtless, because of his own understanding of what publishing in Franco's Spain would entail. Carlos Barral acted somewhat censoriously toward the Colombian author, a move that turned out to be unwise. Many years later, Barral was still claiming that *Cien años de soledad* was not "the best novel of its time" (*Memorias* 576), in an effort to justify his unwise decision.

Once García Márquez settled in Barcelona, however, Barral embraced him, not only as one of the leading Boom authors whom he wished to publish, but also as a key member of the colony of Latin American expatriates who had settled in and around Barcelona and were to participate in Barral's new editorial venture, Barral Editores, where García Márquez's *Eréndira* appeared in 1972. The savvy editor had made a blunder in 1966 but after the success of *Cien años de soledad* on the international market, he clearly wised up and even befriended Gabo. By all accounts their relationship was close and lasted for years.[9] Barral, however, never made it up to García Márquez, and *Cien años de soledad* was not to appear with any of the publishing firms he was to direct after leaving Seix Barral.

2. GARCÍA MÁRQUEZ AND HIS "FAMILIAR" CENSORS

One of the most significant features of García Márquez's literary career (and one of the least studied) is his familiarity with censorship and the masterly skills with which he circumvented it. Early in his career and during the years of *La Violencia* that followed the social unrest triggered by the assassination of Liberal Party presidential candidate Gaitán in 1948, he worked as a journalist. At *El Universal* in Cartagena, where the newspaper room received the daily visit of an official censor, he grew thoroughly accustomed to government censorship. In his memoirs, García Márquez recalls that in addition to this censor he also had to deal with Zabala (the editor in chief of the newspaper), who sometimes acted as censoriously as the official censor. So censorship became part of his everyday life at the paper, to the point that its presence was like an unwanted family visit one has to endure: "un censor del gobierno que se instalaba en un escritorio de la redacción como en casa propia desde la seis de la tarde, con voluntad y mando para no autorizar ni una letra que pudiera rozar el orden público" ["beginning at six o'clock in the evening, a government censor installed himself at a desk in the newsroom as if he were in his own house, with the intention and power not to authorize a single letter that might interfere with public order"] (*Vivir* 387–8/*Living* 322–3). This anecdote, which he reiterates in his latest novel *Memoria de mis putas tristes* [*Memories of My Melancholy Whores*] (2004), can serve as a striking exemplification of his familiarity with censorship ("the censor in his own house"). It suggests too that many Boom writers must have similarly internalized relations with censorship as a normal negotiation that formed part of their creative process.

For us, García Márquez's case is peculiar, however, in that his daily interaction with the censor was quite different from what his fellow Boom writers experienced in Spain. In his case the immediacy of the censorial act, *in situ* at the newsroom, left very little room for the kind of negotiation Boom writers engaged in with their Spanish censors. Another important distinction is that he was first exposed to censorship of the press, which operates under different rules than the censorship of literary works. Authoritarian regimes are wary of the press's power to call for immediate political activism and to generate antigovernment mass movements and protests on the spot. In the case of literary works, there seems to be more opportunity for maneuver, in part because circulation figures are usually smaller and the political impact is not as immediate as printed news can be. (It can also be less ephemeral, of course.) Furthermore, in Franco's Spain the censors of literary works, while concerned with the political agenda of a particular work or writer, tended to focus more stringently on material they saw as indecent and sexually explicit (a focus that, of course, was part of the regime's own political agenda). This difference was important in the case of García Márquez because his training as a journalist took place under the supervision of government censors while for the most part his literary writing in Colombia was freed from censorship. Equally important is that his "familiar" relationship with the government censor resulted in what he calls "a creative challenge." This took the form of finding ways to adhere to the censor's requests in such a way as to circumvent their purpose. He describes *El Universal*'s resident censor as follows:

> Me quedé en la redacción casi dos años publicando hasta dos notas diarias que lograba ganarle a la censura, con firma y sin firma, y *a punto de casarme con la sobrina del censor*. Todavía me pregunto cómo habría sido mi vida sin el lápiz del maestro Zabala y el torniquete de la censura, cuya sola *existencia era un desafío creador*. Pero el censor vivía más en guardia que nosotros por sus delirios de persecución. Las citas de grandes autores le parecían emboscadas sospechosas, como en efecto lo fueron muchas veces. *Veía fantasmas. Era un cervantino de pacotilla que suponía significados imaginarios*. (García Márquez, *Vivir* 388–89; emphasis mine)

> I stayed in the newsroom for almost two years, publishing as many as two daily articles that I managed to get past the censorship, signed and unsigned, until *I was ready to marry the censor's niece*. I still ask myself what my life would have been

without the pencil of Maestro Zabala and the tourniquet of censorship, whose *mere existence was a creative challenge*. But the censor was more on his guard than we were because of his delusions of persecution. Citations from great authors seemed like suspicious ambushes to him, which in fact they often were. *He saw phantoms. He was a second-rate student of Cervantes who inferred imaginary meanings*. (García Márquez, *Living* 324; emphasis mine)

The censor's paranoia seems a logical result of his seeing reporters complying with his requests and apparently working with him, while simultaneously internalizing censorship and learning tricky ways to get around it. Five decades later this censorial experience at the newspaper was to bear fruit in the form of a secondary character in *Memoria de mis putas tristes*, García Márquez's tongue-in-cheek homage to his creative misgivings concerning censorship:

> También estaba allí fuera de horas el censor oficial, don Jerónimo Ortega, a quien llamábamos el *Abominable Hombre de las Nueve* porque llegaba puntual a esa hora de la noche con su lápiz sangriento de sátrapa gordo.... Después de padecerlo por cuatro años, habíamos terminado por aceptarlo como la mala conciencia de nosotros mismos (García Márquez, *Memoria de mis putas tristes* 44)

> Outside of working hours he was also the official censor there, don Jerónimo Ortega, whom we called *The Abominable Nine O'Clock Man* because he arrived at that time each evening with his bloody pencil like a fat despot.... After enduring him for four years, we had finally accepted him as our own bad conscience. (my translation)

This "abominable snowman" of censorship is later described in the novel holding "a pencil like Torquemada" ("con su lápiz de Torquemada") (55), which—however subliminally—links both excerpts (the one from *Vivir* and the one from *Memoria*) to the history of Spanish censorship: the modern censor is seen as a quasi-Inquisitor in the novel, and concurrently as a strict and paranoid Cervantine reader in the memoirs. Taken together, the two excerpts suggest that Spain's history of censorship (particularly in relation to Latin America) was somehow in García Márquez's mind as he wrote, even though at the time these episodes occurred he had not yet attempted to publish in Franco's Spain. (He would have been aware of the restrictions other authors faced under the Franco regime.)

García Márquez's experience with the censors in Colombia was, then, mainly related to his job as reporter. His early novels, *La hojarasca* (1955) and *El coronel no tiene quien le escriba* (1961) appeared at small Colombian presses and were not subjected to the official censorship he faced as a journalist.[10] Arguably, they *were* subjected to a kind of market-driven censorship, since the publishers did not distribute their books very widely. It was as a result of this poor distribution that prospective editors like Barral did not become fully acquainted with his works until after the publication of *Cien años de soledad* and the subsequent reprints of his earlier novels by Sudamericana. But the upshot for García Márquez is that the lack of exposure he received early in his career, together with Barral's blunder, exempted him for the most part from having to undergo the scrutiny of Spanish censorship.

Given that small presses didn't have a wide distribution network, it would have seemed natural for García Márquez to pursue wider distribution and international exposure for his works. Spain's publishing houses were one of the obvious choices. Fortunately for him, however, his first attempt to publish in Spain (well before his dealings with Barral) turned out to be quite disastrous, a fact that meant he did not undergo censorship of the kind most Boom writers experienced there. In 1962, his novel *La mala hora* was awarded the Esso Prize in Colombia, and it was decided to send the book for printing, and apparently for publication, in Spain. (It is unclear if the author or the prize organizers initiated this move.) The chosen printing house was Gráficas Luis Pérez, although García Márquez recalls that the book was sent to Editorial Iberoamericana in Madrid, a firm known for the high quality of their books and competitive distribution. For him, this publication was at first a happy occasion: the book appeared "with a large printing and stellar launching. It was bound in leather, with impeccable print on excellent paper" (*Living* 232). When he checked the text, he thought otherwise.

Before the novel reached the Spanish printer it had already been subjected to some censorial intervention on the part of the president of the Colombian Academy (which sponsored the prize), Father Félix Restrepo. Restrepo intervened to have the work's original title "Este pueblo de mierda" ["This Shit-eating Town"] changed as well as the words "condom" and "masturbation," which he found to be offensive (*Living* 231). These were minor changes and insignificant compared to what García Márquez realized when he looked at the printed book: "The proofreaders at Imprenta Luis Pérez, in Madrid, proceeded—without consulting with the author—to put the text into 'correct Castilian'. They Madrilenized it, removing all Americanisms, replacing phrases or words they found to be obscure, and, as if that weren't enough, they poisoned the novel with typographical errors" (Santana 189).

What remains unclear about this episode is who was behind the changes in the text. There is no record at the *Archivo* showing that *La mala hora* was ever submitted to the censorship authorities, and there is an unaccounted discrepancy between the author's claim that the publisher was Editorial Iberoamericana and the fact that the book is catalogued at the National Library as published by Gráficas Luis Pérez. It is of course possible, although there is no concrete evidence, that—whether formally or informally—the corrections in the book did come from the Spanish censors, and that the printers complied for fear that the book would not be authorized to circulate. However, the Spanish edition met all the necessary legal requirements—"Depósito Legal M. 14738," and "Registro 6506-62"—for distribution in Spain. So the most likely scenario is that Luis Pérez (or, as García Márquez himself indicates, someone else at his firm) took it upon himself to "Hispanicize" or "Madrilenize" the text. After all, this was something the censors had done in the case of other Latin American writers, and publishers and editors were well aware that part of the censors' mission was to maintain the "purity" of the Spanish language. This last scenario seems to be in tune with García Márquez's recollection of the episode, which he calls a "dubbing" of his Indian language into "the purest Madrid dialect" (*Living* 233):

> no conforme con peinar la gramática de los diálogos, el corrector se permitió entrar a mano armada en el estilo, y el libro quedó plagado de parches matritenses que no tenían nada que ver con el original. En consecuencia, no me quedó otro recurso que desautorizar la edición por considerarla adulterada, y recoger e incinerar los ejemplares que aún no se hubieran vendido. La respuesta de los responsables fue el silencio absoluto. (*Vivir para contarla* 279)

> Not content with touching up the grammar in the dialogues, the proofreader permitted himself to change the style with a heavy hand, and the book was filled with Madrilenian patches that had nothing to do with the original. As a consequence, I had no recourse but to withdraw my permission from the edition because I considered it adulterated, and to retrieve and burn the copies that had not yet been sold. The reply of those responsible was absolute silence.[11]] (*Living* 232–33)

To his dismay, then, the edition went forward with a run of five thousand copies (a significant number that indicates it was to be exported), of which, according to the information provided in the book itself, fifty remained in the possession of the author and one hundred seventy in the publishers's hands. This episode is a unique case in the annals of censorship practices in Franco's Spain. For one thing, there is, as I have mentioned, no official record of the 1962 edition of *La mala hora*, and it appears that this submission was simply a printing order from overseas. Is it possible that since the author did not wish to have his name affiliated with such an outrageous edition the printing firm (not the publishing house) finally took responsibility for the work, and published it as a book without the approval of Iberoamericana? The "Madrilenization" of García Márquez's writing was certainly a censorial act on the part of Gráficas Luis Pérez. Such an intervention may seem unimaginable today, but we must bear in mind that one of the clear messages the censors conveyed in their reports was the importance of maintaining the purity of the Spanish (i.e., Castilian) language in addition to supporting good morals and decency and all other tenets of the regime. Perhaps we have here a case of "hyper-corrective censorship," in which the printer went beyond the call of duty and corrected more than what the authorities themselves might have required.

This messy and unusual first attempt at publishing *La mala hora* in Spain perhaps made García Márquez more cautious than his fellow Boom writers about Spanish publishers. It seemed that in Spain he would have to fight not only the kind of official censorship to which he had grown accustomed, but also an unofficial form of censorship on the part of Spanish publishers who wished to "Hispanize" his grammar. Nevertheless, García Márquez did not give up on the idea of publishing his work in Spain. Because of his connection through Balcells with the Catalan publishing industry, it is hard to imagine that this incident in 1962 would have been enough in itself to discourage him altogether from publishing there. And, in fact, by 1965 he had signed a contract with Carmen Balcells that expanded their previous business relationship. Until then, between 1962 and 1965, Balcells had been his agent solely for the translation of his works worldwide. But as of July 7, 1965, she was to represent him in the Spanish-language book market and on both sides of the Atlantic. With this move García Márquez sought to strengthen his connections with the Catalan intelligentsia and the Spanish publishing industry. Thus, it came about that as he was completing *Cien años de soledad*, the opportune letter from Porrúa reached him in Mexico, just as he was poised to publish with Seix Barral. And as we have seen, Porrúa's letter, together with a number of factors that came into play during and after the publication of *Cien años de soledad*, would result in his most famous work being spared from undergoing Franco's censorship, as was his subsequent writing as well.

The commercial and critical success of the novel soon caught the eye of the Spanish authorities (and presumably of Barral also), as García Márquez became an overnight success they could not turn their backs on. The upshot was that from then on he never had to go through the same kind of scrutiny most Latin American authors experienced in Franco's Spain. He appeared on the literary scene as an already consecrated, acclaimed, and economically profitable author, and indeed as one who had published, albeit semi-clandestinely, in Spain. His meteoric publishing career after 1967 made him immune to the Spanish censorship authorities. But he, by then, probably felt quite wary of Spanish presses, and had lost any interest in working with them.

So the Spanish authorities soon began to see a plethora of importation requests for his books. Had he published in Spain, he would clearly have been a great asset to the expansionist policy they sought to implement in the Latin American book market. As the authorities approved the importation of his books, they must have understood that they had lost an author who could win them a very considerable slice of this coveted export market. A quick look at the publishers' requests to import García Márquez's works shows that in 1967 the authorities approved in very small numbers the importation of *La mala hora* (twenty-five copies), *Cien años de soledad* (fifty copies), *El coronel no tiene quien le escriba* (twenty-five copies), and *Los funerales de la Mamá Grande* [*Big Mama's Funeral*] (fifty copies), a total of only two hundred copies. By the following year, however, these requests had increased considerably, with the numbers in the thousands. It would have been clear that Spain had missed a golden opportunity.[12]

As a consequence of the fact that most of García Márquez's works first circulated as imports, his censorship dossier at the *Archivo* is rather thin by comparison with that of other notable Boom writers. The dossier is obviously incomplete. His importation files, though, are impressive in terms of titles and number of requests. Sudamericana and Era were profiting from the book sales of a best-selling author.

Cien años de soledad was first cleared as an imported book in 1967 and, as an international success, later massively distributed in Spain first through EDHASA and later through the book club *Círculo de Lectores*, which made the novel a household item. Since in many cases an import application was a first step toward publishing a

Spanish edition, it is notable that Seix Barral never applied to import *Cien años de soledad*. It was in fact only in 1969 that *any* official authorization to print a book by García Márquez in Spain was approved (perhaps with the exception of *La mala hora* for which there are no official records). The petition came then from EDHASA, the Barcelona publishing house with the closest ties to Sudamericana. On January 29, 1969 EDHASA requested permission to reprint five thousand copies of *Cien años de soledad* at a selling price of one hundred eighty pesetas per book. (Subastas Velázquez auctioned a copy of the first Spanish edition for thirty thousand euros the same day they auctioned the galley proofs of *Cien años de soledad*.)

In its petition EDHASA—which submitted similar petitions to reprint ten thousand copies of *La hojarasca* and another ten thousand of *Cien años de soledad* on April 29, 1969—announced to the Spanish authorities the kind of large-scale reprint that by this time was bound to please them.[13] As in other cases publishers had previously done (Barral, for instance), EDHASA argued that the book market was eager to buy García Márquez's novels. Authorizing EDHASA's petition would not only result in profitable returns for the Spanish printing presses, but also would enhance Hispano-Argentinean cultural exchange, which the government had both cultural and economic reasons to wish to pursue:

> Que dado el éxito alcanzado por la obra de Gabriel García Márquez...y la premura con que nuestros clientes nos solicitan más ejemplares de la misma...y a fin de dar una mayor agilidad a los intercambios culturales con aquella Nación hermana, procurando, al mismo tiempo un incremento de rendimiento laboral para nuestras imprentas...(se) solicita la autorización para imprimir en España....

> Given the success achieved by the work of Gabriel García Márquez...and the urgency with which our clients are asking for more copies of his work...and in order to expedite cultural exchanges with that sister Nation while trying at the same time to increase the productivity of our presses...we request authorization to print in Spain.... (Expediente de *Cien años* January 1969)

Needless to say this petition was quickly approved. The censor's report states that it was an "urgent" request. The novel reached the censor's desk only a day after it had been submitted. A handwritten notation (most likely the censor's) indicated at the end of the report that it had been previously approved as an imported book. This is important for a number of reasons. One, it is very likely that the censor was already familiar with the book and had presumably read it out of his office hours, which would have helped expedite the report. Two, imported books that had been approved numerous times (by then the records show that at least five petitions had been filed) were a shoo-in for approval. And third, successful imports were seen as competition, so that there was a tendency to be more permissive when it came to Spanish editions of books that were already circulating. A couple of weeks after the urgent petition was filed on behalf of EDHASA, February 15 to be precise, the censor had concluded his report on the novel, which was then cleared for publication on February 17, 1969.

Conditioned by the overwhelming approval the novel had received in the importation files, the censor handily concluded that *Cien años de soledad* was indeed a great novel—"Como novela, muy buena." In his view, this was a social novel in which the author depicted the lives of low and middle-class Colombians by exposing matrimonial infidelities, family feuds, their failed businesses, and the high rates of infant mortality and natality. In the picture of this society offered by García Márquez, the censor saw some immoral behavior among members of the family but no endorsement of such behavior on the author's part:

> Moralmente, presenta un ambiente en el que predomina la inmoralidad como cosa de todos los días y sin ulteriores preocupaciones éticas, aunque falten personajes que se planteen problemas de conciencia. Sin embargo, no se incurre en descripciones escabrosas ni inmorales: simplemente, se describen situaciones incovenientes sin aprobarlas ni condenarlas pero produciendo una impresión desfavorable hacia tales situaciones.
>
> Morally speaking, it presents an environment in which immorality predominates as a daily occurrence and without any ulterior ethical preoccupation, even though no character has problems of conscience. However, they are no risqué or immoral descriptions: the novel simply describes unsuitable situations without approving or condemning them, but rather producing an unfavorable impression concerning such situations. (Expediente de *Cien años* January 1969)

The censor's nearly incomprehensible comments on morality reveal nevertheless that the novel's magical realism (which the censor refers to as "como cosa de todos los días" and "se describen situaciones sin aprobarlas ni condenarlas") must have worked as an antidote to his moral concerns. Somewhat oblivious to the magical realist genre (the term itself completely escapes him), the censor argues that García Márquez has written a realist or social novel with the intention of providing "una idea lo más exacta posible de la baja y media sociedad hispanoamericana" ["the most exact idea possible of the low and middle-class Latin American society"]. Even so, he still sees no "particular thesis" in the novel and ultimately no direct call to action on its readers: "Políticamente, la obra no presenta problema ninguno. Ideológicamente tampoco, porque no defiende tesis sino que describe situaciones" ["From a political or ideological standpoint the work does not present any problems because it does not defend a thesis. It just describes situations"] (Expediente de *Cien años* January 1969).

It seems obvious that, had the censor in fact raised significant concerns, the higher-ups at the Ministry would have paid them little attention; their interest in García Márquez's works from that point onwards was now mostly economic. This emerges clearly from a second censor's report, which was issued on May 6, 1969 following EDHASA's petition to print a second Spanish edition of *Cien años de soledad*:

> repetidamente autorizada en ediciones argentinas (cinco de 1967 a 1968). De un notable valor literario, la edición española que ahora se presenta es idéntica en contenido y formato—cubiertas, presentación y paginación—a la última argentina autorizada (en expte. 1184/69) por lo que nuevamente puede autorizarse.
>
> repeatedly authorized in Argentinean editions (five between 1967 and 1968). Of great literary value, the Spanish edition hereby submitted is identical in format and content—book covers, presentation, and pagination—to the last authorized Argentinean edition (see file 1184/69). Therefore it can be authorized again. (Expediente de *Cien años* April 1969)

The approval of this second Spanish edition praises the literary worth of the work and details the economic value of the novel, pointing out the savings on book designs and the number of importations from Argentina that had already been approved. The process, at this point, was virtually automatic.

Still, such leniency did not go unnoticed. On September 24, 1973, the Ministry of Information received a letter from a concerned citizen who was appalled by the wide distribution of *Cien años de soledad* and by the fact that such a "disgusting book" had become mandatory reading in Spanish high schools. As it happens, this amateur censor, by the name of José Vernet Mateu, was a resident of Barcelona's Eixample neighborhood, and his house on Carrer de Córsega was situated only seven blocks away from Paseo de Gracia's *Casa Batlló* (where many years later the galley proofs of *Cien años de soledad* would fail to auction) and two blocks away from Seix Barral's headquarters in Carrer de Provença.

3. A CITIZEN CENSOR

Vernet Mateu's letter is a perfect example of the Francoist government's recruitment of its citizens to perform censorial duties on their own behalf. Indeed, it was one of the underlying principles of the new censorship regulations that came into effect during the *apertura* to move the practice of censorship beyond the Ministry's desks, and displace it onto publishers, writers, and why not, concerned citizens of the regime. Vernet's case is admittedly an extreme one. It is reminiscent of sunny afternoons in bullrings across Spain when amateur matadors (*los espontáneos*) jump into the arena to prove their abilities in the ring. Vernet, you could say, was a "spontaneous censor" and most likely not a welcomed one. His spontaneous leap into the censorship arena was probably motivated by a number of factors. But it mainly sprang out of what must have been obvious to anyone reading this novel in Spain: there were too many infidelities in the Buendía family, too many sexual descriptions and accounts of incest in the novel. To the list he provided one could certainly add the novel's overt political commentary on Spain's colonial past, and its left-leaning political position concerning the imperialist colonization of Macondo. These features had probably not escaped the official censors, who had preferred to look the other way and likewise forgot to investigate the close ties between García Márquez and Castro. But Vernet's letter subsists as a clue to the kind of treatment García Márquez's novel would probably have received had it been first published in Franco's Spain.

Beyond being a formal complaint from a concerned citizen about mandatory reading in Spanish high schools, it does read uncannily like the kind of report the official censors *might* have produced, had the novel been submitted for first publication under the Franco regime. It is not unthinkable that, from what Barral already knew of García Márquez's work (recall that he was perhaps familiar with the Spanish version of *La mala hora*) and his acquaintance with the apparatus of censorship, he anticipated problems with the Spanish authorities very much like the ones outlined by Vernet.

The letter begins with a general critique of the Spanish educational system: "tengo dos hijos en edad escolar y veo que la enseñanza que se les imparte no está de acuerdo con los ideales que informaron el Estado nacido el 18 de julio" ["I have two sons of school age and I see that the education they are receiving is at odds with the ideals that informed the State that was born on July 18"]. Sounding at this point like a disgruntled parent nostalgic for the ideals of Franco's uprising of July 18, 1936 (*Alzamiento Nacional*) that he saw slipping away, he moves quickly to display his skills as a censor, as well as his detailed knowledge of the printing laws that should have prevented the publication and massive distribution of García Márquez's novel:

> voy a referirme tan sólo a un libro que anda de mano en mano entre los estudiantes de COU y aún de cursos anteriores, porque se recomienda en algunos centros docentes y se exige como obligatorio en clases de Literatura española. Se trata de "Cien años de soledad" del escritor colombiano Gabriel García Márquez, y por las fotocopias que acompaño podrá darse V.E. una idea de lo repugnante de su texto.
>
> I am going to refer only to one book that high school seniors (and even students from earlier years) pass from hand to hand because it is recommended in some schools and required in others as compulsory reading for Spanish literature courses. The book is "One Hundred Years of Solitude" by the Colombian writer Gabriel García Márquez, and according to the enclosed photocopies your excellency will get an idea of how repugnant this text really is. (Expediente de *Cien años* 1972)[14]

Unaware though he probably was of the government's policies for expanding the book industry, Vernet's opening statement—couched as it is in pompous prose that is itself redolent of the bureaucracy—performs the conflation of economics and censorship that so clearly drove the regimes's practices. In a manner not dissimilar from what I have found in many official reports on the Boom, his letter describes, on the one hand, the book's alleged immorality (something the official censor had only vaguely pointed out), while on the other, it indirectly addresses the financial returns the novel was bringing in, since it has now become a required or recommended textbook in schools. And he goes on to question why a Colombian author has become part of the Spanish literature canon, a canon that in his view should be closer to the ideals of *Alzamiento Nacional*. Obviously, the inclusion of García Márquez's novel in the high school curriculum is a consequence of the marketing the novel underwent in Spain (marketing that entailed massive Spanish reprints from which Spanish printers benefited), not to mention the endorsement of the Spanish censorship authorities without which this bonanza could not have occurred. And the inclusion of the novel in Spanish literature courses responded to the regime's cultural policies of promoting Spain's heritage and language in the larger community of Spanish speakers in the Americas. Somehow for the authorities, books of great literary value (and great literary "buys") always redounded to the benefit of a Spain that they saw as the cradle of the Hispanic cultural heritage.

Vernet, the fervent *franquista* who believed the regime should stick to its hard-line censorship regulations even in its decaying years, did not seem to be aware that the circulation of books in Spain was a function of these *apertura* policies. He nevertheless was fully aware of the legal steps publishers had to go through in order to gain approval to print and distribute their books. In a surprising show of knowledge concerning these publishing matters, he wonders disingenuously about the legal mechanisms that authorized the printing in Spain of *Cien años de soledad* :

> Yo me pregunto, en mi ignorancia de simple hombre de la calle: ¿Cómo es posible que un libro tan soez, tan demoledor de la moral cristiana, tan embrutecedor, haya encontrado camino expedito para su edición en España, con su "Depósito Legal," su pie de imprenta y todos los requisitos que la Ley exige para que una obra pueda publicarse?

> In my ignorance as a simple man of the streets I wonder how it is possible for a book so obscene, so destructive of Christian morality, so brutalizing, to have found an expeditious way toward publication in Spain, with its "Depósito Legal" and publishing details, everything requisite according to the law. (Expediente de *Cien años* 1972)

To prove his point he enclosed photocopies of the copyright page, along with several passages that in his view demonstrated the novel's obscenity and immorality. He also included photocopies of the back cover where EDHASA listed some of the authors they published and Vernet had circled none other than the playwright Fernando Arrabal, who was a fervent critic of the Franco regime and a prominent member of the exiled community of Spanish intellectuals in France. For the convenience of the Minister of Information, he circled the copyright information where it is clearly stated that the novel is an edition "authorized by Editorial Sudamericana of Buenos Aires" and "published in Barcelona by Editora y Distribuidora Hispano Americana, S.A., (EDHASA), with premises on Avenida Infanta Carlota 129." Finally,

Vernet also circled the "Depósito Legal" information at the bottom of the copyright page, which includes the official registration number for the book and lists the printing press ("Romargraf") that actually put the book together: "Depósito Legal: B.46.618–1972. ROMARGRAF, S.A.—Santa, 387, Barcelona-14" (Expediente de *Cien años*). This was the proof that the book had been printed and distributed in Spain by a duly authorized Spanish firm. This detailed information (which of course the authorities had) suggests that Vernet was dropping heavy hints in hopes that the authorities would launch an inquiry with a view to a possible "sequestration" of the book. Precisely to this end, he had circled the address not only of the printing press (ROMARGRAF) but also of the publisher (EDHASA):

> ¿Es que en el ordenamiento jurídico español no existe algún resorte para evitar la publicación y difusión de libros que ofenden gravemente a la moral, que corrompen a la juventud, que socavan los cimientos de la convivencia entre personas civilizadas? Esto yo no me lo explico. Como tampoco me explico que este libro pueda servir de texto obligatorio a muchachos de 16 años, a los que literalmente corrompe y embrutece.
>
> Is it the case that the Spanish judicial system does not have any recourse that would prevent the publication and distribution of books that are gravely immoral, corrupt youth, and undermine the foundations of social life among civilized people? This I cannot understand. Neither can I understand that this book can serve as a required textbook that literally corrupts and brutalizes sixteen-year-old boys. (Expediente de *Cien años* 1972)

Vernet is resorting once more to his trademark *faux naïf* style. His question falls short of a direct request to the Minister to initiate sequestration procedures, but the implication is evident. This well-informed "spontaneous censor" knew that the authorities had a mechanism in place to remove books from printing presses and bookstores as they saw fit. What would be the point of Vernet's letter if he really thought that nothing could be done to stop the distribution of García Márquez's novel? His closing paragraph makes it perfectly clear that he is pleading for "an opportune remedy" that he trusts the Minister to find and apply:

> ¿Podría darme V.E. una explicación a mis angustiosos interrogantes? ¿Hemos de contemplar cómo se nos pervierte a nues-

tros hijos, por organismos de un Estado que nació de la sangre de millares de españoles que cayeron por una España mejor y más limpia? En espera de que V.E. se dará cuenta de la gravedad del asunto, y pondrá el oportuno remedio, queda de V.E. afmo. Servidor.

Might your excellency provide me with some explanation in response to my anxious questions? Are we to stand by and watch our sons being perverted by the offices of a State that was born from the blood of thousands of Spaniards who died for a better and cleaner Spain? Hoping that your excellency will realize the gravity of this affair and provide the appropriate remedy, I remain your excellency's affectionate servant. (Expediente de *Cien años* 1972)

While Vernet's "spontaneous" reporting is at odds with the Spanish censors' own reporting on the novel, it is worth reiterating that his comments, together with the photocopies of the "censorable" sections enclosed with his letter, offer an indication of the kind of changes the novel would probably have undergone had it been first released in Spain. The sections identified by Vernet the protocensor as "repugnant" and "obscene" are in his words only a small sample, since "from the whole book one could extract numerous pages like the ones reproduced here" ["de todo el libro, podrían sacarse numerosas páginas como las reproducidas"] (Expediente de *Cien años* 1972). Vernet's sampling amounts to nine pages (or sections of pages) of the EDHASA edition of 1969, which as the censorship files show, was identical in format and pagination to the 1967 Sudamericana edition.[15] Most of the selected passages present sexually explicit descriptions or include "offensive" comments on the Catholic church, or both, as in the case of the incest between Aureliano Babilonia and his aunt Amaranta Úrsula, which Vernet places on the top page of his collection of censorable passages:

Aureliano abandonó los pergaminos...y contestaba de cualquier modo las cartas del sabio catalán. Perdieron el sentido de la realidad, la noción del tiempo y el ritmo de los hábitos cotidianos....Mientras él amasaba con claras de huevo los senos eréctiles de Amaranta Úrsula, o suavizaba con manteca de coco sus muslos elásticos...ella jugaba con la portentosa criatura de Aureliano, y le pintaba ojos de payaso con carmín y de labios y bigotes de turco con carboncillo de las cejas...[corresponding to page 341 Sudamericana edition]. (Expediente de *Cien años* 1972)

> Aureliano abandoned the parchments...and carelessly answered the letters from the wise Catalonian. They lost their sense of reality, the notion of time, the rhythm of daily habits.... While he would rub Amaranta Úrsula's erect breast with egg whites or smooth elastic thighs and peachlike stomach with cocoa butter, she would play with Aureliano's portentous creature and give it a Turk's mustache with eyebrow pencil. (*One Hundred Years* 405–6)

While there is no official response to Vernet's letter in García Márquez's dossier, it is possible that the Ministry of Information responded directly. The letter was addressed to the Minister and channeled to the censorship files through the "Secretaría Particular del Sr. Ministro" ["Personal Secretariat of the Minister"], unaccompanied by any instructions or directions. The García Márquez dossier does not include any document written by a censor addressing Vernet's complaints. By 1973 the *official* censors had approved the Spanish edition of *Cien años de soledad* on several occasions. They were understandably not eager to revisit what they must have considered a closed case.

Chapter 5

Betrayed by Censorship

Manuel Puig Declassified

The censor who evaluated Manuel Puig's first novel *La traición de Rita Hayworth* [*Betrayed by Rita Hayworth*] in June 1966 began his confidential report with the following statement: "La lectura de esta novela da la impresión de una leonera llena de cosas heterogéneas e inútiles, todas amontonadas sin orden ni concierto. No tiene casi argumento" ["Reading this novel gives the impression of a lion's den where heterogeneous and useless things are piled up without any order or agreement. It has almost no plot"] (Expediente de *La traición* 1966). This censor, ventriloquizing the rectitude of the Franco regime, sought *orden y concierto* in the assemblage of unmediated dialogues, interior monologues, and excerpts from diaries that makes up *La traición*. To reconstruct the linear story of the novel (as the censor would have liked to do) would be a betrayal of the text's poetics and a form of censorious reading.[1] Irritated by the novel's overt display of voices that prevented him from finding any organizing narrative voice to guide his reading, the censor concluded that little sense could be made of Puig's "cheap novelette" ["novelucho de tres al cuarto"] (Expediente de *La traición* 1966).[2] He did see, however, that the novel attacked the morals of the regime, and therefore refused to allow its publication in Spain. Puzzled by the craft of this seemingly new Catalan writer, "Joan Manuel Puig," and by his subversion of linear narrative, the censor had no choice but to conclude that Puig's novel was "a trash can" ["un cubo de basura"] (Expediente de *La traición* 1966).[3] His most obvious strategy, given that he thought the novel had almost no plot, was to assert that the "foul language" of the adolescents portrayed in the novel made it not only "50 percent pornographic" ["pornográfica en un 50%"] but also "highly obscene" ["soez en alto grado"] (Expediente de *La traición* 1966).

While morals and the preservation of the Spanish language were top priorities for the Spanish censors, it is also revealing that the report on Puig addressed another preoccupation of the Franco authorities: the economic value of literature. The censor stressed that *La traición* had "no value." It was a "pile-up of useless things," a "trash can," and "a cheap novelette" that would be wasteful to publish. His contempt, of course, must be understood within the context of the competition for the Spanish-language book market of the 1960s and 1970s that I have already discussed. Aware of the government's economic interests, the censor argued that if the authorities were to allow the publication of Puig's novel, several corrections would first be needed. He was clearly thinking of the behind-the-scenes negotiations between publishers, censors, and writers that had become commonplace in the publishing industry. In the case of Puig, however, Barral did not seek to negotiate (i.e., to correct or suppress passages in the novel) as he had done with Vargas Llosa or Cabrera Infante, and as the censor had left the door open for him to do. Puig naturally felt betrayed by Barral's failure to negotiate with the authorities: "the book did not get published. A year later I was told it was due to 'censorship,' but that was untrue. So my first encounter with censorship was a confused affair. Dictator Franco wasn't entirely to blame. But it was an indication of things to come" ("Losing Readers" 55).

While Barral was clearly opposed to the censorial practices of the regime, he failed to attend to the censorship he himself practiced as a publisher. As has been noted by critics, the interaction between Puig and Barral was less than cordial; and therefore the process leading to the publication of Puig's first novel by Seix Barral gave rise to suspicions of treachery. Juan Goytisolo remembers that Puig's entry into the Spanish literary market was marked by a series of what he specifically calls betrayals. For example, the jury of the 1965 *Biblioteca Breve* Prize voted in the first ballot to give the award to Puig, but Carlos Barral rejected the results and argued that the novel was too "frivolous" to be awarded the prize. According to Goytisolo, Barral thought that "an effeminate, vulnerable and frail Argentine...did not deserve to appear in the prestigious catalogue of the publishing house" ["un argentino afeminado, vulnerable y frágil...no era digno de figurar en el prestigioso catálogo de la editorial"] (9).

Puig would comment years later that his first encounter with Barral was a "disaster." To begin with, their personal styles clashed: "he was dressed to the nines, I was merely covered; he was rich, a *bon viveur* and a Communist; I was poor, of frugal habits, and only a Socialist" ("Losing Readers" 55). Barral did not like Puig's "relaxed appearance," nor did he enjoy Puig's criticism of the Castro regime. This last was perhaps a miscalculation on Puig's part given that Barral's alliance with one of Cuba's most prominent cultural institutions, *Casa de las Américas*, was widely known. To make things worse for Puig, as it turned out, Barral had just returned from Cuba.

Being rejected in this manner by one of the most established publishers in the field, Puig realized that official censorship was not the only form of censorship hindering his literary career. It was evident that, even before being exposed to the official censorship of the Franco regime, his writing had already been subjected to a form of gender-based censorship, which applied as well to his persona. Jaime Manrique comments that after the publication of Puig's masterpiece *El beso de la mujer araña*, "the literary establishment could not forgive a major author of the 'boom' for coming out with a gay novel," one in which the "revolutionary hero," Molina, was a child molester and a queen (43). While Manrique's assessment of the reception of *El beso* is debatable, it *is* worth remembering that recognized figures of the literary establishment such as Jorge Luis Borges had expressed disdain for Puig à la Barral well before the publication of Puig's most openly gay novel: "Imagine a book that has lipstick on its cover," the erudite Borges commented about *Boquitas pintadas* [*Heartbreak Tango*] (Levine 231). (The elegant jacket of the Seix Barral edition of *Boquitas* comments eloquently on Borges's disdain; [Fig. 5.1]). Similarly, Puig was snubbed by the Latin American intelligentsia and by his prospective publishers for the "provocative" titles of his novels: Borges found *Boquitas* to be a "horrible" title (and possibly a horrible book), and the Latin American acquisitions person at Editions du Seuil in France proposed the more normative title of *Personnages* [*Characters*] for *La traición*, which could almost have been a response to the Spanish censor's demand for *orden y concierto*. Goytisolo claims that it was he who "discovered" the title *La traición de Rita Hayworth* after reading the novel for a possible edition by the French publisher Gallimard: "'La traición de Rita Hayworth'... fue la frase que me cautivó: tal era, debía ser, el título. Así, éste fue obra de Manuel Puig, pero su descubrimiento mío" ["The betrayal of Rita Hayworth... was the phrase that captivated me: that was it, that should be the title. Thus, Puig created the title but I discovered it"] (9). Here as often, Puig's title is exquisitely emblematic of the "faggotry" that permeates his fictions. His titles are for the most part intriguing phrases—that is, "the kiss of the spider woman," "pubis angelical," "the Buenos Aires affair," "eternal curse on the reader of these pages"—that give a foretaste of the ambiguity, nonconformity, and populist character of his writing. Of course, when critics used labels like "provocative" and "frivolous" for these titles (and the fictions behind them), they were code words for gay, and Puig would interpret them as homophobic remarks (Levine 222). The Spanish censors also picked up on the campiness of Puig's fiction, but were somehow unable to articulate this particular concern, even in terms of frivolity and glamour.

Even though no censor ever directly labeled Puig a gay author or claimed that he had written a gay novel, it is clear that they entertained this suspicion. But, as we know, their decision making in 1960s and 1970s was driven mainly by their desire to see an economic expansion of the book trade, and both ideology and morals consequently played a secondary role when revenues were at stake. This must have become quite clear to Puig when he experienced rejection from publishers and from the Spanish censors in the late 1960s and then the promotion and recognition of his works in the 1970s—ironically enough, by those who had previously rejected them. In this way, Puig's publishing trajectory is very illustrative of the economic and ideological tensions that dominated the Latin American Boom. Furthermore, as is so frequently the case with other Boom writers, Puig's novels often provide us with a reflection of such tensions in their own concerns, so that they are themselves very illustrative of the interrelatedness of economics and censorship. So I propose in this chapter to "declassify" the censorship imposed on Puig by publishers, writers, and official censors, and simultaneously to explore the important role played by censorial practices as a motif that is linked to the idea of betrayal in Puig's writing.

In particular, I will examine the publishing trajectory of *La traición* as an exemplary case study of Puig's dealings with the various forms of censorship he faced in his literary career. In tracing this trajectory, I declassify not only the Spanish government reports on Puig, but as well the economic and censorial cultural tensions that impeded Puig's entry into the book market and that also inform his novels. Economics and censorship *inform* Puig's literary career and literary production both in the sense that they "give form or character to" them and in the sense that they "disclose information about" them (*American Heritage Dictionary*). And, as I will show later, economics and censorship are key themes and organizing principles in *La traición*, where the Casals' discussion of the family economy mirrors the textual economy of Puig's

Fig. 5.1: Book cover. Manuel Puig's *Boquitas pintadas*. 2nd reprint (Barcelona: Seix Barral, 1976).

writing. In this novel (and in others by Puig), information is "economized," in the sense that family genealogies and relationships are omitted, characters barely outlined, and linear narratives dispersed. Puig's parsimonious approach to information was a complicating factor in his attempts to publish his early works, which, as I have noted, came under suspicious scrutiny for their apparent reticence, their practice of signifying something that went unspecified—for not saying more. This reticence made Puig's novels interpretable as "treacherous" texts in the sense that they were not to be trusted.

1. BETRAYED BY THE MARKETPLACE

The publication history of *La traición* is a cogent example of the scrutiny Puig endured in the 1960s book market. Once it was published in June 1968 by a small press in Buenos Aires, Editorial Jorge Álvarez, both the Spanish censorship authorities and Barral himself were forced to reconsider the value of Puig's work. The dilemma faced by censors became one of moral rectitude (the book was immoral and obscene) vs. economic profit (the book was published by a competitor). Similarly, the dilemma faced by Barral was one of queer aesthetics (his dislike of Puig's overt display of "faggotry") vs. publishing competition (in 1970 Jorge Álvarez ceded the Puig contract to Editorial Sudamericana). As had been the case with other Latin American novels, the Franco regime would not allow Puig's novels to be published in Spain until the case for their "usefulness" and profitability could be clearly made. This is not to say that profit making overruled the prohibition on publishing any work that the censors rejected. But economic success and international market recognition became helpful tools with which publishers like Barral could negotiate. Fortunately, Puig's belated appearance on Spain's literary market coincided with the implementation of the new censorship rules. As we have seen, for fervent *franquistas* such as Vernet, the regime's relaxation of these rules was *itself* a betrayal of the guiding principles of *Alzamiento Nacional*, which had been "revised" during the 1960's economic expansion (Labanyi 207).

These tensions between censorship and economics, which became endemic to the publishing industry of the 1960s, and, in the end, determined Puig's literary career, were summarized in the Spanish censor's report of 1966. Puig himself tried to "cash in" on having been censored in Spain. When he saw the manuscript Barral had submitted back from the censors "all underlined in red," he anticipated that the fact of having been censored in Franco's Spain would work elsewhere as a symbolic badge of honor. It was "a conflict [that] had created some curiosity" and would generate interest in his work on the part of other publishers (Puig, "Writers and Repression" 30–31). This proved to be the case when he first sought to publish his novel in England, Mexico, Argentina, and the United States. There *was* "curiosity" in all these places. But as the months went by, Puig was to realize that the symbolic capital derived from having been censored in Franco's Spain was, in the end, not necessarily sufficient or even helpful. Prospective publishers in London (Hamilton) and New York (Knopf) not only disagreed about the investment value attached to censorship; they also concurred with the Spanish censor's evaluation of the novel. As Puig confessed in a letter to the renowned literary critic Emir Rodríguez Monegal, the publishers' reactions to his novel did not differ from the Spanish censors': "according to them the novel was unbearably confusing, filled with characters that are impossible to follow, since you can't tell if they're speaking or thinking.... What sort of divine donkeys are these people who are in charge?" (Levine 186).

Why was it so important to these readers to be able to decode *La traición*? Why did the "divine donkeys" need all the characters and story lines in the novel to be fully and clearly identifiable? Certainly, Puig was not the only Latin American author who made use of fragmented narratives, nor was he the only one who resorted to multiple narrative perspectives. The fact that the Spanish censor's report and prospective publishers elsewhere concurred in viewing Puig's novel with a degree of suspicion perhaps indicates that the grounds for their dislike for Puig lay elsewhere. As is often the case when people write reports on books, what is said in the report is not necessarily what the reporter had in mind. Reports of this kind, in other words, are subject to self-censorship, and those that Puig was subjected to need to be looked at in the clear light of day and what they don't explicitly say about his work taken into account. They need to be declassified. For instance, the Spanish censor's report focused on the lack of *orden y concierto* in Puig's novel. But in fact it was chapter XI that he found to be the most problematic section of the novel, describing it as "a crime against decency" ["delito contra la honestidad"] that was "nauseating to read" ["da nauseas (sic) leerlo"] (Expediente de *La traición* 1966). In chapter XI, to which I will return later for a longer discussion, two of Toto's classmates reveal their sexual interest in him. To the censor, the chapter was "nauseating to read," but no further details are given as to what exactly produced this nausea. He could not bring himself to write the word homosexuality, it seems. Complaining about the lack of *orden y concierto* in the novel, he evidently intended "order" to mean "norm"—the heteronormativity that, it is true, Puig's text did not advocate.

What then made it possible, in due course, to publish *La traición* in Spain, even though in 1966 a censor had clearly seen what was "unnormal" about Puig's text and recommended that it be rejected on grounds of indecency? A first attempt to unblock the publication of Puig's novel occurred in August 1968, when the Spanish publisher Visor Libros requested permission to import ten copies of the Jorge Álvarez edition. The censors rejected this petition, on the grounds that the novel was still "immoral" (Expediente I-1268-68). Ten copies circulating in Spain would not have made a significant dent in the moral rectitude the censorship authorities wished to maintain, but giving clearance to import the novel from overseas would have allowed Spanish firms an opening in order to pursue its publication locally—something that, as the authorities were well aware, they were signaling that they wished to do. (Requests of this kind to import books from Latin American countries into Spain were frequently geared toward a possible Spanish edition of the books in question, and such requests often ranged between ten and fifty copies, as a way of testing the waters without alarming the regime.) So, although *La traición* was not published in Spain until 1971, one can assume that meanwhile both the Franco regime and, certainly, Barral kept a close eye on developments in Argentina, where Puig had finally managed to place his novel.

As recounted in Jill Levine's biography of Puig, the publication of *La traición* in Buenos Aires did not make Puig an overnight literary sensation. On the contrary, Puig felt "a thrill and a horror" when he realized first that the Álvarez edition was full of typos, and then that influential Argentinean journals and newspapers were refusing to advertise the novel and disapproved of its portrayal of frustrated housewives and "depraved" adolescents (Levine 205–207). If in Spain Puig had endured official censorship, in Argentina it was the market that imposed a censorship of its own. Puig himself reports that, even though there was no official censorship under the Onganía regime (1966–1970), de facto censorship was carried out in Argentina by publishers, who feared seizures of books and even their own incarceration if they printed material the regime found to be pornographic or obscene. In Argentina seizures at bookstores and a certain degree of intimidation of booksellers and printing presses who handled supposedly obscene material were common. The League of Mothers, Puig recalls, fought for (and won) the removal of *La traición* from bookstores in Buenos Aires in January 1974 ("Writers and Repression" 31). Also a report in the newspaper *La Nación* states that in 1974 the

Division of Morality of the Federal Police raided several downtown bookshops in Buenos Aires (Fausto, Atlántida, Rivero, and Santa Fe), where they seized, among other books, Puig's *The Buenos Aires Affair*, and detained the employees of these stores for a short while (Avellaneda 114).[4]

Thus, when Paco Porrúa—the first publisher willing to take a risk on Puig's novel—sent the galleys of *La traición* to the press, the "linotype operator noticed the abundance of four-letter words and stopped the work" ("Losing Readers" 55). Puig had then looked for another publisher, who did get his novel into print. But the Álvarez edition went for the most part unnoticed, and to Puig's disappointment the publisher did not respond by advertising the novel more aggressively. Thus, the release of *La traición* in Argentina was censored mostly by the agents (in the broader sense of the term) of the literary market. Puig also failed to convince Joaquín Mortiz, Seix Barral's partner in Mexico to publish it (Levine 199, 220).

His first real breakthrough in the literary market came in 1969, when the prestigious publisher Gallimard launched *La trahison de Rita Hayworth* in France to great popular and critical acclaim. The novel made it into *Le Monde*'s list of best novels of the year (Levine 219). That same year Puig completed his second novel *Boquitas pintadas*, which Editorial Sudamericana in Buenos Aires had agreed to publish. These two very significant publishing successes made Puig a best-selling author, so that his name began to be associated with economic profits. Thus it was that in 1969 the Spanish authorities, taking note of Puig's successful career, allowed the importation of Sudamericana's edition of *Boquitas* in 1969 *and* approved their request to reprint five thousand copies of Puig's second novel in Spain. This is only apparently inconsistent with the Spanish government's protectionist policies; notice the terms in which EDHASA (Editora y Distribuidora Hispanoamericana Sociedad Anónima), Sudamericana's affiliate in Spain, convinced them to allow the novel to be printed in Spain under the Sudamericana label:

> Dado el éxito alcanzado por la obra de Manuel Puig *Boquitas pintadas* editada por nuestra representada Editorial Sudamericana de Buenos Aires y la premura con que nuestros clientes nos solicitan más ejemplares de la misma... [y] habida cuenta del retraso que representa su envío desde la República Argentina, hemos solicitado de nuestra representada autorización para proceder en su nombre... a la impresión en España de una nueva edición que constaría de unos cinco mil (5000) ejemplares y que sería puesta a la venta al

mismo precio de 190 pesetas.... En su virtud y a fin de dar una mayor agilidad a los intercambios culturales con aquella Naciónhermana [sic] procurando al mismo tiempo, un incremento de rendimiento laboral para nuestras imprentas.

Given the success achieved by Manuel Puig's *Heartbreak Tango* published by our affiliate Editorial Sudamericana of Buenos Aires and the urgency with which our clients demand more copies of this novel... [and] being aware of the delay in shipments from the Republic of Argentina, we request... authorization to proceed with the printing of a new edition of 5,000 copies in Spain to be priced at 190 pesetas. In order to expedite cultural exchanges with this sister nation and to simultaneously increase the returns on labor from our printing presses we request permission to print 5,000 copies of the aforementioned work. (Ordenación editorial 1969)

Puig's works, as noted in the request, had now overcome the initial deficit of being perceived as "useless" or "trash," and were in demand. Important returns for Spanish printers could be anticipated should the request be approved. EDHASA also dutifully "borrowed" the argument that the regime had used since 1959 to intensify commercial exchanges with Latin American countries: Spain had a moral responsibility to foster cultural relations with the sister nations of the Americas, and to preserve the Spanish language worldwide. The deal would promote "bona fide" cultural exchange, and conveniently prove profitable also as a commercial enterprise. Two birds with one stone.

While *La traición* was still censored and unpublished in Spain, government officials were aware, then, of the successful reception and commercialization of *Boquitas*. Likewise, they were aware that Puig's success was permitting Sudamericana's books to make inroads into the Spanish market, as EDHASA foresaw in its petition. Carlos Barral, for his part, also took note of Puig's literary success. According to Suzanne Jill Levine, Barral now pushed for an "emergency edition" of *Boquitas*, and requested that Puig make "personal appearances" in Barcelona in an effort to gain notoriety in Spanish publishing circles. Puig was delighted and yet resentful: "the new Seix Barral is trying to imitate Universal and its well-remembered super production 'Three Wise Girls Smart Up'" (Levine 225).[5]

Barral also decided at this time to resubmit *La traición* to the Spanish censors. Argentinean editions of *La traición* were not authorized in Spain until 1976, and between 1968 and 1971 requests from book importers and distributors to import even small quantities ranging from ten to fifty copies were routinely denied (Expediente I-1268–68, Expediente 347–69, Expediente, 1384–71, Expediente, 671–73, Expediente, 776–73, Expediente, 20–76). The reason why *Boquitas* was authorized in 1969, three years before the Seix Barral edition of *La traición*, lies in the fact that it was actually printed in Spain under Sudamericana's imprint (Ordenación editorial 1969). Nevertheless, in November 1971 Manuel Puig's (no longer Joan Manuel Puig's) *La traición* again reached the censor's desk.

This time, Puig had a record with the Spanish authorities, so the censor in charge of reporting on the novel began his evaluation with the 1966 report on file.[6] Not surprisingly, he concurred with the previous evaluation of *La traición*, and as good as reproduced the opening sentence of the 1966 report: "Esto es un increíble cajón de sastre de difícil lectura" ["This is an incredible mess, difficult to read"] (Expediente de *La traición* 1971). This censor's "tailor's drawer" ["cajón de sastre"] echoes the lack of "orden y concierto" that the 1966 report had complained of.

There was a difference, though, in the reading abilities of these two censors. The 1971 censor was more perceptive, and perhaps less irritated, also, by Puig's style. He tried to place Puig within the literary trends of the Latin American Boom, which meant that in reflecting on *La traición*'s status as a Boom novel, he was implicitly addressing it as a potential best seller:

> Pretende encuadrarse en la nueva narrativa latinoamericana con toda clase de licencias no sólo literarias sino morales. Está compuesta por escena contadas a través de varias épocas de distintos personajes, abundando las impresiones de adolescentes, que agravan la impresión definitiva de la novela.
>
> [It] has an ambition to be considered part of the Latin American new novel with all sorts of licenses, both literary and moral. It comprises several scenes narrated by various characters at different points in time, with an abundance of adolescents' impressions [or: portrayals of adolescents], which detract from the overall impression of the novel. (Expediente de *La traición* 1971)

Unlike his colleague in 1966, this censor understood Puig's novel as a montage, then. But he was, to say the least, suspicious of it. What—and who—hides behind the unmediated voices in the novel? he seemed to wonder. To him, Puig was a Boom writer, but an unusual one, who allowed himself too many "literary and moral licenses" and, therefore, should not be trusted, much less published. He too was more concerned than he explicitly says about the atmosphere of homosexuality that permeates *La traición*. The supposedly unusual character of Puig's fiction and the difficulty of formulating an "impresión definitiva" are coded ways of referring to the "impression" of campy queerness that the novel exudes. While the 1966 report had not referred directly to the homosexuality of Puig's protagonist, chapter XI had already been flagged as "nauseating," so that the 1971 censor would have been pretty much forced to reexamine it. The 1966 censor was tantalizingly frugal in his remarks: "Particularmente el capítulo XI, desde la página 222 a la 240, da nauseas (sic) leerlo ["Particularly chapter XI, from pages 222 to 240, is nauseating to read"] (Expediente de *La traición* 1966).[7]

In the chapter in question, Cobito, the school's "wanna-be gangster," tells of his fixation on Toto and his plan to commit the perfect crime. He has assumed the voice and the role of another character, Deadly Joe, acting the part of a tough guy whose plan is to "rape" Toto and blame another classmate for the crime:

> ¡carajo!... de haber sabido que había una salida abierta en el corredor de las aulas de dibujo no se nos escapaba Casals, con las ganas de coger que tengo, me cago en Casals. El crimen perfecto, hay que prepararlo con tiempo, es como un reloj que funciona sin atrasar nunca, Colombo el calentón quiso agarrarlo el domingo de salida.... (*La traición* 1971, 197)

> shit! If I'd only known in time that there was a way out of the art rooms Casals wouldn't have gotten away, and me wanting a fuck so bad, damn Casals. The perfect murder takes time to prepare, it must be like a watch that never slows down, hot-pants Colombo wanted to grab him that very Sunday.... (*Betrayed* 148)[8]

The 1966 censor avoided all mention in his report of Deadly Joe's desire for Toto and of the violence with which it is expressed. Instead, his homophobic disgust is displaced into an attack on Puig's "foul language." What "nauseated" him, he says, is that the chapter is filled with words like "son of a bitch, motherfucker, asshole, fuck, shit, and so forth (for example, pages 231 and 232)" ["hijo de puta, la madre que te parió, cabrón, joderla, la mierda de, cagar (ejemplo, en págs. 231 y 232)"] (Expediente de *La traición* 1966). The 1971 censor, however, read this chapter, and the entire novel, in greater and more specific detail, concluding not only that Puig's novel was as "trashy" and "useless" as his predecessor had declared, but also that the novel's overt depiction of homosexuality was grounds for rejection: "Además de la pobreza literaria, rezuma mal gusto, abundando de manera reiterada las expresiones obscenas, de mal gusto, descripciones de homosexuales y toda clase de atrevimiento entre jóvenes de distinto sexo" ["Besides its literary poverty, the novel oozes bad taste, abounding in reiterated obscenities, expressions of poor taste, descriptions of homosexuals, and all sorts of audacities among youngsters of both sexes"] (Expediente de *La traición* 1971).

The "literary poverty" of *La traición*, he seemed to argue, was of a piece with its "abundance" of "poor taste," "audacities," and sexual encounters. In so doing, he made perfectly clear what the 1966 censor had meant by the "nauseating" effect of chapter XI. He uncensored his colleague's remarks and by stating what the other had failed to mention—that the novel is filled with "descriptions of homosexuals"—he officially "outed" Puig for the benefit of his superiors.

This second attempt to publish *La traición* in Spain was due in large part to tactical maneuvering on the part of Barral, who, according to the 1971 censor, had "softened or omitted some passages and expressions" ["suavizado o suprimido algunos pasajes y expresiones"] (Expediente de *La traición* 1971), and who shrewdly chose the option of *depósito* as his method of submission. Chancy as it was for him to invest in the production costs of a novel the censors had rejected in 1966, he took advantage of this legal option in order to present the authorities with a final product that was ready to be marketed. He was well aware that, after the successful publication in Argentina of *Boquitas* and a reprint of *La traición*, the fact that Puig's market standing was now so strong would provide a powerful enough motivation for the Spanish authorities to reconsider their initial rejection, and perhaps tolerate the "abundance of trash" and homosexuals in the novel.

Despite the predictable profitability of Puig's first novel, the 1971 censor concluded, however, that the deposit should not be accepted and that the Special Judge of the Press should intervene to block its distribution and to sequester, if necessary, Seix Barral's run of three thousand copies held at "Gráficas Diamantes, 83 Zamora Street, Barcelona" (Expediente de *La traición* 1971). The judge in Madrid, for his part, did not process the censor's request and instead transferred the file to the Special Judge of the Press in Barcelona, who decided not to pursue the sequestration and, in effect, allowed the novel to be published and distributed. Most likely, Barral was aware that he had a better chance of succeeding in his attempt to publish *La traición* by following the tactics he had employed for other best-selling novels like Vargas Llosa's *La ciudad y los perros*. He relied on the power of the judge in Barcelona to override the censor's recommendation, which the Director of the Censorship Division had seconded, and since no further opposition was forthcoming from the authorities in Madrid, Puig's first novel finally came out on the Spanish book market. The information about the transfer of Puig's file to Barcelona appears in the 1973 report issued upon Seix Barral's request to publish a second run of three thousand copies of *La traición*. Given that the book had been published in 1971, the censor who examined the request for deposit of the second run briefly summarized the above-mentioned legal proceedings as follows:

> Fue presentada a depósito con algunas modificaciones a todas luces insuficientes. Denunciada, sin secuestro previo administrativo, el 18-11-71, al Juez Especial de Prensa de Madrid, quien posteriormente, y por razón de competencia, remitió las actuaciones al Juez Especial de Prensa de Barcelona. Sin noticias posteriores. Como existen indicios racionales de que las actuaciones finalizaron con sobreseimiento, parece procedente aplicar a esta segunda edición el SILENCIO.

> (The novel) was deposited with several modifications which were clearly insufficient. On November 18, 1971 prior to any sequestration effort the novel was reported to the Special Judge of the Press in Madrid, who transferred the file, due to issues of jurisdiction, to the Special Judge of the Press in Barcelona. No further news. Given that it is reasonable to assume that this judge dismissed the case, it seems proper to declare SILENCE on this second edition. (Expediente de *La traición* 1973)

The novel that appeared in Spain in 1971 following this tacit authorization was the "edited" version that Barral had presented to the censorship authorities. Seix Barral's definitive edition of *La traición* did not reach the bookstands until 1977, two years after Franco's demise, and almost a decade after the first Argentinean edition. Likewise, it was not until 1977 that Seix Barral managed to publish Puig's third novel, *The Buenos Aires Affair*, which the censors vetoed in 1973 and 1974 for its "obscenity and eroticism," and in 1975 for its "abundant pornography" (Expediente I-877-73, Expediente I-698-75). As for *El beso de la mujer araña*, Barral was able to publish it in 1976 without delay. This, of course, was in the early days of Spain's transition into democracy after Franco's death. Barral found *El beso* to be more political, and perhaps less frivolous than *La traición*, so his own brand of publisher's self-censorship was less an issue too.

2. BETRAYED BY AUNT CLARA

The frivolity and glamour that the earliest readers of Puig's *La traición* thought trivial and offensive was an effect of a desire, on their part, for *orden y concierto*. They sought to impose a fixed linear structure on the novel, in defiance of the "queer aesthetics" to which they were sufficiently sensitive to be disturbed by. *La traición* was read censoriously by those who tried to disambiguate the ambiguities in Puig's narrative out of a need for clarity. But its apparent lack of authority (of *orden y concierto*) originated in Puig's intentional omission of what had been designed to be its first chapter, "Aunt Clara" ["La tía Clara"], which Puig self-censored precisely in order to enhance the apparent *desorden y desconcierto* of the novel.[9] His intention in omitting "Aunt Clara" was to emphasize the narrative's appropriation of the styles of others and to blur any authoritative or dominant voice. But the effect of this omission was to further complicate the titular *traición*, a word whose various meanings and nuances in Spanish—betrayal, treachery, deception, and disappointment in their active and passive senses—are fully exploited in the novel and, in addition, are closely tied to censorship as Puig had experienced it. Puig's characters, in both the published novel and the omitted chapter, experience *traición* in all its various senses. To Puig himself, the marketplace's rejection of his novel felt like a *traición*, a huge disappointment that in part had its origins in his own deliberate omission of "Aunt Clara." And if the omission of this chapter was an act of self-censorship on Puig's part, it was an act of treachery for his prospective readers, and one of deception for the Spanish censors. The chapter's suppression, though, needs to be understood as a function of the general textual economy designed by Puig, that is, within his desire to produce what the censors described as a "pile-up" or a "tailor's drawer," a desire that turned out to be likewise misunderstood by Puig's prospective publishers.[10]

Certainly, "Aunt Clara" would have pleased those who felt deceived (or perhaps disappointed) by the novel's narrative dispersion and wanted to read a more clearly defined linear narrative.[11] But also aunt Clara is perhaps the most outspoken member of the Casals family, and the inclusion of this chapter might have resulted in an even more troublesome experience for Puig with the Spanish censors. Not coincidentally, her name means "clear, bright, transparent," and the information she provides would have brought a "clarity" to the novel that the latter would probably have appreciated in one way, but would have been scandalized by in another.

In this respect, aunt Clara's monologue contains several potential stumbling blocks. The most significant of these is her portrayal of the Spanish immigrants of Coronel Vallejos, mostly owners of small businesses like the pharmacy where Mita works, and wanna-be entrepreneurs like Berto Casals, whom Mita will end up marrying. Clara voices her concerns about the way of life of Spaniards in Argentina, showing a mixture of resentment and admiration. The *"gallegos"* in the novel ("Galicians," as Spaniards are called in Argentina) own property, small businesses, and lend money to the locals, reproducing the colonial presence of Spain in the economic structure of the remote rural town of Coronel Vallejos. By metonymy, Galicia, Spain's most northwestern region and birthplace of Francisco Franco, came to represent Spain in many Latin American countries; it was (and is) the place of origin of the vast majority of Spanish immigrants in Argentina. By contrast, Clara's mother comes from a small town on the River Po in Italy, and was forced to move to La Plata after marriage. Clara's contrasting of these two immigrant communities concludes that Spaniards are not to be trusted:

> ya se sabe que estos medios gallegos no son de nuestra modalidad, a la italiana, somos más tranquilos, más de confianza. Los españoles tienen esos arrebatos y esa mugre en la casa, y por ahí se salen con desplantes de los más desagradables. Hoy te adoran y mañana te odian, según como sople el viento...eso sí tienen estos españoles, y es que nuncan olvidan su tierra, extrañan como locos.
>
> It is well known that these half-Galicians are not of our kind, as Italians we are more tranquil, more trustworthy. Spaniards have fits of rage and filth in their homes, and every now and then they come up with imprudent remarks of the most unpleasant kind. Today they love you, tomorrow they hate you, depending on which direction the wind blows...but what is true about these Spaniards is that they never forget their homeland, they are crazy about it. (Amícola, *materiales* 244)

In Coronel Vallejos, as it happens, the pharmacy owner and the bank manager are from two other Northern regions in Spain, Asturias and the Basque Country, respectively. This does not prevent them from being included in Clara's scathing remarks about *gallegos*. The pharmacist she views as a pitiful drunkard who migrated from Asturias and married a woman of Spanish descent, described by Clara as "this woman who turned out to be so sickly and was the daughter of Spaniards" ["esta mujer que le salió tan enferma y que era hija de españoles"] (Amícola, *materiales* 245). The association of disease with the Spanish presence in Coronel Vallejos hints perhaps at the colonial past.

Clara's unflattering opinion of *gallegos* leads her to blur the real geographical and cultural differences between Catalans, Basques, and Galicians—something that Franco's censors might have appreciated. Clara favors the term "*medios gallegos*" ["half-Galicians"] a catch-all for the Spanish bourgeoisie that controls the economy in Coronel Vallejos. Of particular significance in this respect is the scene where Mita agrees to play a Catalan woman on stage for a social function organized by the Spanish colony in Coronel Vallejos:

> Mita tuvo uno de los mejores papeles, y hacía de catalana. Claro, Mita había visto a tantas artistas buenas en el teatro... cuando le dieron un poquito de soga se robó la obra y dicen que en Vallejos no se olvidan más los catalanes que la vieron.... Y ahí parece que Berto le echó el lente.
>
> Mita had one of the best roles, she played a Catalan woman. Of course, Mita had seen so many great female artists in the theatre... when they gave her a small chance she stole the show, and in Vallejos they say that Catalans who saw her performance will never forget it.... Since then Berto apparently had his eyes on her. (Amícola, *materiales* 255)

Mita's acclaimed performance stirs a craving in her would-be husband, Berto, for "una catalana" in the isolated town, a response that could have looked to the censors like a sign of regional nationalism. So if the omission of Clara's monologue eliminated her unfavorable portrayal of "gallegos," it also eliminates a potential mitigating element that would have softened the significance of Berto's preference for his fellow Catalans over, for example, Basques. Despite her disparaging remarks about Spaniards, Clara does not question the unity of Spain, for in her view these *medios gallegos* are all the same, they all come from the same place and represent the same national identity. "They never forget their homeland," she reminds us, as if to underscore the unified national identity that *gallegos* and *medios gallegos* share. Albeit in a pejorative tone ("Spaniards have fits of rage and filth in their homes"), Clara thus seems to echo the regime's view of Spain as "Una, Grande, Libre" ["One, Grand, and Free Nation"], and its claim that regional differences are valid as long as they don't pose a threat to national unity. This is ultimately the very same call for unity or oneness that also permeates the censor's report on Puig's novel. Its alleged lack of order was ideologically offensive as an undoing of such wholeness.

The "Catalanization" of Mita in "Aunt Clara" also serves as a link between two intertwined motifs that do appear in the novel, betrayal and economics. Berto anticipates that Mita will make a conscientious homemaker, given that she can convincingly impersonate "una catalana." But she turns out, of course, to disappoint Berto's expectations: "Mita que está gastadora.... Vicios y vicios, de revistas y qué tanta crema para la cara" ["That Mita is such a spender.... Vices and vices, magazines, and what is with all the face lotion"] (Amícola, *materiales* 257). He feels betrayed. By contrast, Clara sees in Berto a careful and devoted businessman who "does not buy anything and does not even spend money on candy" ["no se compra nada y no gasta ni en confitería"] (Amícola, *materiales* 264). This opposition between Berto as saver and Mita as spender responds to two distinct modes of textual economy. While "Aunt Clara" presents an "economical" (or condensed) version of the novel, corresponding to Berto's view on expenditure, the novel's narrative actually follows Mita's more extravagant spending habits, which result in the display of an array of texts and discourses without apparent unity.[12]

Another "economical" effort appears in Clara's censoring of her letter to Mita, in which she voices her concerns about Berto's handling of "family affairs": "Yo en una carta se la había mandado a decir a "Mita"/ pero mamá me lo hizo tachar todo bien con cuidado porque era peor que Berto se hubiese puesto a leer debajo de las rayas que le hice" ["I was determined to tell "Mita" in a letter all about it/ but mom made me cross out everything very carefully, because it was worse if Berto had been able to read through my scratching out in the letter"] (Amícola, *materiales* 263).

While other family members voice their concerns about Mita's and Berto's marriage in the novel, Clara follows her mother's instructions and blanks out all reference to her dislike of Berto, which could certainly make things worse for Mita. She prefers good order to honesty and frankness. Even though this censored letter ended up not being mentioned in the novel, the story does anticipate two other instances in which the narrative introduces letters that undergo censorship.

Mita's letter to Mr. and Mrs. Mansur requesting permission for her servant Delia to marry their son, the Turk Yamil (chapter VII), and Berto's letter to Jaime (chapter XVI), in which the relationship between betrayal and the family economy is finally specified are reproduced only partially. Both letters remind us that in Puig's novels the "more informative" passages, which are particularly valuable in helping the reader to decode the story, tend to appear in a document format—letters, police reports (*El beso*), newspapers cuttings (*Buenos Aires*), and so forth.

Thus, in Berto's letter, we learn that Berto has been betrayed by Jaime, his older brother, who is responsible for his having to leave school as well as for the economic shortages the Casals had to face: "Cuando me viene a la mente la plata que perdimos aquel año porque no me quisiste hacer caso, me golpearía la cabeza contra la pared" ["When I think of the cash we lost that year because you didn't want to listen to me, I could knock my head against the wall"] (*La traición* 1971, 293/*Betrayed* 218). But Jaime's betrayal also goes beyond these economic losses. Berto similarly censures Jaime's abandonment of his son Héctor, who remains in the care of Berto and Mita for the entire novel, while Jaime has relocated to Spain and stopped writing the family back in Argentina. Jaime's move to Spain is also seen as betrayal by Berto, since it is clear that Jaime is not a returning emigrant and that he has little interest in keeping the family ties in either Argentina or Spain: "y no te perdono si te volvés del paseo sin ir a ver a los parientes en Barcelona, quiero que al volver me cuentes todo hasta el último detalle, y si se parecen a mamá y a nosotros" ["... and I'll never forgive you if you come back from the trip without seeing our relatives in Barcelona, when you're back I want you to tell me all about it, right to the last detail, if they look like Mom and us"] (*La traición* 1971, 296/*Betrayed* 220).

This letter is subjected to Berto's own censorship, as he decides in the end that it is not worth investing in mailing it since he does not expect a letter from Jaime in return: "no te puedo perdonar, Jaime, no te puedo perdonar.... Esta carta va al tacho de la basura, para vos no pienso en gastar un centavo en estampillas" ["I can't forgive you, Jaime, I cannot forgive you.... This letter is going into the wastepaper basket, I wouldn't spend a cent on stamps for you"] (*La traición* 1971, 299/*Betrayed* 222). But this self-censorship is also a sort of betrayal for the disappointed reader who learns in chapter II of the novel that the letter has been destroyed. Puig's display of the censored letter is aimed at surprising the reader and clarifying Jaime's betrayal, which echoes the titular betrayal of Rita Hayworth. One of the servants says: "—Señor, yo no sabía que usted estaba escribiendo una carta, yo creía que estaba haciendo cuentas.... No tengo que ir al correo porque el señor rompió la carta que estaba escribiendo" ["—Sir, I didn't know you were writing a letter. I thought you were doing accounts.... I don't have to go to the post office because Mister Berto tore up the letter he was writing"] (*La traición* 1971, 28/*Betrayed* 22).[13]

As we have seen, censorship is tied up with economics. While the servant makes a distinction between Berto's accounts and personal affairs, this distinction does not seem so clear to Berto, who is always engaged in "family business" of one kind or another. In a sense, his refusal to waste money on the stamps for his letter is another point of intersection between betrayal and economics, and one that can be read in light of the Spanish censors' appraisal of Puig's novels from an economic standpoint. To a degree, the destruction of the letter can also be read in terms of what Berto considers "wasteful writing," writing that needs to be discarded and disposed of. While Puig maintained the chapter "Berto's Letter" as a part of the novel, he intentionally displaced it, or rather delayed its appearance in the novel.[14]

Berto's letter is relevant as a whole by virtue of the thematics of betrayal; the absence of "Aunt Clara" points us to a more fundamental option, however, concerning the texture of the novel's writing. As we have noted, Puig's omission of "Aunt Clara" resulted in the omission of information about what goes on in the novel and about who is who. Whether Barral or the Spanish censors ever saw this chapter is not clear. (Amícola estimates that *La traición* was written between 1963 and 1966, a near-final version of the novel having been presented in the fall of 1965 to the judges of the Seix Barral *Biblioteca Breve* Prize [*materiales* 22]). It is evident that to the Spanish censors this omitted chapter, unlike "Berto's Letter," would have been another "nauseating" chapter to read, if only for its unfavorable opinion and its sharp-tongued representation of *gallegos*. As for Barral, his Catalan nationalism might well have been a factor. Clara's outspoken criticism of the Casals family and of Berto's machismo toward Mita did not reflect well on Catalans: "de los Casals puede sacar quién sabe qué rarezas, qué gente más difícil" ["coming from the Casals one can expect all sorts of oddities, what a difficult bunch they are"] (Amícola, *materiales* 252).

Clara's openness would have eased the treachery Spanish censors felt in Puig's "tailor's drawer" ["cajón de sastre"], but would have also brought more clarity to the novel, and not of the kind of the censors were looking for. Puig's omission of this first section and subsequent silencing of Clara's voice (she is barely heard in the novel) is crucial to keeping Toto's homosexuality under wraps until chapters XI and XIV of the novel. Had "Aunt Clara" remained as chapter I of the novel, Toto's "outing" would have become part of the reader's apprehension of him from the start. Clara begins with a relatively vague statement about Toto—"How outrageous are some of the things Toto comes up with...." ["Toto es una barbaridad con las cosas que sale a veces"]

(Amícola, *materiales* 233), but goes on to voice a more specific opinion about his sexuality:

> Pero el "Toto" qué manera de salir maniático del cine y de todo lo que sea funciones, o de cine o de teatro y hasta de bailes, que creo que es lo que más le gusta, las danzas. Pero eso es feo que se ponen tan mujercitas, y este chico que "Mita" lo tiene tan criado con ella todo el día.

> "Toto" is so passionate about movies and all kinds of performances, film, theater and even dance, which is what he truly likes, I think, the dancing. But this is an ugly matter, because kids like that turn into little women, and Mita spoils this kid having him by her side all day long. (Amícola, *materiales* 253)

In the absence of this heavy hint, not only about Toto's sexual orientation, but also about his mother's supposed responsibility for it, his homosexuality remains coded for most of the novel. While Toto's fixation on Hollywood divas works in a similar way, the actual denunciation of his sexuality takes place as late in the novel as chapter XIV. It comes via the "Anonymous Note Sent to the Dean of Students of George Washington High School, 1947," which works like the remarks in "Aunt Clara" in that it is through someone else's voice, not by Toto's own avowal, that we learn of Toto's desires, with the consequence that here too the mode of disclosure is that of insinuation. It is through someone else's voice—that of Cobito—that we learn of Toto's sexual desires:

> Bueno, volvamos al pendejo Casals, ese degenaradito que además es adicto a costumbres raras y si no preguntale a Adhemar, que está podrido de que el pibe le diga que quiere ser igual que él... y el pibe Casals le pregunta cómo hizo para desarrollar el pecho y los músculos y le pregunta a Adhemar cuántas pajas hay que hacerse por semana. (*La traición* 1971, 261)

> Anyway, getting back to Casals the brat, that little louse also happens to be addicted to strange habits, if you don't believe me ask Adhemar, who's sick and tired of that kid telling him he wants to be just like him.... And good-boy Casals looks at him and asks him what he did to develop his chest and muscles and he asks Adhemar how many times a week he jerks off *so that his prick will grow as big as his*. (*Betrayed* 198; emphasis mine)

Toto's "strange habits," which aunt Clara saw as one of the many "oddities" that characterize the Casals family, are by now pretty clear.

However, many readers did not see these "strange habits" fully disclosed, since the 1971 Seix Barral edition, quoted above, omitted the last clause in the passage. As noted by the 1971 censor, the publisher had softened some passages in the novel out of respect for the concerns the censorship authorities would be likely to have about Puig's first novel. This omitted phrase—"para que le crezca la pija igual que a él" (*La traición* 1982, 266)—reappears only in Seix Barral's definitive edition which is about five or six pages longer than the previous Seix Barral editions. (The jackets of the 1971 and 1982 editions reflect these changes: the latter cover is notably sexier and more provocative than the former; [Figs. 5.2, 5.3]). Whether Puig was aware of Barral's editorial interventions prior to sending the novel to the censors is not known, but we do know that Puig never fully approved of Barral's handling of his novels. He recalled his early dealings with the censorship authorities in Spain as a "confused affair," in which, as we have seen, Barral failed to fight for approval of his novel with the necessary vigor and ingenuity. (Even so, it is safe to assume that like many of his fellow Latin American writers, he tacitly agreed with Barral's behind-the-scenes maneuvering to accomplish the publication of their works.)

In the end, the omission of the phrase would perhaps have changed very little in the way readers of the novel, like its characters, perceived Toto's homosexuality. For even to Toto himself, homosexuality always presents itself in coded form, most notably through his fascination with women's films ["películas de mujeres"] and the stories of passion and betrayal they portray. In campy fashion, he sees these Hollywood divas as "heroines that represent stereotypes of femininity" (Campos, "películas" 61–62; [translation mine]). Perhaps there is an element of self-censorship in this preference for fictional feminity over the world of Coronel Vallejos. Even Toto's apparent refusal to grow up could be seen as a way of denying the significance of his sexuality, as if in adolescence he was clinging to the supposed innocence of childhood.[15]

It is precisely this innocence of childhood that caught one censor's attention. He was outraged by the fact that "a first-year high school student would have done a better job of writing most of the chapters" ["la mayoría de los capítulos los escribiría mejor un niño de Ingreso de Bachillerato"] (Expediente de *La traición* 1971). But Puig's intention was precisely to reproduce the writing of a school kid, and to appropriate the naïveté of his style, something, of course, that the 1966 censor, like many of Puig's prospective publishers, disapproved of and mistook for incompetence: "está escrita en un estilo que pretende ser moderno, pero que resulta sosísimo e insorportable" ["(the novel is) written in a style that pretends to be modern, but turns out to be dreary and

Fig. 5.2: Book cover. Manuel Puig's *La traición de Rita Hayworth*. 1st ed. (Barcelona: Seix Barral, 1971).

Fig. 5.3: Book cover. Manuel Puig's *La traición de Rita Hayworth*. 1st ed. *Biblioteca Formentor* (Barcelona: Seix Barral, 1982). [*edición completa*; uncensored version]

unbearable"] (Expediente de *La traición* 1966). Thus, the censor recognized Puig's literary craft as typical of the "modern" novel, but failing to appreciate its point, could not see that Puig merited membership in the select group of the Latin American Boom. And as we have seen, the 1971 censor would make the same case even more forcefully, stating that the novel had the "pretension" of being part of the Latin American new novel. Even in 1971 Puig's literary success, in the censor's eye, did not fully justify consideration of *La traición* as a Boom novel, despite the fact that by then his publishing successes in Argentina and France in the late 1960s had given the lie both to the censor's verdict and to the opinion of those publishers, including Barral, who continued to be reticent.

3. "PLAYING 'TORO'": BETRAYED BY MS. HAYWORTH

Puig bore a grudge against Carlos Barral, apparently for the rest of his life, over the latter's tepid support of *La traición* in 1966 and his editorial modifications to the text. On the occasion of their last encounter at a book fair in Caracas in 1980 Puig's comment about the publisher was: "She's such an evil woman that she's gotten old" (Levine 184). But Barral did not bear the brunt of the author's queenly wit alone; the whole of the literary establishment that for years read Puig's "frivolous" novels so censoriously was also a target. As Jaime Manrique puts it, Puig was known for appropriating "queeny bitchery, [and] turning it into a valid instrument of critical discourse" (40). A particularly fine example of such bitchery was displayed in Puig's conceit of reading the Boom as a Hollywood affair, where stars compete for fame and awards (Levine 200–201), thus "playing up" the Bourdieu model of jockeying for position that is characteristic of cultural production.

Cabrera Infante remembered this conceit in an article titled "La última traición de Manuel Puig" ["The Ultimate Betrayal of Manuel Puig"] which appeared in *El País* on July 24, 1990, two days after Puig's death:

> me regaló una lista extraordinaria. Eran los escritores hispanos haciendo el papel de estrellas de la Metro, con un comentario *ad hoc*. Borges, ciego, era Norma Shearer, la de los ojos bizcos. Comentario: "Oh, qué digna". Carpentier era Joan Crawford: "Oh tan fiera." Asturias era Greta Garbo: "Sólo por ese favor del Nobel." Juan Rulfo era Greer Garson. Cortázar era Hedy Lamarr: "Tan helada y remota." Lezama

era, ¡sorpresa! Lana Turner, y Vivien Leigh "tan temperamental y enferma" era Sábato. Vargas Llosa era Esther Williams, "tan disciplinada", y Carlos Fuentes era Ava Gardner a quien le rodeaba el *glamour*, aunque Puig preguntaba: "Pero ¿podrá actuar?" García Márquez era Elizabeth Taylor: "Bella cara pero un cuerpo terrible." Ya en los sesenta, Severo Sarduy era Vanessa Redgrave y Manuel incorporaba a Julie Christie...

He gave me an extraordinary list of Hispanic writers playing the parts of MGM stars. It included an *ad hoc* commentary. Blind Borges was Norma Shearer, she of the cross eyes. Carpentier was Joan Crawford, "such a spitfire." Asturias was Greta Garbo, "as a favor for having won the Nobel Prize." Juan Rulfo was Greer Garson. Cortázar was Hedy Lamarr, such a cold fish and so distant. Lezama, surprise, surprise, was Lana Turner, Vivien Leigh, "so sickly and such a creature of temperament" was Sábato. Vargas Llosa was the "always disciplined" Esther Williams, and Carlos Fuentes was Ava Gardner surrounded by glamour, though Puig wondered: "Can s/he act?" García Márquez was Elizabeth Taylor, "beautiful face but terrible body." In the 1970s, Severo Sarduy was Vanessa Redgrave and Manuel played Julie Christie.... (Cabrera Infante, "La última traición" 22–23)

Puig obviously viewed the intersections of Latin American literature with Hollywood as going well beyond what Latin American writers have borrowed from the movie capital for their fictions (think of Cortázar's *Queremos tanto a Glenda* or Puig's own recreations of Hollywood classics). His list also suggests that the parallel star systems in his star map share a language, or more precisely a code, a code that Puig himself had appropriated for his fictions and that shows us the way in which he understood literary success.

Setting aside what may seem to be a certain degree of arbitrariness here and there, it is clear that Puig's comparisons between literary and film stars were generally well thought-out. In Cabrera Infante's words: "la lista revelaba que Manuel no era sólo una cara linda del cine sino un crítico literario agudo y penetrante como un estilete" ["the list revealed that Manuel was not only a pretty face in the movies but also a sharp and poignant literary critic with a knife-like thrust"] (22). Puig's cataloguing of the stars of publishing is another attempt, like José Donoso's food-related comparisons in *Historia personal* (128), at explaining the Boom phenomenon, albeit not simply metaphorically, but also in a more coded way than what other writers have proposed.

Even so, his appropriation of the Hollywood star system to talk about the Boom is not unique. Jean Franco has explored the implications of the "star status" of contemporary Latin American writers, the so-called *super-estrellas* in an age of mass-consumption; and the Catalan writer Juan Benet in "El efecto Barral" also echoes Puig's inventive Sally: "Seix Barral era en la Barcelona de los últimos sesenta lo que la Metro o la Paramount podían ser para Los Ángeles en los años inventivos del cinema" ["In late 1960's Barcelona Seix Barral became equivalent to what Metro or Paramount meant for Los Angeles in the founding years of cinema"] (22).

Using the feminine gender in reference to the Boom actresses-writers ["ellas"] as well as to Barral ("an evil woman"), and referring to himself as "this dame" ["esta mujer"], Puig glamorized and arguably feminized the Boom (something that might have pleased Ferré's bitchy opposite numbers, Fina and Franca). He was reacting in his own way to the self-imposed straitjacket of masculinity worn by the members of the boys' club that would be known as the Boom. His "queenly bitchery" was a device to combat the imposition of the same "straight-" jacket, which publishers, official censors, and literary agents, so it seemed, all wanted him to wear himself: "cuando conocí a Manuel, seguía siendo Sally, mucho después de ser famoso...todo el mundo tenía nombre de mujer, todas las relaciones eran de mujer a mujer y sus dioses tutelares eran diosas: Greta Garbo, naturalmente, pero también Lana Turner y Susan Hayward" ["When I met Manuel he was still being Sally, even after he became famous...everybody had a woman's name, all the relationships were woman to woman and their protective gods were goddesses: Greta Garbo, naturally, but also Lana Turner and Susan Hayward"] (Cabrera Infante, "última traición" 22). His "map of the stars" can be seen, then, as a critique of the all-male star system publishers and agents seemed to perpetuate in the 1960s.

One might speculate, too, that Puig's fascination with Hollywood female stars helped him channel the sense of exclusion he felt in the early years of his publishing career. He obviously lived his own publishing career as that of a movie star. Puig managed to become an up-and coming star of publishing—and along the way he made critics and fans alike more aware of the parallels between Latin American literature and the Hollywood films he recreated, and of the star qualities of contemporary Latin American literature in the world of books. His witty insight invites us to consider that Hollywood and contemporary Latin American literature share not only icons, adaptations of novels into film, and narrative techniques, but also, and perhaps more importantly, *traiciones*, stories of failure, betrayal, and success. Stories that are very illustrative of the importance of stardom in the literary markets of the last thirty years, which have been primarily controlled by mass consumption and competition among the stars of publishing.

The glamour Puig imposed on his fictions and his own persona did not fare well with official censors and other specialized readers (publishers, literary critics), who often looked for a "straighter" version of his novels. While the Spanish censors objected to the heterogeneous nature of his work—"the pile-up", "the tailor's drawer"—, his prospective publishers did not know what to make of the marginality of his characters and his narratives. Something similar was also true of the Latin American intelligentsia, which dismissed Puig's version of the Latin American intellectual. If in *La traición* Toto, the gay youngster who experiences the isolation of rural Argentina, represents the writer as an adolescent, Molina, the queen-turned-revolutionary in *El beso*, updates this figure into maturity. It seems symptomatic that both Toto and Molina "come out" of their respective confinements, Coronel Vallejos and a dismal prison, by glamorizing Hollywood movies and recreating their lives through them. Through them Puig's fictions advocate a different kind of creation, one in which the figure of the writer appears far removed from the elitism of Cortázar's Morelli or Borges's erudite Menard. Puig's Toto does not attempt to write *Don Quixote* in the twentieth century like Menard or propose a theory of the novel à la Morelli. Toto simply writes about something apparently trivial and frivolous, his fascination with Hollywood divas, their glamour, and the betrayals they commit.

The most obvious reason for Toto's fascination with female Hollywood stars is summed up in Rita Hayworth's *Blood and Sand*. This 1941 film is an adaptation of the Spanish writer Vicente Blasco Ibáñez's novel *Sangre y arena* (1908) and a remake of the 1922 silent version with Rudolph Valentino. The story is, needless to say, one of betrayal and deceit. And it is also the story of a man who marries a submissive woman but desires an extravagant and rebellious one. In *Blood and Sand*, a young and impressionable bullfighter, Juan Gallardo (that is, John the Brave), falls for Doña Sol (Ms. Sun), a wealthy socialite and known seductress. Trapped by his passion for Sol, Gallardo ruins his career and his marriage, and loses his fortune. Penniless and abandoned by Sol, he reconciles at last with his wife and returns to the arena, only to be fatally gored by a bull while Sol watches, unmoved and indifferent.

The novel focuses on one particular scene of the film, in which Gallardo plays the role of a bull being fought by Sol at her luxurious estate. Their love game is interrupted by the unannounced visit of

Gallardo's wife, Carmen, who pleads with Sol to give Gallardo up. While the two women converse in the living room, Gallardo, unaware of his wife's presence, remains on the terrace. Soon after hearing Carmen's plea for her to withdraw from the affair, Sol interrupts their conversation and calls to Gallardo by saying simply "toro, toro." Gallardo responds to Sol's call, and the lovers embrace in a long and passionate kiss. It is only then that, to his dismay, Gallardo realizes that his wife is in the room, and that Sol has deliberately betrayed him. This scene is Berto's favorite, and the one that Toto remembers in his own monologue (*La traición* 1971, 82/*Betrayed* 64).

Interestingly, in Puig's novel, it is the Spanish colony in Vallejos that is responsible for bringing the movie to town. As Toto recalls it, the *gallego* Fernández came to his home to sell tickets for a showing of the movie sponsored by the Spanish Society of Vallejos, which is responsible for nurturing Hispanic culture, but also tends to commercialize it.[16] It is clear, in any case, that this movie experience has a profound impact on Toto. This is so not simply because his dad has chosen Rita Hayworth as the actress he likes "better than any other actress," but also and more significantly because it is through the movie that he feels closer to his father: "y a mí me empieza a gustar más que ninguna también... y así íbamos a hablar toda la cena de la cinta" ["I'm starting to like her better than any other too.... And Dad, tell me about other parts you liked... in this way we could talk all during supper"] (*La traición* 1971, 82/*Betrayed* 63). The movie also introduces Toto (and the rest of the family members) to the kind of kitschy, folkloric Spain that was promoted during the Franco regime: "Voy a escribir en letras grandes R. de Rita y H. en letras grandes, le dibujo de fondo un peinetón y algunas castañuelas" ["I'm going to write in big letters the R of Rita and H in big letters, for background I'll draw a mantilla comb and some castanets"] (*La traición* 1971, 83/*Betrayed* 64).

Finally, *Blood and Sand* exemplifies, of course, the novel's titular theme of "Rita Hayworth's betrayal," embedding it in the Casals family's story, with all its "oddities," and associating it, in the process, with Spain. Toto's father's favorite betrayal by Rita Hayworth is precisely the scene in which Tyrone Power "becomes her bull" in a playful love game that inverts the bullfighter's role from agent of treachery to receiver: "a papá le gusta cuando le hacía 'toro, toro' a Tyrone Power, él arrodillado como un bobo y ella de ropa transparente... al final lo deja" ["Dad likes when she did 'toro, toro' to Tyrone Power, him kneeling down and her with a transparent dress... and she came right up close to him to play toro... and in the end she leaves him"] (*La traición* 1971, 82/*Betrayed* 63).[17] As Lucille Kerr has pointed out, "the betrayal of Rita Hayworth" ["la traición de Rita Hayworth"] is an ambiguous phrase, since it is unclear whether Rita Hayworth betrays or is betrayed (*Suspended* 28). Similarly, the actions of most of the characters in the novel oscillate between betraying and being betrayed. However, in Toto's view, Rita Hayworth's appeal lies pretty much in the fact that it is she who is the generator of betrayal(s), which then the family members reenact: "Y a veces pone cara de mala, es una artista linda pero que hace traiciones" ["And sometimes she looks wicked, she's a pretty actress but she's always betraying somebody"] (*La traición* 1971, 82/*Betrayed* 63).

But there is more. Rita Hayworth's novelistic and filmic betrayal came home to roost for Puig when the two finally met in 1971, the year Seix Barral finally published the novel. Their meeting took place in Mexico City, where the diva was filming a movie. Rita Hayworth claimed to have read the novel and, following their meeting, wrote Puig a nice thank you note: "I don't really believe you were betrayed by me." But, according to Vicente Leñero, the Mexican novelist who won the 1963 Seix Barral *Biblioteca Breve* Prize and was instrumental in arranging the encounter, the diva was rather cold and distant toward Puig at the actual meeting, and he felt betrayed by her indifference (Levine 227–28). He was perhaps predisposed to do so by the fact that Rita Hayworth had already "betrayed" him as early as 1966. On February 24 of that year, and following the advice of Carlos Barral, Puig had written to the star to ask permission to use her name in the title of the novel Seix Barral was then about to publish, possibly as the winner of the *Biblioteca Breve* award. Rita Hayworth's response was a business-like letter of acknowledgement from her lawyer, which disappointed the starstruck author cruelly (Levine 17).

Puig's letter to "Miss Hayworth" reads as if it was intended to be a fan letter as well as a request for permission to use the diva's name. He included also a summary of the novel, an interpretation of Rita Hayworth's role in it, and a rather optimistic assessment of its likely market success:

> This novel concerns you in [a] very special way. To my surprise it was a strong competitor in the December 65 "Biblioteca Breve" award, the most important award given in Spain, by the avant-garde publishing house "Seix Barral" of Barcelona. Immediately the editor asked me for the rights to publish the spanish (sic) version, and "Einaudi" of Rome and "Gallimard" of Paris did the same for the respective translations. "Hamish Hamilton" of London also seemed to be inter-

ested.... The name of the novel is "La traición de Rita Hayworth" ("The Betrayal of Rita Hayworth"). I had suggested this title to "Seix Barral" most timidly, but everybody loved it right away. For them it's exciting in a pop-art way, etc. Before anything else I would like to assure you that your name is used in the title only as [a] symbol of screen seduction and that the novel in no ways (sic) deals with your personal life and neither does it attempt to evaluate you as an actress. Mr. Barral mentioned too that he had met you in Barcelona and thought that you were a lovely person and that you wouldn't object to such a thing.... The publication will take place in September. I would gladly come to Los Angeles to meet you next month and show you the manuscript and the pages where you're mentioned (Amícola, *materiales* 433–434)

In implying the likelihood of publication in four countries, Puig was obviously attempting to ensure Rita Hayworth's approval. So he avoided all mention of the many difficulties he was having with publishers and censors, and made no reference to the mixed reactions his preferred title had received; instead he held out the prospect of publication with prominent firms like Seix Barral, Einaudi, Gallimard, and Hamilton. His novel was "avant-garde" and its title appealing in a "pop-art way." In the event, though, none of the publishers he mentioned turned out to be willing to take the risk of publishing it. Perhaps involuntarily, they had been "playing toro" with Puig. And we know that, like the Spanish censors, they did not think positively of Puig's avant-gardism and had no idea what to make of the assemblage of popular discursive forms in the novel. Disingenously Puig failed to foresee any such problems in his letter, or in any case did not mention them. He also disregarded the possibility of "betrayal" on Rita Hayworth's part. Had not Barral himself met her in Barcelona, and concluded that she would be receptive to Puig's request? When the diva did not engage with him in the way he had hoped for, and failed even to respond personally to his letter, much less to meet him in Los Angeles, he must have concluded that his own creation, "the betrayal of Rita Hayworth," had turned against him.

What then, in conclusion, are we to make of this phrase: "the betrayal of Rita Hayworth?" It encapsulates Puig's own sense of being betrayed by censors, publishers, and other specialized readers who did not know what to make of the novel's own enactments of betrayal. But it also summarizes, therefore, the way in which Puig himself "played toro" on the literary market with a novel that combined self-concealment with provocation. To declassify Puig, as I have suggested, it is not enough to decode the censor's reports of Francoist Spain or to gather information about book seizures in Argentina. It also entails an examination of Puig's publication trajectory in light of the economic and censorial tensions that permeate the novels themselves. This is not to imply that Puig intentionally fictionalizes his dealings with publishers and censors, or that his works simply mirror the censorship practices he was subjected to. Rather, Puig seems to be telling us that his prospective readers are bound to be betrayed (and to betray) if they insist on declassifying the multilayered fictions he proposes by reading linear narratives into, or out of, complex textual assemblages. For to read Puig in such fashion is to read him censoriously also and thus constitutes a betrayal. To read Puig without betraying him is to agree to "play toro," and to take the risk—as well as to enjoy the thrill—of textual treachery.

In the novel, it is as if Rita Hayworth's "playing toro" betrays Toto by "making him gay." But to be gay is also to commit a thrilling act of betrayal, as Rita Hayworth does: she becomes a seductress, smoldering and sexy, and dangerous to the men with whom she "plays toro." When Rita Hayworth in real life, following Barral and the censorship authorities in Spain and Argentina, repeats the "betrayal of Rita Hayworth," all these players in the Hollywood Boom are thus confirming the novel's own gayness/queerness and its own Rita-like powers of seduction, which lie in the way it "betrays" the normative values of literature (and more specifically Boom literature). The irony is that this mode of implied acknowledgement of the novel's real literary character (its gay identity) also entails putting real difficulties in the way of its publication.

Epilogue

Legends of the Boom

Latin American Publishing Revisited

Carmen Balcells, who had been an almost mythic figure of the Boom and its most visible literary agent, took center stage again in Hispanic publishing when she announced her retirement in March 2000. Critics and journalists revisited her role in the promotion of Latin American literature in the 1960s and 1970s, and the "Balcells legend" (*la leyenda Balcells*) became the stock phrase that summed up her distinguished career and the crucial role she played in the promotion of Latin American literature in Spain, the Americas, and beyond. The plethora of newspaper articles and personal testimonies that appeared in the print media in 2000 presented an inviting occasion to reexamine the publishing history of the 1960s and 1970s, when Latin America's literary production made its appearance on the international scene.[1] The appellatives invented to describe Balcells are reminiscent of some of the Boom's own literary creations, and reinforce her status as a mythic and legendary figure. Mario Vargas Llosa, for example, called her "Barcelona's Big Mama" ("El jubileo" 1) or "The Big Mama of the Latin American novel" (Saldívar, *viaje a la semilla* 458); the journal *Quimera* labeled her "the alchemist of the book" (Riera 23); and the French daily *Le Monde* describes a woman with the character of the Buendía matriarchs: "astuta como una campesina, generosa como una madre de familia, dispuesta a defender a sus autores a base sobre todo de intuición" ["as wily as a peasant woman, as generous as the mother of a brood of children, and above all given to defending her authors mainly according to the dictates of her intuition"] (Mora, "Generosa" 1). These descriptions caught my eye not only because they bring back to life the same literary creations (such as García Márquez's Big Mama) that Balcells helped bring to light in the Boom years, but also because they now seem to supplant the real personality of the distinguished Catalan agent. Over time, the "literary mother of the Boom," whom some also call an "editorial terrorist," has acquired larger-than-life features that surpass the literary characters she herself helped to market in the 1960s and 1970s (Mora, "Generosa" 1). In this spirit, Juan Cruz, the director of Alfaguara (the leading publisher of Latin American literature today), describes Balcells as a "literary superagent with a license to kill like James Bond," and able to pull out from "her office desk's top drawer the pistol Vargas Llosa had as a cadet at Leoncio Prado, which he gave her" ("La Balcells" 2).

These recent descriptions of Balcells, however, are not the new phenomenon one might think. As early as 1972, in his *Historia personal*, José Donoso had already described the materno-cannibalistic approach Carmen Balcells had toward Latin American writers entering the Spanish book market in the 1960s: "reclinada sobre los pulposos cojines de un diván, se relamía revolviendo los ingredientes de este sabroso guiso literario... quizá con admiración, quizá con hambre, quizá con una mezcla de ambas cosas" (124) ["reclining against the well-stuffed cushions of a divan, she would lick her lips repeatedly as she stirred the ingredients of this tasty literary stew... perhaps out of admiration, perhaps out of hunger, perhaps out of a mixture of both"]. Ten years after the first edition of *Historia personal*, Donoso would remember Balcells as "todavía refugiada en su modesta guarida de la calle Urgel sin el lujoso velito que ahora caracterizaba su cabeza" (216) ["nevertheless still curled up in her modest lair on Urgel Street minus the luxurious veil that now graced her head"], contrasting this picture with the new Balcells "en sus versallescas instalaciones de la Diagonal" ["in her Versaillesque quarters on Diagonal Avenue"] (219). This is the powerful and manipulative figure of the publishing industry, part literary mother and part devouring editorial creature, who inspired Donoso's character Núria Monclús, Balcells' *alter ego* in *El jardín de al lado* (44). The monstrous Monclús, incidentally, was responsible for Isabel Allende's submission of *La casa de los espíritus* [*House of the Spirits*] to Balcells in the early 1980s, as the author herself confessed in a 1996 interview. It may seem like an incident typical of the publication history of a Boom novel, but Allende claims that, after reading the characterization of the Catalan agent in Donoso's novel, she sent her manuscript to Balcells' address in Barcelona in two packages. Only the second part of the novel reached its destination, but this did not prevent the almighty Balcells from "smelling a huge success" (Gómez, "El retiro").

The visionary and intuitive Balcells is often contrasted with the spiritual matriarch and heartless businesswoman (à la Eréndira's grandmother). This persistence in representing Balcells as a character drawn from the same Latin American novels that she helped promote (and benefited from financially) clearly has to do with what Patricia Meyer Spacks in *Gossip* calls "a community's principles of continuity" (230). Such principles tend to produce a sense of unity by giving substance to the mythic character of the shared stories into which collective memories become incorporated. I mean that the publishing history of the Boom has taken shape and substance from a sense of continuity and nostalgia that derive from a set of oft-repeated anecdotes. These have become the constitutive myths of a literary community, whose values are thus sustained. All the repetitions of the "Balcells legend," Barral's famous refusal to publish *Cien años de soledad*, for instance, or the alleged fistfight between García Márquez and Vargas Llosa over a marital dispute (a favorite item of Boom gossip), create and perpetuate the literary community of the Boom.[2]

No doubt this repetition of legends and myths has contributed not only to building a particular literary community, but to perpetuating a common book trade tradition for Spain and Latin America as well. The gossip often invites us to consider the ambiguous postcolonial turns that linked Spain and Latin America in the 1960s book market, and also to wonder whether and to what extent the ongoing mythification of the Boom has not surpassed the original efforts to construct it. That it is authors of the caliber of García Márquez, Donoso and Vargas Llosa who insist on presenting Balcells as an emblem of magical realism is significant: we should not forget that these gossipy communal stories were spread by the original Boom writers. They tend to explain the authors' literary success as if it too were a supernatural or inexplicable phenomenon like the superagent Balcells. So it seems that her legend sums up all the myths concerning Spain's colonization of the Spanish-language book market that have been created by authors, publishers, and scholars of the Boom, and reflexively invites us, therefore, to reexamine the myths that we in Spain have constructed for Latin America, that is to say, the self-interested representations the subcontinent has endured for centuries. These accounts are evidence that Latin America continues to be somewhat subjugated to a maternal figure who, on the one hand, protects and caresses it, and, on the other hand, exploits and utilizes it for purposes of her own. To view Balcells through characters such as Big Mama and Eréndira's heartless grandmother is to construct an allegory that reevaluates (or parodies through grotesque exaggeration) the conventional theme of Spain as the motherland (*madre patria*) of Latin America.

So it is understandable, in light of these literary revisions of the relationship between Spain and Latin America, that the Boom writers who themselves "colonized" the Spanish book market during the Franco regime suggest in their reminiscences of the period that, thanks to agents like Balcells and publishers like Carlos Barral, they managed to turn the tables somewhat by making Spain their own "literary homeland" (*patria literaria*). Juan Cruz, on the theme of Spain the motherland, sees Balcells' case as exemplifying the idea that "a literary agent is a homeland and therefore the most desired of agents are female agents" ("La Balcells" 2).[3] Balcells stands both for the prestige of Spain as a literary motherland, and, as Vargas Llosa reminds us, for a treacherous, materialistic and "money-driven literary assassin" (*una pesetera literaturicida*), representative of a country that helped itself to the profits earned by Latin American writing ("El jubileo" 2). An example of both those profits and Latin American table turning would be the reported figures surrounding García Márquez's royalties. In the Boom gossip, García Márquez's revenues are a staple of its legendary continuity: "las cifras que se barajan en torno a las obras de García Márquez, por ejemplo, han entrado en la leyenda y nadie, salvos los interesados, puede saber si son ciertas o no" ["the numbers that are bandied about for García Márquez's works have entered into the realm of legend and no one, except the parties involved, can know for sure if these numbers are accurate or not"] (Mora, "Generosa").

According to the ongoing legend, the Colombian author received one million dollars for *El amor en los tiempos del cólera*, and ten million dollars for *El general en su laberinto* [*The General in His Labyrinth*] and a similar amount for his memoirs (Mora, "Generosa"). Undoubtedly, these numbers invite skepticism, if only for the reason that Balcells has earned the reputation of being a discreet businesswoman who never reveals any money amounts or other details pertaining to book contracts (Riera 23-4). In the case of García Márquez, she did once mention a sum of money when asked a hypothetical question one day about what the price would be for a novel by the best-known Boom author. She responded that "it would be valued at more than 10 million dollars" (Mora, "Generosa"). This comment, misinterpreted by the French daily *Le Monde*, was accepted as an actual amount (Martínez 65). More recently, the advances paid to Vargas Llosa for his novels published by Alfaguara—*Los cuadernos de Don Rigoberto* and

La fiesta del chivo—have been the object of similar gossip. And Juan Cruz justifies Alfaguara's generosity by pointing out that "all the fantasies and criticisms surrounding Vargas Llosa's contract" do not take into account the fact that the royalties paid to an author include the Spanish-language book market worldwide, "which changes things quite a bit" ("No tener miedo" 20).

What these exorbitant sums, assuming them to be at least roughly accurate, *do* prove is that Balcells won a certain battle against publishers in the early 1960s, and that Latin American authors benefited from her achievement. At that time publishers agreed to provide her authors money advances and time-limited contracts, the result being an unprecedented professionalization of the Latin American writer, who rapidly moved from struggling in obscurity in the first half of the twentieth century to a new status as "superstar author" in the Boom years and beyond. The "superstar author," according to Jean Franco, is an emblematic outcome of phenomena, such as the presence of agents and the importance of translation and movie rights, that became significant elements in Latin American literary culture in the 1960s and beyond.

Naturally the "Big Mama" of the Boom has evoked García Márquez's Macondo and its myth of creation and destruction, which offers another indirect way to reflect on the Spanish publishing industry as a whole and the role Latin America plays in it.[4] Balcells' bipolar mothering of her authors suggests a double view of Spain's mothering of Latin America—one in which the continent figures on the one hand as a source of innovation and aesthetic renewal and on the other as a lucrative cash cow. Carlos Barral acknowledges that he and his business partner Víctor Seix were interested in "the Ibero-American side of the publishing business" and the "exportation and diverse mechanisms for the delivery, reprinting, and distribution of books" (*Cuando las horas veloces* 73), making no secret of the revenues his firm expected from Latin America. Balcells in turn has noted that from the beginning she saw that the publishing industry was a huge operation, but one in which there was a disconnect between literary creation and economic profit taking: "Esta industria tiene una materia prima que, según los editores, es el papel, yo creo, en cambio, que la materia prima indispensable es el autor" ["According to publishers this industry has one raw material, paper, but I think that the indispensable raw material is the author"] (Riera 27).

If there was a tug-of-war between "paper" and "the author"—financial profit and literary creativity—the evidence is that the Franco regime, which sought to overhaul the decaying Spanish paper industry in the late 1950s and early 1960s, was much more interested in the former than in the latter. Paper was a key component of its policies for expanding and promoting the Spanish book trade in the Americas, even though its importance as raw material is rarely mentioned in the extensive memorializing of the Boom.[5] Scholars too seem to have forgotten the crucial role paper had in those years, but the documents I have unearthed from the *Archivo* tell another story. They clearly show that at an early stage of the market competition for the profitable Boom writers Spain's National Book Institute saw an urgent need to reform the paper industry, so as to be able to increase the presence of Spanish books on the Latin American market. Such a reform was part and parcel of a broad economic plan that included government-sponsored loans for export, the reduction of postal rates, and tax breaks for the use of paper by publishers, all of which were implemented at the same time as the *apertura* was making lenient censorship practices possible. One cogent example of the government's efforts to overhaul the paper industry would be a 1963 confidential report in which the National Book Institute proposed "that the importation of paper for publishing be permitted under optimal conditions of quality and price... by means of which Spanish publishers will be able to compete—at least as far as paper is concerned—with their foreign counterparts. This is one of the measures that will have the most decisive importance" ["que se permita la importación de papeles editoriales en condiciones óptimas de calidad y precio... con lo cual los editores españoles podrán situarse en condiciones competitivas (al menos en lo que se refiere al papel) respecto de sus colegas extranjeros. Esta (sic) es una de las medidas que tendrá... más decisiva importancia"] (Informe sobre el comercio 21).

But some of the Spanish government's confidential reports during this period read like some kind of book trade alchemy, obsessively detailing meticulous studies on raw bisulfate, a chemical compound that is essential for making paper paste. This component was scarce in Franco's Spain. In 1958 the lack of bisulfate obliged Papelera Española to cut its production by 50 percent, and prompted the government to create a Subcomission for Paper (Subcomisión del Papel) with a mandate to analyze the economic impact of Spain's lack of bisulfate and to report on the possibility of importing it from Sweden, Finland, and Austria (Papelera Española 1). If Balcells saw paper as a secondary raw material of the publishing industry, for Spanish officials at the National Book Institute, and consequently for Spanish publishers too as they cashed in on government subventions for paper, it became a supremely precious commodity.

According to the Subcomission's calculations paper accounted for 1.2 percent of Spain's commercial income in 1963 with a net value estimated at 6,260 million pesetas, of which 55 percent represented books and related items. These figures were closely relevant to the export trade in books, since imported paper for publishing was taxed at the rate of 24 percent to 28 percent, to which a 15 percent fiscal and custom tax was added for a grand total of 42.5 to 47 percent. This disadvantage to Spanish publishers competing in the export markets was considerable, as a 1962 government report noted: "algunos gobiernos iberoamericanos priman los papeles editoriales para favorecer el desarrollo de la industria del libro en su respectivo territorio" ["some Ibero-American governments subsidize paper for publishing in order to benefit the development of their book industry in their respective territories"] (Breve comentario 1). This report clearly endorsed one of the publishers' and book exporters' demands: a full refund of the tariffs imposed on paper for the printing of books to be sold abroad. The 1946 Book Law (which remained "on the books" until 1975) foresaw a possible refund to publishers, but according to the publishers' accounts had never really been put into effect. This was a law that sought to remedy the "unfavorable conditions and the abandonment of the Spanish book" and to establish "the groundwork for the future expansion Spanish books are destined to enjoy in Latin America, by virtue of the universality of our language and our Catholic spirit" (Ley de 18 de diciembre de 1946).[6]

These were the lofty goals (long enshrined in the law but never fully enacted) that now moved the regime to overhaul Spain's paper industry. During the Boom years paper would become a much-coveted good like gold in colonial times. The Franco government made efforts to resolve the scarcity of paper and to provide the necessary conditions for Spanish publishers and book exporters to compete with profit on the international market. The 1946 law had been only "a first step in a much larger policy of protection" (Ley de 18 de diciembre). The effort became more concrete with a tax exemption given to publishing houses so that they could expand their facilities and improve their economic standing, and was later reaffirmed with tax refunds of about 5 percent to cover exportation tariffs on paper (Devolución del impuesto). Whether by sheer coincidence or not, the refund policy did not take full effect until 1962, a key date for the Boom: Vargas Llosa's *La ciudad y los perros* won the *Biblioteca Breve* Prize that year, and Fraga Iribarne became Minister of Information with a mandate to relax the rules of censorship and expand the Spanish book market overseas. Now, after negotiations with publishers, the regime issued a Ministerial Order on June 25 which finally implemented fiscal refunds on paper tariffs for the export of books recognized by the law. According to the reports at the *Archivo*, such refunds had not been applicable between 1947 and 1960, and were only granted once to three publishers in 1961 (Devolución del impuesto).

Paper, then, became the centerpiece of the regime's overhaul of publishing in the 1960s. Raw bisulfate was the alchemist's ingredient that was to bring about the desired book trade overseas. In more prosaic and less literary fashion, paper's delivery and refund cost likewise accounted for a great deal of the detail in these government reports. For instance, in 1962, it cost the government fourteen pesetas for every four kilos of books sent to Buenos Aires or Havana, which amounted to a yearly cost of fifty million pesetas. However, the cost in discounted postal rates, in the government's view, was clearly compensated for by the revenues generated by exports to Latin America, which in 1959 amounted to 577 million pesetas for Argentina, Chile, and Cuba and by 1962 had jumped to 15,600 million pesetas (Datos de la Exportación de Libros).

Given these figures, it seems natural that the records of the Subcomission for Paper also looked into the paper industry in Latin America.[7] It *is* somewhat surprising, however, that in the memoirs of publishers and Boom writers, there is no mention of these all-important raw materials. Among the writers, all the emphasis is on manufactured goods, the books; for example, Seix Barral's cutting-edge book covers (Donoso, *Historia personal* 85). In the same line of thinking, Carlos Barral remembers the Boom years as a "period of decline for humanistic publishing in Latin America." That, he says, was why Seix Barral's publishing policy was designed to "impose...the literary content of that period on the Spanish-language book market" by means of an "intelligent and convincing" presentation of the books (*Los años* 138). And such was clearly the objective of the *Biblioteca Breve* collection, conceived under the auspices of the same language as a "transatlantic bridge" to facilitate "the unification of an authors' market in the same linguistic environment" (*Cuando las horas* 78–9).

The success of the Seix Barral publishing policy in Latin America is as legendary as Balcells, and like her it has generated a plethora of references in the reminiscences of the 1960s and beyond. Vargas Llosa declared in an interview with José Miguel Oviedo that "without the support of Carlos Barral...the Boom would not have had the diffusion [distribution] and recognition it deserved" (Vargas Llosa and Oviedo 6). If the Balcells legend sees her as the mother of the Boom, it becomes inevitable therefore for Barral to be perceived as the Boom's father figure. Jorge Herralde, the founder and editor of Anagrama, calls him "something more than a publisher and an editor," an exceptional figure who "concocted the famous Boom" (195); for Mario Muchnik, director of Anaya and Taller de Muchnik, he represents the "publisher's paternal feeling" toward his authors (*Lo peor* 40). This fatherly image reaches its apotheosis in the comments made by Donoso's wife, María Pilar, in her own "domestic version" of the Boom; she speculates about the royal favors Carlos Barral earned during the Boom years for his services to the Spanish crown: "mucho se dice en España que el rey Don Juan Carlos tiene pensado ennoblecer a Barral dándole el título de vizconde de Calafell" ["it is rumored in Spain that king Juan Carlos is thinking about conferring the title of Viscount of Calafell upon Barral"] (Donoso, *Historia personal* 173).[8] Barral's putative ennoblement never took place, but its plausibility at the level of gossip does at least show the extent of the commercial success publishing houses like Seix Barral enjoyed, and the significant contribution they made to overhauling the decaying Spanish book industry in the 1940s and 1950s, and the degree of personal esteem enjoyed by the man thought to have been the Boom's progenitor.

Spanish publishing did not completely lose national importance with the end of the Boom. The legends and myths generated by it remain in the memory of contemporary writers. The Spanish publishing industry (albeit as part of the multinational conglomerates) still leads the Spanish-language book market as a direct outcome of the Franco regime's policies, as Rafael Mérida Jiménez, formerly of *Círculo de Lectores*, suggests: "todavía heredera editorial de los modelos precedentes, como confirma el papel estratégico desempeñado por Seix Barral" ["it is still heir to the earlier industry models, as is confirmed by Seix Barral's strategic role"] (56). What the Boom memoirs have generated is not only legends and myths about publishing, then, but also the idea that Spain and Latin America are united in what Jesús Polanco, the director of the Santillana Publishing Group (which comprises Alfaguara), calls "a cultural universe" and describes in a slightly odd turn of phrase: "lo que te encuentras en Latinoamérica es parte de tu familia y no sólo en el aspecto cultural... a golpe de libros se ha consolidado el entendimiento entre España y América Latina" ["what one finds in Latin America is part of your family and not only from a cultural point of view... thanks to books the *entente* between Spain and Latin America has been consolidated"] (Aznárez). His idiomatic expression "a golpe de libros" or "by wielding books," used in reference to the cultural universe that is supposedly shared on both sides of the Hispanic world, situates his remarks as "heir to" the attitude I have found in the Franco regime's confidential reports on the publishing industry. To cite only one further example of this utilitarian—not to say cynical and more than a little militaristic—approach to books, Santiago Salvat, founder of Editorial Salvat (a publishing enterprise that achieved fame and a wide audience with its inexpensive paperback editions during the *apertura*), openly expressed Spain's neocolonial ideological tendencies in a 1963 letter to Robles Piquer, Director of Censorship Services: "lo más importante sería una política estatal que en su conjunto viniera a colaborar con los esfuerzos que los editores venimos realizando desde hace mucho años para *la conquista y mantenimiento de aquellos mercados*" ["the most important state policy would be one that would fully complement the repeated efforts publishers have been making for many years *to conquer and keep those markets*"] (Informes sobre las dificultades 3; emphasis mine)

A strategic "wielding" of books and "the conquest" have long been uppermost in Spanish publishers' minds when it comes to Latin America. Fernando Lafuente, Spain's former General Director for Books, echoes this old tradition of colonial expansion. Lafuente, who offers some data on the Spanish book industry in the 1990s, situates its export figures around fifty million pesetas, averaging fifty-two thousand titles and more than two hundred eight million manufactured books. Lafuente appreciates that Spain nowadays needs the Latin American market just as it did under the previous regime: "La gran salida para el libro español, o para el libro en español...es Iberoamérica....En cuanto a España, su destino natural es Iberoamérica" ["the great gateway for Spanish books or the Spanish-language book is Ibero-America. Spain's natural destiny is Ibero-America"] (Alfieri 12–13). So here is another legend spawned by the memory of the Boom. The projected figures, excessive as they often are nowadays (and were already under the Franco regime), create unrealistic book market expectations for the Spanish industry in Latin America. While it is true that Spain's publishers put out about fifty-two thousand titles per year, Pío Serrano, director of Editorial Verbum, clarifies that this figure is somewhat deceptive because it includes any "book" that qualifies as such under the law: that is, any printed material of "16 or 32 pages," with printing runs that can fluctuate anywhere between "500 or one million" (38). These numbers for production and distribution begin to look no less exorbitant than the sums certain Boom authors are alleged to have received as royalties.

In a strictly commercial perspective, these legends pinpoint "a feudalization of the Spanish publishing world," one that depends on a reliable distribution network by means of which the Spanish book invades Latin America, just as the expansionist plans devised by the Franco regime in the 1960s foresaw (Mérida Jiménez 51). Today's neocolonial enterprise is not undertaken by wielding arms, but by the deployment of books. The neocolonial situation in which Latin American publishing now finds itself has been the object of fierce criticism on the part of small and independent publishers who are unable to compete with the international conglomerates. Mario Muchnik argues that "an extremely hermetic economic and political system has been set up and remains closed by virtue of a tacit agreement between agents in the publishing and political worlds" ["se ha montado un sistema económico-político muy hermético, muy cerrado [por] una especie de acuerdo tácito entre los agentes del mundo editorial y político"] ("La mala salud" 25). The closedness of the book trade is driven by novelty, "almost everything is new.... Tusquets is new, Anagrama, Lumen, Alianza, the Anaya Group, Santilla, Planeta" (Martínez Alés 31). The craze for novelty in the market and the attendant disappearance of independent publishers is an outcome of the "spectacular and quasi-cancerous expansion" the multinational book companies have imposed on the market economy (Serrano 37). A case in point would be the almighty Bertelsmann group, which comprises the great publishers of the Boom (Sudamericana, Planeta/Seix Barral).

Where does all this leave Latin America? From the 1960s to the present, and at the same time as its vast market has remained one of the greatest bulwarks of the book industry, the legends and myths perpetuated by the Boom and its players have constructed Latin America as a vast land of opportunities. The autumnal patriarchs of publishing, the alchemists of the book and other figures of Latin American narrative reinforced and recreated the Balcells and Barral legends, and these legends, in turn, have helped to create a myth of the book industry in which Latin America is legendary in both its capacity to imagine and its market possibilities, while Spain is legendary in its powerful publishing figures, its astute publishers and agents, its solid distribution, and perhaps the production of literary prestige. Vargas Llosa's words pertaining to the Balcells legend best sum up the view of Spanish-Latin American relations that has stuck in the collective memory of the Boom: "a condición de aceptar su imperio benevolente, de ser dócil y sumiso, uno era feliz" ["provided one accepted her benevolent empire and became docile and submissive one was happy"] ("El jubileo" 3). Latin America manages to publish its books internationally, provided only that it accepts the reign of Spanish publishing houses, and remains docile and submissive to the publishing conglomerates that dominate the publishing industry today.

Aptly enough, the sense that it is Latin America's destiny to be dominated in the world of publishing was revived with the announcement of

Balcells' retirement. Some have taken this announcement with a grain of salt, as Vargas Llosa does when he warns authors: "¡Qué nadie aspire mientras la Balcells respire!" ["So long as Balcells breathes, let everyone hold their breaths!"] (Vázquez Montalbán 2). He is echoed by Juan Cruz, who believes Balcells' move is a strategic retreat: "desde las alturas de su torre de merengue y acero acecha los nuevos horizontes tecnólogicos de la edición" ["from the heights of her meringue and steel tower she lies in readiness to ambush the new technological horizons of publishing"] ("La Balcells" 3). The Big Mama of the Boom, he suggests, aspires to become the "Cyber Mama" of Hispanic publishing, infiltrating the world of digital book production. Future generations may not remember her. But it is a safe bet that they will create magnates and cold-blooded literary agents of their own—as well as a long list of excluded players to bitch about them.

Notes

CHAPTER 1: PUBLISHING MATTERS

1. For my discussion of this law, *Ley de Prensa e Imprenta*, I follow *Prensa e Imprenta*, the annotated edition for legal scholars, which includes the complete law authored by Fraga, the documentation of its approval process, and the regulations that followed its implementation up to 1968. The 1966 law overturned the obsolete 1938 *Ley de Prensa*, issued by Franco during the Spanish Civil War. Upon his arrival at the Ministry of Information and Tourism in 1962, Fraga took charge of drafting the law and changing the rules of censorship at the Ministry. A 1964 draft of the law was given to the National Press Council and the National Book Institute for review, and it was finally introduced in the Franco-controlled parliament on August 13, 1965 (*Prensa e Imprenta* 44). [All translations are mine unless otherwise indicated. My practice is to quote the original Spanish first except when it would disrupt the flow of an English sentence].

2. The *Archivo*'s payroll records that have been declassified show only seventeen "readers" on the payroll (*lectores fijos*). Their work hours were from 9:00 a.m. to 2:30 p.m., and then from 4:30 p.m. to 9:30 p.m., and their salaries range from six thousand to eight thousand pesetas, typical of what civil servants would make around that time. Most of these *lectores* held law degrees, some were priests, and others did not have any university education according to the available documentation. In many cases it is hard to identify censors' signatures in the reports. This was not a privacy protection measure, simply a reflection of the fact that most people in Spain sign their names illegibly. Manuel Abellán reproduces a list of the personnel working in 1954, which does not fully correspond to the 1961 records I have scrutinized (*Censura* 288).

3. Likewise, Maider Dravasa estimates that in 1969, about nine hundred publishers were registered in Spain, and more than 82 percent of the books printed in Spain were headed for Latin America, mainly Argentina (18 percent), Mexico (13 percent), Venezuela (10 percent), and Chile (10 percent) (212–16). [see also Downing 76–111].

4. However, it is not until 1957 that the National Book Institute is transferred to the Ministry of Information in an effort to coordinate censorship and book production under one single administrative unit (Decreto de 28 de junio). The 1943 Decree had granted supervision of the Institute to the Minister and Secretary of the FET and JONS (*Falange Española Tradicionalista y Juntas de Ofensivas Nacional Sindicalistas*, Franco's political party). Under the Ministry of Information, it became very active, and as early as 1957 issued a step-by-step manual for Spanish editors, *Editores españoles: guía comercial* [*Spanish Publishers: Commercial Guide*], which included specific information for the exportation of books to Brazil, Bolivia, Colombia, Costa Rica, Chile, The Philippines, and Mexico (369–75). In 1965, it published another key manual for Spanish editors, *Recomendaciones para tener en cuenta en la redacción de los contratos de edición* [*Recommendations to be Taken into Account in the Writing of Publishing Contracts*].

5. In their studies of the legal implications of "silencio administrativo negativo" [negative official silence] and "silencio administrativo positivo" [positive official silence], Guillén Pérez and Ernesto García-Trevijano point out that the 1956 *Ley Reguladora de la Jurisdicción* [Law of Judicial Regulation] included a three-month waiting period for the petitioner to appeal official silence, after which time the petition was deemed rejected. Their respective essays show that from 1958 on, the authorities began to clarify the legal implications of official silence in several procedural laws. The 1966 printing law, as quoted above, associated official silence with a positive outcome of a petitioner's request (García-Trevijano 96-107; Guillén Pérez 53–81).

6. For Robert C. Post, Michel Foucault's concept of "productive censorship"—constructive of knowledge and social practices—gives a precise account of regulatory practices of censorship such as *consulta voluntaria* (2).

7. Mario Santana borrows "wheat and chaff" from the Jesuit J. M. Aicado who in 1905 argued: "There on the American continent there is much of Spanish, much that is ours: seeds sown by the conquering and civilizing spirit of the Catholic Kings and the House of Austria that have produced a vast wheat, which—although mixed with foreign chaff—is nevertheless essentially ours" (135). A more contemporary reference is to Jean Paulhan's essay *De la paille et du grain* [*Of Wheat and Chaff*] against the blacklisting of authors who collaborated with the Germans in World War II.

8. In the same interview, Pere Gimferrer (who had been involved in Seix Barral since the 1960s and became its director in the 1990s) responded testily to my question about the economic success of the firm: "I only know about the literary aspects of our publishing house, I know *nothing* about marketing." What is most intriguing about this reaction, in my view, is not his outright denial of knowledge in economic matters (something he reiterated during the course of interview), but his insistence on drawing a clear-cut distinction between the aesthetic and economic programs of the firm.

9. Ángel Rama sees the Boom as a movement toward the globalization of Latin America based on advertising strategies, and David Viñas as lacking any aesthetic common denominator among its writers. For Emir Rodríguez Monegal the initial link between the Boom writers' support for the Cuban revolution and their "revolutionary" use of language was transformed into a publishing phenomenon: "the result of a decision in the industry to launch a product they thought they could sell, the new Latin American prose fiction" (Mac Adam 30). Rodríguez Monegal refers to three factors that generated this movement of oscillation between a cultural revolution and an industrial boom: the role of Seix Barral, the creation of literary journals such as *Marcha, Primera Plana, Mundo Nuevo,* and *Libre,* and the increasing number of translations and film adaptations of Latin American novels. Carlos Fuentes avoids the term Boom and focuses on *nueva novela,* defined by the modernization of Latin American fiction and its renovation of language, themes, and narrative structures. [see also Tola de Habich]

10. In this connection, an ad for Barral Editores in the second issue of *Libre,* clearly showed the continuation of Carlos Barral's line of symbolic investment in literary success: "Manténganse en Vanguardia, siga a Barral" ["Keep up with the Avant-Garde, Follow Barral"] (*Libre* 2, 1971–72).

11. The Formentor and International Prizes were created by a consortium of six publishers from France (Gallimard), Spain (Seix Barral), Italy (Einaudi), England (Weidenfeld & Nicholson), Germany (Rowohlt Verlag), and the United States (Grove Press)—who were later joined by seven more publishers from Portugal, Canada, the Netherlands, and the Scandinavian countries. They met once a year at the Formentor Hotel in Majorca to award the Formentor Prize to the best unpublished manuscript, and the *Prix International* to an established author of world stature. Each prize carried a $10,000 award and the publication of the author's work by the thirteen publishers. The *Premio Biblioteca Breve*—which carried an award of less than $2,000 and the publication of the winning manuscript—was officially open to literary works from Spain and Latin America without restriction. In reality the selection of manuscripts by members of the jury (Joan Petit, José María Castellet, Luis Goytisolo) was subject to internal recommendations as well as the editorial policies of Carlos Barral (see p. 80–on, *Cuando las horas veloces)* [*When the Hours Are Fast*]. It is no surprise that Barral's supervision of the prize between 1959 and 1969 resulted in five Latin American winners and two finalists (see Chronology; end of chapter).

12. In recent years, Seix Barral has relaunched its *Biblioteca Breve* Prize. Several up-and-coming Latin Americans have received the award: Chilean Mauricio Electorat for his *Burla del tiempo* [*Kidding Time*] (2004), Colombian Mario Mendoza for *Satanás* [*Satan*] (2002), Argentinean Gonzalo Garcés for *Los impacientes* [*The Impacients*] (2000), and Mexican Jorge Volpi for *En busca de Klingsor* [*Looking for Klingsor*] (1999). The "new" new Seix Barral has redesigned its book covers and upgraded the quality of its printing paper.

13. Seix Barral published eleven titles by José Donoso and two editions of his memoirs *Historia personal del boom* (1972, 1983) [*The Boom in Spanish American Literature: A Personal History*].

14. The novel is set during the early years of the *transición* (121), but there are several references to the Franco regime (18) and the word *censura* (15) does appear a few times. Censorship, however, is never mentioned in connection with the Boom writers' publishing careers.

15. In a letter from his agent, Donoso learns that the regime authorities continue to oppose the publication of *El lugar sin límites* in Spain. Carmen Balcells recommends authorizing the reprinting of the novel with Mexico's Joaquín Mortiz (Letter from Balcells to Donoso, May 29, 1971). Seix Barral's request for permission to import this novel in 1967 was rejected: "por su carácter inmoral, ya que el argumento se desarrolla...en un ambiente de prostitución, sin que figure una sola frase en que se repruebe, en que se desapruebe, la conducta inmoral de los protagonistas" ["owing to its immoral character, since the novel takes place in a world of prostitution and there is not a single sentence of reproach or disapproval of its protagonists' immoral conduct"] (Expediente I-326-67).

16. The fictional Julio Méndez brings to mind the importance of political exiles in the production of Latin American literature; for her part, Gloria reminds us that translations are a key element in the promotion of Boom authors, particularly in publishing centers like New York and Paris. I thank the press's readers for their helpful suggestion that I explore the international context in which the Boom emerged. Unfortunately, due to length limitations, it is impossible to address this question in any substantive way. For the importance of translations, see Balderston's and Schwartz's *Voice-Overs: Translation and Latin American Literature*.

17. There are two versions of this text. It first appeared in 1990 in Puerto Rico, and four years later a condensed version was published in *Quimera* and illustrated with drawings of several "bitches." The 1990 version, from which I am quoting here, included additional sections on René Marqués, Luis Rafael Sánchez, Edgardo Rodríguez Juliá, Clara Lair, and Ana Lydia Vega, and was published in Puerto Rico's Editorial Cultural.

18. See Burkhard Pohl for complete listings of Seix Barral and Barral Editores collections and awards (438-59).

CHAPTER 2: THE WRITER IN THE BARRACKS

1. The works of Mario Vargas Llosa (1936–) are closely linked to the Spanish literary market and to Seix Barral, despite the fact that his most recent novels—*La fiesta del chivo* [*Feast of the Goat*] (2000) and *Los cuadernos de*

Don Rigoberto [*The Notebooks of Rigoberto*] (1997)—have been published by Alfaguara, the global publishing enterprise affiliated with Random House and the Bertelsmann Group. Under the Franco regime, Seix Barral published six titles by Vargas Llosa, and Barral Editores published his essay *García Márquez: historia de un deicidio* [*García Márquez: The Story of a God-Killer*] in 1971, and José Miguel Oviedo's 1970 seminal work on Vargas Llosa, *La invención de una realidad* [*The Invention of a Reality*]. Vargas Llosa's memoirs were published by Seix Barral in 1993 (*El pez en el agua* [A *Fish in the Water*]).

2. The novel competed with eighty-one manuscripts, thirty of which came from Latin America. The jury members—José María Castellet, José María Valverde, Víctor Seix, Carlos Barral, and Joan Petit—unanimously selected *La ciudad y los perros* in the first round of voting, something unheard of in the history of the prize (Oviedo, *La invención* 30–31).

3. In addition, Vargas Llosa was awarded the *Premio Internacional de Literatura Rómulo Gallegos* in 1967, the *Planeta* Prize in 1993 for *Lituma en los Andes* [*Death in the Andes*], the *Premio Príncipe de Asturias de las Letras* in 1986, and the 1994 *Premio Cervantes*, the so-called Nobel Prize of Hispanic Letters.

4. In 1974, Vargas Llosa wrote an essay entitled "La censura y el cine" ["Censorship and Film"], in which he criticizes the Peruvian government's decree ("decreto-ley 205574") prohibiting the display of "sex and violence" in films. Many of his remarks on censorship in this piece originate in his experience under the Franco regime, as he insists that the decree's rules ("reglamento") must be abolished ("La censura y el cine").

5. Even though Vargas Llosa had resided in Barcelona during several years of the *apertura*, the law required two years of residence prior to naturalization. The law, at article 21, allows the government to grant citizenship by Royal Decree under "exceptional circumstances" (*Código Civil*).

6. Robles Piquer was General Director of Information at the Ministry of Information from 1962 until 1969, when he became General Director of Popular Culture and Theatre. After holding several political appointments during the transition, he became a member of the European Parliament from 1986 until 1999. During his years as the head of censorship services he implemented the so-called semi-official censorship [*censura oficiosa*], by which he personally read manuscripts prior to their being "officially" submitted to the authorities (Cisquella 28). In the case of Vargas Llosa's *La ciudad y los perros*, it appears that he intervened after the censors had evaluated and rejected the novel.

7. This possibility is also backed by the "definitive editions" ["ediciones definitivas"] of his novels published in Alfaguara's collection "Biblioteca Mario Vargas Llosa," which includes, among others, *La ciudad y los perros*, *La casa verde*, *Conversación en la catedral*, and *Pantaleón y las visitadoras*.

8. However, the censor categorically rejected any inclusion of Julio Cortázar's commentary, which is literally crossed out with a red pen: "En el centro mismo de *La ciudad y los perros* late como un corazón colérico la denuncia de una inautenticidad; mejor aún, de las formas por las cuales se desemboca en esa inautenticidad que pesa trágicamente en el panorama del Perú, es decir, de toda Sudamérica. Pero esa denuncia no tendría el valor catártico que alcanzará algún día si no estuviera escrita como sabe hacerlo Mario Vargas. Implacable testigo del infierno, su alucinante experiencia puede ser también fórmula de redención el día en que nuestros pueblos descubran la libertad profunda que su hora enterrada al pie de las estatuas ecuestres de las plazas" ["At the very core of *La ciudad y los perros*, the condemnation of inauthenticity beats like a choleric heart; or better, the denunciation of the forms that channel this inauthenticity, that weighs so tragically on the outlook of Peru, that is, that of Latin America. But this condemnation would not have such cathartic value had it not been written as only Mario Vargas knows how. Relentlessly bearing witness to hell, his hallucinatory experience may also be the formula for redemption on the day in which our people discover the deep liberty that lies buried beneath the equestrian statues in our squares"] (Expediente de *La ciudad y los perros*).

9. Argentine artist Ernesto Diera, in what I see as a response to the censorship authorities' resistance to Carlos Mensa's work, created six etchings inspired by *Pantaleón y las visitadoras*. Vargas Llosa prefaced the exhibition with a brief essay entitled "Las aguafuertes excesivas de Ernesto Diera" ["The Excessive Etchings of Ernesto Diera"].

10. In order to keep his mission secret, Pantaleón renames the Army's river boat *Pachitea* and hydroplane *Requena* as "Eve" ["Eva"] and "Delilah" ["Dalila"] respectively (*Pantaleón* 1995, 86–7, 93).

11. Carlos Mensa (Barcelona, 1936–1982), founder of the *Grupo Síntesis* in the 1960s, used a combination of surrealist and pop culture motifs in his paintings (www.artque.com). The painting in question was part of Rodríguez Aguilera's collection.

12. Sara Castro-Klarén has argued that Pantoja's detailed and almost absurd evaluations must be understood as a parody of the *huachafo*, the Peruvian version of the pseudo-refined, pretentious, and vulgar (137–8). [see also Oviedo, *La invención* 273.]

CHAPTER 3: CUBAN NIGHTS FALLING

1. I am drawing here on Michel Foucault's view of censorship as a repressive and productive form of power (*Discipline and Punish* 3–31) and on Judith Butler's assertion that "censorship is a productive form of power" that is not "merely privative, but formative as well" ("Ruled Out" 252).

2. "Metafinal" is the alternative ending to *Tres tristes tigres* that the author published in 1970 (also included in *Ella cantaba boleros* [*She Sang Boleros*]) and the 1972 "Epilogue" is a final commentary on the novel. These addenda to *Tres tristes tigres* indicate the author's view that the published novel was somehow an incomplete text.

3. The English version of the "cronología" was published in *Review* (*Center for Inter-American Relations*) 72 (Winter 71/Spring 72) by the author and with the title "(C)ave Attemptor! A Chronology of GCI (After Laurence Sterne's)." The issue also includes the "Epilogue for Late(nt) Readers" (4–32). The "cronología" has been reprinted in Cabrera Infante's *O* (Seix Barral 1975), and in Pereda (1978). In recent editions of *Tres tristes tigres* the "cronología" is more extensive and covers the writer's life up to 1998. The updated version has a less pompous title, "Orígenes: una cronología llamada: un autor se presenta" ["Origins: A Chronology Called: An Author Presents Himself"] (Cabrera Infante, *Tres tristes tigres* 1999, 496–520)

4. Years later in Spain, when Seix Barral submitted *Así en la paz* for clearance in 1971, the Spanish censors concurred with Ediciones R's assessment, perceiving that "the work's objective" was "to praise the Cuban Revolution" (Expediente de *Así en la paz como en la guerra*).

5. For Cabrera Infante's description of the film, see his essay titled "La peliculita culpable" ["The Guilty Little Film"] (*Mea Cuba*, 68) or "P.M. means Post Mortem" in the English version of *Mea Cuba* (53). "P.M" is now available in *Censuré à Cuba*, a collection of short Cuban films released by FNAC in 2002.

6. In "Las fuentes de la narración," an interview by Rodríguez Monegal published in *Mundo nuevo*, Cabrera Infante explains that the first title was "La noche es un hueco sin borde" ["Night is a borderless void"], a title the author discarded because it was "terribly pretentious" ["terriblemente pretencioso"] (48).

7. The playful reference to Charles Baudelaire's preface to *The Flowers of Evil*, "Au Lecteur" ["To the Reader"], underscores a fraternal relation of hypocrisy between the writer and the reader that Baudelaire saw as key to modernity (and hence literary modernism). Hypocrisy, Chambers argues, is the form of censorship that unites the otherwise critical writer with the self-deceiving reader under the tyrannical regime of Satan: "—Hypocrite reader, —mon semblable, mon frère—!" ["—Hypocrite reader, —fellowman—, my twin!"] (6–7). See Chambers' *Writing of Melancholy*.

8. The reference to James Joyce's "silence" and "cunning" comes from *Portrait of the Artist*: "and I will try to express myself in some mode of life or art as freely as I can as wholly as I can, using for my defence the only arms I allow myself to use—silence, exile and cunning" (213). Interestingly, in his appropriation of the Joycean motto "writing from the outside," Cabrera Infante leaves out "exile."

9. Similarly, when José Lezama Lima tried to publish *Esfera imagen* [*Sphere Image*] in Spain, the censors had at their disposal a brief biography of the Cuban writer: "Es un hombre de gran humanismo, espiritual y físico, pues mide 1.90 mts y pesa más de 100 Kgs, y está enfermo de asma. Parece ser que no tiene implicaciones políticas y que, incluso, no es simpatizante de Fidel Castro, aunque la revolución le ha respetado por su gran prestigio literario.... Lo cierto es que no ha tenido ni tiene cargos oficiales...." ["He is man of great humanism in a spiritual and physical sense, since he is 1,90 meters tall and weighs over 100 kilograms, and he suffers from asthma. It appears he is not involved in politics and he is not even a sympathizer of Fidel Castro, even though the Revolution has respected him because of his literary prestige.... It is true that he has not held nor is he holding any official position...."] (Expediente de *Esfera imagen* 1969). Lezama Lima's literary prestige, however, did not preclude the sequestration proceedings ordered by Fraga himself when in 1968 Equipo Editorial, a small Basque publishing firm, tried to release *Paradiso* [*Paradise*], which would not be authorized in Spain until 1973 (Expediente de *Paradiso*).

10. *Lunes* became a major bastion of the Revolution's cultural apparatus despite its short-lived existence from March 1959 until November 1961, rapidly expanding from a run of about 100,000 issues to about 250,000 after the Bay of Pigs. For a complete listing of all the essays included in these two special issues see Luis (*Lunes* 55–135). The 1961 issue of *Lunes* was reprinted as a collection of essays titled *La España rebelde* [*Rebellious Spain*] that Guillermo Cabrera Infante edited and published the same year at Movimiento Universitario Revolucionario (Lima, Peru). This reprint also includes an open letter addressed to the Spanish Minister of Information (signed by "240 intellectuals from Madrid and Barcelona") demanding the overhaul of censorship procedures in Spain, namely, the right of appeal and the release of the censors' names (15–17).

11. Scare-quotes for the verb "to silence" are appropiate since I use it in a slightly different sense than the dictionary's definition: "1. To make silent or bring to silence. 2. To curtail the expression of; suppress" (*American Heritage*).

12. The approval of *El siglo de las luces* required the intervention of Robles Piquer, given that in November 1964, when the censors first evaluated the novel, they objected to its "irreverent" attitude toward Spain's Catholicism. In July 1965, Robles Piquer authorized a "corrected" version that was finally cleared on December 30, 1965 (Expediente de *El siglo de las luces*). In 1966 Seix Barral submitted Carpentier's *El reino de este mundo* [*The Kingdom of this World*] to the censors, and gained rapid approval for it, the censors having no problem with the novel's "circumstantial remarks" on Cuba and Spain (Expediente de *El reino*).

13. Barral appropiates for his appeal the same questions censors had to answer in their reports and reproduces them almost verbatim in the *alega-*

ciones: "¿Ataca al dogma?, ¿a la moral?, ¿a la Iglesia y sus Ministros?, ¿al Régimen y a sus instituciones?" ["Does it attack the dogma, morals, the Church and its Ministers, the Regime and its institutions?"] (Expediente de "Vista" 1965).

14. The reference is to the Surrealists' game of *cadavre exquis* or exquisite corpse.

15. The censor provides an inventory of the pages in *Tres tristes tigres* that required "supresión de párrafos" ["paragraph deletions"] for obscenity, antimilitaristic stances, and for political content, pages 119 through 138—corresponding to the added new section on Trotsky (Expediente de *Tres tristes tigres* 1966). Only some of these corrections were made for the 1967 edition.

16. "Vista" consists of the following sections: "Prólogo" (1–11); "Los debutantes" (3–14); "Ella cantaba boleros" (14–21, 29–32, 44–46, 72–76, 87–92); "Mapa dibujado por un espía" (21–29); "Crepúsculos en la casa de los espejos" (32–44); "Nights in Havana: el camino de Santa Fe" (46–50); "Historia un bastón y algunos reparos de Mrs. Campbell" (50–57), "Seseribó" (58–72); "El último show" (76–83), and the political vignettes (intersected in pages 6 through 92, and as a block in 92–105). *Tres tristes tigres* does not include "Mapa dibujado," "Havana Nights," "El último show," or any of the political vignettes.

17. The 1971 English version *Three Trapped Tigers* (a translation "from the Cuban" the author considers a completely different book) and the 1972 addendum "Epilogue for Late(nt) Readers" also contributed to *Tres tristes tigres*' international visibility in the 1970s. For González Echevarría *Tres tristes tigres* must be understood as a composite text made of the original "Vista," the published version in 1967, the 1970 "Metafinal," the English version of 1971, and the 1972 "Epilogue for Late(nt) Readers" (225).

18. The censorship cuts ("cortes de censura") listed in the Ayacucho edition correspond to the ones I found in the October 1966 censor's report. These cuts are primarily related to the "explicit language" the censors saw in the description of sexual encounters in *Tres tristes tigres* (1990: 19, 54, 56, 85, 86, 113–14, 123, 124, 132, 150, 171, 173, and 296). The 1999 Seix Barral edition incorporates these omitted passages as well (1999: 29–30, 83–99, 86, 127, 167–168, 183–84, 184, 195, 225, 251, 255, and 434).

19. Emir Rodríguez Monegal, an advocate of Cabrera Infante's early works in the pages of *Mundo Nuevo*, argues that the Latin American Boom novels present a "revolutionary writing" which is to be understood as revolutionary in its aesthetic innovations, in its left-leaning ideals, and early support of the Cuban Revolution, the one historical event that both unites and separates the Boom writers. This is particularly true for Cabrera Infante (Rodríguez Monegal, "A Revolutionary Writing").

20. Two vignettes from the 1965 "Vista" (the manuscript held in Alcalá de Henares)—"Era un abogado del pueblo" (the story of poet-lawyer who is executed for a play he wrote titled "The Immortal Heroes: A Patriotic Tragedy in Five Acts"), and "El hijo regresó del trabajo" (the story of a son who returns from work to find his father dead) ("Vista" 1965, 94–96)—do not appear in the 1974 *Vista* (Seix Barral), or in any of its four drafts held at the Princeton Library.

21. It is worth noting that the Princeton Library drafts of *Vista* do not include any of the author's own cutouts of the 1965 "Vista" galley proofs that had been extensively marked by the Spanish censors. Clearly the author had these cutouts in his possession as he used them for the composition of the 1966 manuscript "Tres tristes tigres" held at Princeton. This is another indication on the author's intention to hide the most compromising of his dealings with the Spanish censors.

22. The first page of the censor's report lists "Vista" as consisting of 220 pages, which presumably corresponds to the actual number of printed pages once the 105 pages of legal-size galley proofs were reformatted into book-size pages (Expediente de "Vista" 1965).

CHAPTER 4: FROM MELQUÍADES TO VERNET

1. Subastas Velázquez also put up for sale several photographs of García Márquez with friends in Mexico, personal letters, and first editions of his works. Among these are: *La hojarasca* [*Leaf Storm*] (opening price, $1,000), *La mala hora* [*In Evil Hour*] (opening price $1,000), the French translation *Cent ans de solitude* (opening price, $450), the Catalan translation *Cent anys de solitud* (opening price, $300), *Crónica de una muerte anunciada* [*Chronicle of a Death Foretold*] (opening price, $1,500), and *El amor en los tiempos del cólera* [*Love in the Times of Cholera*] (opening price, $300).

2. García Márquez sees literary techniques as "secret craftsmanship": "Muchas de las novelas que entonces leía y admiraba sólo me interesaban por sus enseñanzas técnicas. Es decir, por su carpintería secreta" ["Many of the novels I was reading then, which I admired, interested me only because of their technical lessons. That is: their secret carpentry"] (*Vivir* 324/*Living* 271). This "secret carpentry" is literalized in "La prodigiosa tarde de Balthazar," in the craftsmanship of a brilliant carpenter who creates a magnificent wooden birdcage that is described as "an adventure of the imagination" ["una aventura de la imaginación" (*Funerales* 69/*Collected Stories* 140).

3. In a letter addressed to Vargas Llosa, García Márquez explains his decision to keep changes on the galley proofs to a minimum: "Acabo de corre-

gir las pruebas de imprenta de *Cien años de soledad*. Ya no me sabe a nada, así que en vez de cambiarlo todo, como era mi deseo en las noches de insomnio, decidí dejarlo todo como estaba" ["I just finished correcting the galley proofs of *One Hundred Years of Solitude*. It has no taste for me now, so I decided that instead of changing everything, as was my desire during my nights of insomnia, I would leave everything as it was"] (Letter to Vargas Llosa, March 20, 1967). [Given that Subastas Velázquez has gone out of business, I have been unable to get the necessary permission to reproduce here a page showing sample galleys from the auction's catalogue.]

  4. The catalogue reproduces two full pages of the galleys and sections of another ten that show additions and typographical corrections (Subastas 12, 14, 16). As a big selling point the catalogue includes the first page with the autographed dedication and one page from the penultimate section of novel in which García Márquez adds a missing phrase that the compositors omitted: "Amaranta Úrsula le había asignado una suma para sus gastos personales" (page 322 of the Sudamericana edition) ["Amaranta Úrsula had assigned him a sum for his personal expenses"].

  5. The auction's catalogue does not directly refer to the existence of other typescripts of the novel, but it does include a long list of handwritten changes to the typescript to prove the uniqueness of the document being auctioned: "the butterflies have to be 'amarillas,' the 'Opera Magna' is 'Alquimia,' the 'fenómenos' are 'cambios,' 'la prodigalidad' becomes 'el desprecio,' 'La Bella' becomes 'la sobrina,'...'voluntad' is 'salud,' 'troglodita' is 'atarván.'...There are many similar examples which change the first draft considerably" (Subastas Velázquez 19).

  6. Santana reminds us that the "figure of the wise Catalonian" has been long considered a "fictional transposition of Ramon Vinyes, to whom the character, according to García Márquez, pays homage" (148, see also note 49, 202). In *Escribir en Barranquilla*, Illán Bacca describes "Don Ramón's presence" ["la presencia de don Ramón"] as an inspiring force in the "Barranquilla Group of which García Márquez was a member in the 1950s (488). They devoted their time to literary conversations in the Café Colombia (see also Saldívar, *viaje a la semilla*, 234–243; García Márquez, *Vivir* 522; and Joset, *Cien años* 488).

  7. Eligio quotes a survey among publishers conducted by *La cultura de México* in 1964 in which Neus Espresate details Era's policies for the publication of novels, poetry, and essays. In all cases they published very small runs, ranging from five hundred copies for works of poetry, one thousand for novels and short stories, and three thousand for political essays (50). This editorial policy did not please García Márquez, and by 1968 he had taken his books from Era to Sudamericana without the consent of the Mexican firm, as he explains in a letter to José Donoso: "firmé con Sudamericana por los libros que Era tenía congelados y no quería ceder. A Era le dije simplemente que me llevaran a los

tribunales. No pasó nada. ["I signed up with Sudamericana for the books Era was holding in deep freeze and did not want to let go. I dared Era to take me to court. Nothing happened"] (Letter to José Donoso, 1968).

    8. Sudamericana's launching of the novel was quite modest. There was some promotion in *Primera Plana*, where there was a small note announcing the "Amadís of Colombia" but the reasons for its success lie primarily in the expectations the novel had built up among scholars and critics since *Mundo nuevo* had published one chapter in August 1966 and a second one in March 1967. In the pages of *Mundo nuevo*, Rodríguez Monegal became the "greatest propagandist" of the novel, as he confessed to García Márquez in 1966 (Letter to García Márquez). By June 1967 it had been acclaimed as the "great novel of America" (García Márquez, *Tras las claves* 26–7).

    9. After the publication of *Cien años de soledad* was settled, Barral and García Márquez let bygones be bygones and the Colombian author soon enjoyed full membership in the Catalan intelligentsia: "Estamos en Barcelona como si tuviéramos muchos años aquí" ["We are in Barcelona as if we had been here for many years"] (Letter to José Donoso, January 5, 1968).

    10. *La hojarasca* appeared in Ediciones S.L.B ("Sipa Limitada, Bogotá") in 1955, and *El coronel* in Aguerri Editor in Medellín (1961). These were very small presses with limited circulation and low-end printing and costs. Reprints of *La hojarasca* appeared at minor presses with the exception of Sudamericana, which relaunched the novel worldwide. These are the reprints between 1955 and 1975: Organización Continental de los Festivales del Libro (Caracas 1958, 1969); ARCA (Montevideo 1965); Sudamericana (Buenos Aires 1969, 1971, 1972, 1973, and 1975); Gráficas Guada (Barcelona 1974); and Plaza & Janés (Esplugas de Llobregrat, Barcelona 1975). *El coronel* first appeared in *Mito* IV, n. 19 (1958), and as a volume in 1961. Reprints include: Ediciones Era (Mexico 1961, 1963, 1966, 1967, 1969, 1970, 1972, 1973, and 1974); Sudamericana (Buenos Aires 1968, 1969, 1970, 1971, and 1973); and Plaza & Janés (Esplugas de Llobregrat, Barcelona 1974).

    11. The 1966 edition includes a preliminary note by the author in which he rejects the Spanish edition and claims the Mexican edition to be the true first edition (García Márquez, *La mala hora* 1966, 6). [See also Joset, "*mala hora*"]

    12. All the petitions to import García Márquez's books were approved with the exception of *Cuando era feliz e indocumentado* [*When I Was Happily Illegal*]. In it the importation department found "insults against the Franco regime" ["injurias al régimen de Franco"] (Expediente I–1764–70). In a letter to Cobo Borda, García Márquez explains that this book was written under censorship: "el libro demostrará que en mis mocedades fui muy mal periodista. Pero una cosa debe quedar clara: todo fue escrito bajo un régimen de censura" ["the book will demonstrate that I was a very bad journalist in my youth. But one thing must remain clear: I wrote it all under a censorship regime"] (Letter to Cobo Borda).

13. The authorities rubber-stamped these two petitions in a day, and generated a rush report on *La hojarasca* in which they basically summarized the plot, very clumsily, and the narrative techniques used by the author (Expediente de *La hojarasca*).

14. Vernet's letter is dated September 24, 1973, but it is included in the 1972 dossier for *Cien años de soledad*. Apparently the censorship authorities opted for filing it in the most current dossier for the novel.

15. Vernet's selection includes the following passages: Aureliano's sexual encounter with a mulatto adolescent girl who was forced into prostitution by her grandmother (51)—which García Márquez would rewrite in *Eréndira* (1971); Father Nicanor's use of miracles as a way to collect money to build the biggest temple in the world (77); the scene where José Arcadio is auctioned off by women (84); the quasi-incestuous relationship between José Arcadio and Rebeca, who are cousins but are raised as brother and sister (85–6); Sacristan Pretonio's comment to José Arcadio: "Es que hay cristianos corrompidos que hacen sus cosas con las burras" ["There are some corrupt Christians who do their business with female donkeys"] (163/186); the disclosure of Fernanda's sexual habits and her refusal to consummate her marriage to Aureliano Segundo (181–2); Petra Cotés' love affair with the identical twins Aureliano and José Arcadio (298); and the incestuous relationship between Aureliano Babibolina and his aunt Amaranta Úrsula (341).

CHAPTER 5: BETRAYED BY CENSORSHIP

1. The novel presents sixteen chapters or life sketches about a middle-class Argentinean family of Catalan origin, the Casals. These chapters are intended to reproduce fragments of their lives in a remote provincial town called Coronel Vallejos, where the characters' dull and mundane existence is both contrasted with and informed by the glamour of Hollywood films of the 1930s and 1940s.

2. The Spanish expression "tres al cuarto" [literally, "three units per quarter"] is of some significance here because it is a reminder that censors often read the literary qualities of novels in economic terms: "locución adjetiva con que se denota y pondera la poca estimación, aprecio y valor de una cosa" ["adjectival phrase with which one denotes and weighs the low estimate, appraisal or value of something"] *(Diccionario de la Lengua Española)*.

3. In the first censorship file on Puig, dated June 7, 1966, his name appears in Catalan, "Joan Manuel Puig" (usually pronounced in Spain as "puch"). Seix Barral, the publishing house that would later publish all of Puig's works, submitted his name in Catalan to the censorship authorities in 1966, but corrected to "Manuel Puig" in the subsequent petitions to publish his works in 1971, 1973, and 1976. The fact that the censorship authorities had

accepted and filed a request with a Catalan name was also a significant change in their procedures. Often, Catalan names in the censorship documents housed at the National Archive appear in Spanish. This procedure changed during the *apertura* years of the early 1960s.

    4. Vittoria Martinetto claims that Puig had a copy of the third edition of *The Buenos Aires Affair* that was published by Editorial Sudamericana in 1973. This edition was seized by Argentinean authorities and somehow Puig found a copy in a second-hand bookstore in New York City and kept it as "a fetish" for years until handing it to Martinetto in 1987. Martinetto reveals that the authorities blanked out the sexually explicit passages in chapter VI of the novel, but disregarded those passages with a political or "revolutionary message": "lo que la censura no ha conseguido entender es que el mensaje revolucionario de la novela va mucho más lejos de un discurso positivo sobre la homosexualidad o uno negativo sobre el peronismo" ["censors did not manage to understand that the revolutionary message in the novel goes much further than a positive discourse about homosexuality or a negative discourse on Peronism"] (Amícola and Speranza 220–221).

    5. The movie reference here is Deanna Durbin's classics, the 1937 *Three Smart Girls* and the 1939 *Three Smart Girls Grow Up*.

    6. The signatures on the 1966 and 1971 reports do not match, but it is obvious that the second censor had access to the first report on *La traición*.

    7. The pagination in the censor's report corresponds to pages 193 through 213 in the 1971 edition by Seix Barral.

    8. I follow here Jonathan Tittler's interpretation of chapter XI (19–20) and Suzanne Jill Levine's English translation, which was published by Dutton in 1971.

    9. As revealed by José Amícola, "Aunt Clara" was the first chapter of a novel then entitled *Pájaros en la cabeza* [*Birds in the Head*] (Amícola, *materiales* 232–265). Through the eyes of Clara, this chapter presents an overview of all the main characters and themes in *La traición*. It is, above all, a condensed version of the main motifs and major plot lines as well as a general panorama of who's who in the novel. Even though the chapter was never published as part of the novel, some of the phrases and motifs in "Aunt Clara" were later incorporated into other chapters.

    10. I would also argue that Puig writes in a similarly "economical" way about the movies mentioned in *La traición*. With the exception of *Blood and Sand* and *The Great Waltz*, the rest of the movies are only referred to in snippets and not as fully incorporated into the characters' lives. Puig's economical incorporation of the 1930s and 1940s Hollywood is exemplified in the novel's scattered references, among others, to *Snow White* (33, 38), *Romeo and Juliet* (37), *In Old Chicago* (69), *Weekend in Havana* (79, 81), *Intermezzo* (110), *Wuthering Heights* (92, 82, 106), *The Constant Nymph* (125), *The Great*

Man's Lady (138), and *For Whom the Bell Tolls* (235) [all quotations are from the 1971 Spanish edition of *La traición*]. See also Lucille Kerr's (*Suspended* 79) and Campos' proposed filmography (*Espejos* 181–182).

11. Clara remains a character in the novel, but her role is very minor. With the exception of chapter I, the unmediated dialogue at Mita's parents' house, Puig does not allow her voice into the text, so that her character is constructed through the voice of others. The omitted "Aunt Clara" chapter would have inverted this relationship between Clara and the other members of the Casals family, since Clara's would have been the opening voice that sets up the rest of the novel. Amícola's examination of Puig's manuscripts concludes that "La tía" ["the Aunt"] was the initial chapter in Puig's index for *La traición*. "Aunt Clara" was eliminated, and the novel became a fourteen-chapter text. Finally, Puig later added the closing letter ("Berto's Letter, 1933," chapter XVI) and the anonymous note ("Cobito, Spring, 1946," chapter XI) that constitute the sixteen chapters of the novel. Interestingly, the Seix Barral editions of *La traición* included the final version of the index, and the 1971 English translation omitted it.

12. I draw here on Julia Romero's proposal to read another textual economy in Mita's and Toto's similar syntactical constructions, and on Graciela Goldchluk's interpretation of Puig's "zero narrator" whose "expenditures govern the economy of the text" (Amícola, *materiales* 298, 373, 472).

13. In his reconstruction of Puig's manuscript of *La traición*, Amícola indicates that Berto's letter was not found with the rest of the chapters of the novel, but in a box that contained newspaper articles. Amícola argues that the separation of the letter from the body of the novel represents "another rupture with Puig's initial prohibition on showing the letter," which Puig himself intentionally separated from the original manuscript. Thus, "this implicit prohibition," as Amícola calls it, "censors the showing of the letter," underscoring the importance of censorship and betrayal in the novel, and I would add, in Puig's literary career (*materiales* 421).

14. Given that the letter is dated 1933, it belongs chronologically at the beginning of the novel, along with "Mita's Parents' Place, La Plata, 1933" (chapter I) and "At Berto's, Vallejos, 1993" (chapter II). Kerr argues that this temporal inversion circumvents the apparently "final figure of authority" and "renders powerless the vow of negation and closure with which Berto's text ends" (*Suspended* 37-38).

15. Mita and Delia often remark on the stunting of his physical growth: "because Toto didn't grow and still uses last year's [clothes]. Héctor outgrew everything" (*Betrayed* 96). In parallel fashion, Toto fails to "develop" a passion for soccer like his cousin Héctor. For this reason, the novel has been read as a failed *bildungsroman*, "a novel about upbringing and education, but restricted to childhood and adolescence" (Echevarren 18). The impossibility of placing the novel in a particular genre, in my view, has to do with the

nonnormative character that Puig gives most of his novels, which are, in sum, queer texts. Censors and publishers alike rejected such queerness.

16. *Blood and Sand* encodes Hispanic culture in two different ways. Not only is the movie an adaptation of Blasco Ibáñez's *Sangre y arena*, but also the lead actress, Rita Hayworth, is of Spanish descent. She was born Margarita Carmen Cansino (Brooklyn, NY 1918–New York, NY 1987) and was the daughter of a Spanish dancer, Eduardo Cansino, who migrated to the United States in 1913. At the age of twelve, she joined her father's dancing troupe and at the age of sixteen signed a contract with Fox (Internet Movie Data Base, http://us.imdb.com/).

17. The scene in which Rita Hayworth "does toro," also closes the omitted chapter "Aunt Clara." In it, however, Clara presents a very different movie experience. Her attempt to watch the "betrayal of Rita Hayworth" is interrupted by her son Tito's obsession with the bull in the movie: "el otro día en "Sangre y Arena" no me dejó ver nada, que empezaba "¿dónde esta el torito? ¿dónde está el torito?" cada vez que no salía el toro y cuando aparecía se ponía a llorar "¿qué le hacen al torito? ¿Mami, qué le hacen al torito?", una lata" ["The other day at "Blood and Sand" he did not let me see a thing. Whenever the bull was not on the screen he started up with "where's the little bull?, where is the little bull?," and when it was on he cried "what are they doing to the little bull? Mommie, what are they doing to the little bull?," what a pest"] (Amícola, *materiales* 265). Tito's obsession with the "little bull" and consequent interruption of Clara's viewing of the movie substitutes for the scene of the betrayal. Aunt Clara's final remark—"what a pest"—dramatizes her disapproval of Tito's fixation on the bull, a disapproved that, in a coded way ("he did not let me see a thing"), anticipates the Casals family's tacit dislike for Toto's obsession with betrayals.

EPILOGUE

1. I refer here to the articles written by Juan Cruz, Manuel Vázquez Montalbán, Rosa Mora and Mario Vargas Llosa. They appeared in the *El País* in May 2000, coinciding with Balcells' retirement and her being awarded Spain's Gold Medal of Fine Arts. Meanwhile in Latin America Balcells' role was recognized in Argentina (Ezequiel Martínez) and in Chile (Andrés Gómez). As was the case in Spain, these articles reiterate the legendary character of Balcells' literary interventions, which encompass a stellar roster of Latin American writers such as Mario Vargas Llosa, Gabriel García Márquez, José Donoso, Guillermo Cabrera Infante, Carlos Fuentes, Augusto Roa Bastos, Isabel Allende, Antonio Skármeta, Alfredo Bryce Echenique, Jorge Edwards, and Pablo Neruda.

2. María Eugenia Mudrovcic argues that this fistfight resulted in Vargas Llosa's refusal to allow the reprinting of his essay *García Márquez: historia de un deicidio* published by Barral Editores in 1971 ("algunas lecciones" 130–1).

3. For further reading on the role of female literary agents in contemporary Spanish book market, see "Mujeres del Libro" by Rosa Mora. See also Christine Henseler's *Contemporary Spanish Women's Narrative and the Publishing Industry*.

4. Ezequiel Martínez titles his article on Balcells "The Autumn of Big Mama." And Vargas Llosa calls Balcells the "woman crying on Diagonal Avenue" in reference to the dedication García Márquez wrote for her in *De amor y otros demonios* [*Of Love and Other Demons*]: "For Balcells, bathed in tears" ("El jubileo" 2).

5. Joaquín Díaz Canedo, the founder of México's Editorial Joaquín Mortiz, is the exception: "Otro de los grandes problemas en México es el papel, nunca ha sido bueno ni hemos tenido la variedad que hay en otros países" ["Another big problem we face in Mexico is paper. It has never had a good quality and we don't have the variety other countries have"] (Vargas 59). Barral's memoirs and Rostagno's essay on the promotion of Latin American writers by Knopf, Harper & Row, Straus & Giroux make no direct mention of the importance of paper.

6. Editora Nacional, the regime's own publishing house, became an integral part of this expansionary policy.

7. The Subcomission's report lists twenty-three publications and presentations on the Spanish paper industry. Among these are José Luis Asenjo Martínez's "El Papel y su fabricación" (INLE 1961) and "Necesidades de capital en la industria papelera y pastera española (período 1961/1973)" published in *De Economía* 80 in Madrid in 1962 (Inventario de la información existente en el sector de la fabricación de pastas de papel, papel y cartón [included in Subcomisión del papel 19]).

8. See "El 'boom' doméstico" by María Pilar Donoso, which is a short essay included in the final version of Donoso's *Historia personal del boom*. Calafell is the fisherman's town that became a legendary meeting point for the Boom writers and Carlos Barral (and the inspiration for the fictional town in *Penúltimos castigos*): "A lo largo de los años sesenta y durante la década siguiente... mi viejo pueblo se convertía en un pasillo de visitas literarias y editoriales, y en los períodos largos en residencia de amigos y colaboradores" ["During the sixties and the following decade... my old town would become a corridor for literary and publishing-related visits, and in periods of largesse a residence for my friends and collaborators"] (*Cuando las horas* 155).

Works Cited

Abellán, Manuel. *Censura y creación literaria en España (1939–1976)*. Barcelona: Ediciones Península, 1980.

———. "La censura franquista y los escritores latinoamericanos." *Letras Peninsulares* (Spring 1992): 11–21.

Alfieri, Carlos. "Entrevista con Fernando R. Lafuente." *Cuadernos hispanoamericanos* 564 (1997): 7–17.

Allende, Isabel. Interview. *Espejo de escritores*. Videocassette. Hanover, NH: Ediciones del Norte, 1986.

American Heritage Dictionary. Vers 4.0. CD-ROM. Soft-Key International, 1995.

Amícola, José, ed. *Manuel Puig: materiales iniciales para La traición de Rita Hayworth*. Buenos Aires: Centro de Estudios de Teoría y Crítica Literaria, 1996.

Amícola, José, and Graciela Speranza, eds. *Encuentro Internacional Manuel Puig*. Buenos Aires: Beatriz Viterbo Editora, 1998.

Anderson, Danny J. "Creating Cultural Prestige: *Editorial Joaquín Mortiz*." *Latin American Research Review* 31.2 (1996): 3–41.

Armas Marcelo, J. J. *Vargas Llosa: el vicio de escribir*. Madrid: Temas de Hoy, 1991.

Artque España. http://www.artque.com

Avellaneda, Andrés. *Censura, autoritarismo y cultura: Argentina 1960–1983*. Buenos Aires: Centro Editor de América Latina, 1986.

Aznárez, Juan Jesús. "Polanco recibe un homenaje en México por su intensa labor latinoamericanista." *El País*. 1 Decemeber 1998: http://www.elpais.es.

Balcells, Carmen. Letter to José Donoso. 29 May 1971. Papers of José Donoso. Firestone Library. Princeton University.

———. Letter to Mario Vargas Llosa. 21 April 1970. Papers of Mario Vargas Llosa. Firestone Library. Princeton University.

Balderston, Daniel, and Marcy Schwartz, eds. *Voice-Overs: Translation and Latin American Literature*. Albany: State University of New York Press, 2002.

Barral, Carlos. *Almanaque*. Valladolid: Cuatro, 2000.

———. *Años de penitencia*. Barcelona: Plaza & Janés, 1994.

———. *Los años sin excusa*. Barcelona: Plaza & Janés, 1994.

———. Carta a Robles Piquer. 30 July 1963. Archivo General de la Administración, Alcalá de Henares.

———. *Cuando las horas veloces*. Barcelona: Tusquets, 1988.

———. Letter to José Donoso. 11 May 1973. Papers of José Donoso. Firestone Library. Princeton University.

———. *Memorias*. Barcelona: Península, 2001.

———. *Penúltimos castigos*. Barcelona: Plarza & Janés, 1994.

Baudelaire, Charles. *The Flowers of Evil*. Trans. James McGowan. New York: Oxford UP, 1993.

Benet, Juan. "El efecto Barral." *Revista de Occidente* 110–111 (July–August 1990): 11–15.

Blood and Sand. Dir. Rouben Mamoulian. Perf. Tyrone Power, Rita Hayworth, and Linda Darnell. Twentieth-Century Fox, 1941.

Bourdieu, Pierre. *The Field of Cultural Production*. Ed. and Trans. Randal Johnson. Gainesville: Polity Press, 1993.

———. "Censorship and the Imposition of Form." *Language and Symbolic Power*. Ed. John Thompson. Trans. Gino Raymond and Matthew Adamson. Cambridge: Harvard UP, 1994.

Breu Història de la Editorial Seix Barral, S.A. Dossier. Departamento de Promoción. Barcelona: Seix Barral, undated.

Breve comentario al informe sobre dificultades con que tropieza en varios países de la América española la exportación de libros. 1962. Archivo General de la Administración, Alcalá de Henares.

Butler, Judith. "Ruled Out: Vocabularies of the Censor." *Censorship and Silencing: Practices of Cultural Regulation*. Ed. Robert C. Post. Los Angeles: The Getty Research Institute Publications and Exhibitions Program, 1998. 247–59.

Cabrera Infante, Guillermo. *Así en la paz como en la guerra*. La Habana: Ediciones R, 1964.

———. *Así en la paz como en la guerra*. Barcelona: Seix Barral, 1971.

———. Carta a Robles Piquer. 3 February 1966. Archivo General de la Administración, Alcalá de Henares.

———. "(C)ave Attemptor! A Chronology of GCI (After Laurence Sterne's)." *Review* 72 (Winter 1971/Spring 1972): 5–9.

———. *Ella cantaba boleros*. Madrid: Alfaguara, 1996.

———. "Epilogue for Late(nt) Readers." *Review* 72 (Winter 1971/Spring 1972): 23–32.

———. *¡La España rebelde! (Ensayos selectos)*. Lima: Movimiento Universitario Revolucionario, 1961.

———. "Las fuentes de la narración." *Mundo nuevo* 25 (1968): 41–58.

———. *Infantería*. Ed. Montenegro, Nivia and Enrico Mario Santí. México: FCE, 1999.

———. Letter to Mario Vargas Llosa. 29 December 1966. Papers of Mario Vargas Llosa. Firestone Library. Princeton Library.

———. *Mea Cuba*. Madrid: Alfaguara, 1994.

———. *Mea Cuba*. Trans. Kenneth Hall and Cabrera Infante. London, UK: Faber & Faber, 1994.

———. "Metafinal." *Alacrán Azul* 1 (1970): 18–22.

———. *O*. Barcelona: Seix Barral, 1975.

———. *Un oficio del siglo XX*. La Habana: Ediciones R, 1963.

———. "Lo que la censura no ve" (photographs). *Lunes de Revolución*. 20 February 1961.

———. *Tres tristes tigres*. Barcelona: Seix Barral, 1967.

———. *Three Trapped Tigers*. Trans. Suzanne Jill Levine. New York: Harper & Row, 1971.

———. *Tres tristes tigres*. Barcelona: Seix Barral, 1981.

———. *Tres tristes tigres*. Caracas: Editorial Ayacucho, 1990.

———. *Tres tristes tigres*. Barcelona: Seix Barral, 1999.

———. "La última traición de Manuel Puig." *El País*. 24 July 1990. 22–23.

———. "Las vértebras de España." *Lunes de Revolución*. 20 February 1961. 2–3.

———. *View of Dawn in the Tropics*. Trans. Suzane Jill Levine. New York: Harper & Row, 1978.

———. "Vista del amanecer en el trópico." 1965. Archivo General de la Administración, Alcalá de Henares.

———. *Vista del amanecer en el trópico (Relatos)*. Barcelona: Seix Barral, 1974.

———. *Vista del amanecer en el trópico*. Barcelona: Plaza & Janés, 1984.

———. *Writes of Passage*. Trans. John Brookesmith, Peggy Boyers, Guillermo Cabrera Infante. London: Faber and Faber, 1993.

Campos, René. *Espejos : la textura cinemática en La traición de Rita Hayworth*. Madrid : Pliegos, 1985.

———. "Las 'películas de mujeres' y *La traición de Rita Hayworth*." *Literature and Popular Culture in the Hispanic World*. Ed. Rose S. Minc. Montclair State College: Ediciones Hispamérica, 1981.

Cano Gaviria, Ricardo. *El buitre y el ave fénix: conversaciones con Mario Vargas Llosa*. Barcelona: Anagrama, 1972.

Castro-Klarén, Sara. *Understanding Vargas Llosa*. Columbia: U of South Carolina P, 1990.

Catálogo General de Publicaciones. Barcelona: Seix Barral, 1969.

Censuré à Cuba. DVD. Compiled by Zoé Valdés and Ricardo Vega. Editions de Montparnasse/FNAC, 2002.

Cervantes, Miguel de. *Novelas ejemplares*. Madrid: Castalia, 1997.

Chambers, Ross. *Room for Maneuver. Reading (the) Oppositional (in) Narrative*. U of Chicago P, 1991.

———. *The Writing of Melancholy: Modes of Opposition in Early French Modernism*. The U of Chicago P, 1993.

Cisquella, Georgina et al. *Diez años de represión cultural: la censura de libros durante la Ley de Prensa (1966-76)*. Barcelona: Anagrama, 1977.

Cobo Borda, Juan Gustavo. *Para llegar a García Márquez*. Santa Fé de Bogota: Tema de Hoy, 1997.

Código Civil de España. Art. 21. Sec. 1. 1993.

Coetzee, J. M. *Giving Offense. Essays on Censorship*. Chicago: U of Chicago P, 1996.

Conclusiones de la Primera Exposición Itinerante del Libro Español. 1970. Archivo General de la Administración, Alcalá de Henares.

Cortázar, Julio. *Queremos tanto a Glenda*. Buenos Aires: Alfaguara, 1996.

Créditos a la Exportación de Libros. 1962. Archivo General de la Administración, Alcalá de Henares.

Cruz, Juan. "La Balcells." *El País*. 27 May 2000: http://www.el pais. es.

———. "No tener miedo a la concentración." *Cuadernos hispanoamericanos* 564 (1997): 19–23.

Datos de la Exportación de Libros, 1959–1962. Archivo General de la Administración, Alcalá de Henares.

Decreto de 6 de abril. Reglamento del Instituto Nacional del Libro. Boletín Oficial del Estado. April 23, 1943.

Decreto de 28 de junio. Reorganización de los servicios de la Dirección General de Información. Boletín Oficial del Estado. July 18, 1957.

Devolución del impuesto sobre el gasto que grava el papel exportado en forma de libros. 1962. Archivo General de la Administración, Alcalá de Henares.

Diccionario de la Lengua Española. Real Academia. Madrid: Espasa–Calpe, 1992.

Donoso, José. *The Boom in Spanish America Literature: A Personal History.* Trans. Gregory Kolovakos. New York: Columbia UP, 1977.

———. *Coronación.* Barcelona: Seix Barral, 1968.

———. *Donde van a morir los elefantes.* Madrid: Alfaguara, 1995.

———. *Este domingo.* Barcelona: Seix Barral, 1976.

———. *Historia personal del "boom."* Santiago, Chile: Alfaguara, 1998.

———. *El jardín de al lado.* Barcelona: Seix Barral, 1981.

———. *El lugar sin límites.* Mexico: Joaquin Mortiz, 1966.

———. *El obsceno pájaro de la noche.* Barcelona: Seix Barral: 1970.

———. *Tres novelitas burguesas.* Barcelona: Seix Barral, 1973.

"Dossier: el libro español." *Cuadernos Hispanoamericanos* 564 (1997): 7–51.

Downing, Gloria Romero. "Latin American Writers and the Franco Censorship: 1939–1976." Diss. University of Nebraska-Lincoln, 1992.

Dravasa, Maider. "El 'Boom' y Barcelona: literatura y poder." Diss. Yale U, 1991.

Echevarren, Roberto, and Enrique Giordano. *Manuel Puig: montaje y alteridad del sujeto.* Santiago de Chile: Instituto Profesional del Pacífico, 1986.

Editores españoles: guía comercial. Madrid: Instituto Nacional del Libro Español, 1957.

Epstein, Jason. *Book Business. Publishing Past, Present, and Future.* New York: N.W. Norton Co., Inc. 2001.

España pierde su mercado librero en América. September 1963. Archivo General de la Administración, Alcalá de Henares.

Expediente de *Así en la paz como en la guerra*. 19 October 1971. Archivo General de la Administración, Alcalá de Henares.

Expediente de *Las buenas conciencias*. 19 October 1960. Archivo General de la Administración, Alcalá de Henares.

Expediente de *Los cachorros*. 21 February 1967. Archivo General de la Administración, Alcalá de Henares.

Expediente de *La casa verde*. 21 January 1966. Archivo General de la Administración, Alcalá de Henares.

Expediente de *La casilla de los Morelli*. 19 February 1973. Archivo General de la Administración, Alcalá de Henares.

Expediente de *Catálogo General de Publicaciones de Seix Barral*. 13 June 1969. Archivo General de la Administración, Alcalá de Henares.

Expediente de *Cien años de soledad*. 10 May 1976. Archivo General de la Administración, Alcalá de Henares.

Expediente de *Cien años de soledad*. 9 January 1976. Archivo General de la Administración, Alcalá de Henares.

Expediente de *Cien años de soledad*. 19 July 1975. Archivo General de la Administración, Alcalá de Henares.

Expediente de *Cien años de soledad*. 12 June 1975. Archivo General de la Administración, Alcalá de Henares.

Expediente de *Cien años de soledad*. 28 April 1975. Archivo General de la Administración, Alcalá de Henares.

Expediente de *Cien años de soledad*. 7 June 1972. Archivo General de la Administración, Alcalá de Henares.

Expediente de *Cien años de soledad*. 13 March 1971. Archivo General de la Administración, Alcalá de Henares.

Expediente de *Cien años de soledad*. 29 April 1969. Archivo General de la Administración, Alcalá de Henares.

Expediente de *Cien años de soledad*. 30 January 1969. Archivo General de la Administración, Alcalá de Henares.

Expediente de *La ciudad y los perros*. 27 September 1963. Archivo General de la Administración, Alcalá de Henares.

Expediente de *Conversación en la catedral*. 1 December 1969. Archivo General de la Administración, Alcalá de Henares.

Expediente de *Coronación*. 11 October 1967. Archivo General de la Administración, Alcalá de Henares.

Expediente de *Día de ceniza*. 20 March 1973. Archivo General de la Administración, Alcalá de Henares.

Expediente de *Diario de la guerra del cerdo*. 20 March 1973. Archivo General de la Administración, Alcalá de Henares.

Expediente de *Eréndira*. 8 July 1977. Archivo General de la Admnistración, Alcalá de Henares.

Expediente de *Esfera imagen*. 29 October 1969. Archivo General de la Administración, Alcalá de Henares.

Expediente de *Este domingo*. 22 April 1971. Archivo General de la Administración, Alcalá de Henares.

Expediente de *García Márquez: Historia de un deicidio*. 26 December 1971. Archivo General de la Administración, Alcalá de Henares.

Expediente de *Gracias por el fuego*. 4 December 1964. Archivo General de la Administración, Alcalá de Henares.

Expediente de *El hacedor*. 21 March 1963. Archivo General de la Administración, Alcalá de Henares.

Expediente de *Historia personal del boom*. 2 December 1972. Archivo General de la Administración, Alcalá de Henares.

Expediente de *Historia secreta de una novela*. 5 October 1971. Archivo General de la Administración, Alcalá de Henares.

Expediente de *Huerto cerrado*. 15 April 1972. Archivo General de la Administración, Alcalá de Henares.

Expediente de *Los jefes*. 26 March 1959. Archivo General de la Administración, Alcalá de Henares.

Expediente de *Libro de Manuel*. 10 December 1973. Archivo General de la Administración, Alcalá de Henares.

Expediente de *La mala hora*. 1 December 1962. Archivo General de la Administración, Alcalá de Henares.

Expediente de *El mundo alucinante*. 1970. Archivo General de la Administración, Alcalá de Henares.

Expediente de *La nueva novela hispanoamericana*. 12 November 1969. Archivo General de la Administración, Alcalá de Henares.

Expediente de *El obsceno pájaro de la noche*. 7 July 1971. Archivo General de la Administración, Alcalá de Henares.

Expediente de *Oficio del siglo XX*. 4 May 1973. Archivo General de la Administración, Alcalá de Henares.

Expediente de *Pantaleón y las visitadoras*. 10 May 1973. Archivo General de la Administración, Alcalá de Henares.

Expediente de *Paradiso*. 24 September 1973. Archivo General de la Administración, Alcalá de Henares.

Expediente de *La región más transparente*. 17 May 1973. Archivo General de la Administración, Alcalá de Henares.

Expediente de *El reino de este mundo*. 19 November 1966. Archivo General de la Administración, Alcalá de Henares.

Expediente de *Los reinos originarios*. 3 June 1971. Archivo General de la Administración, Alcalá de Henares.

Expediente de *El siglo de las luces*. 9 October 1964. Archivo General de la Administración, Alcalá de Henares.

Expediente de *Sobre héroes y tumbas*. 27 January 1970. Archivo General de la Administración, Alcalá de Henares.

Expediente de *Summa de Maqroll*. 26 May 1973. Archivo General de la Administración, Alcalá de Henares.

Expediente de *La traición de Rita Hayworth*. 7 June 1966. Archivo General de la Administración, Alcalá de Henares.

Expediente de *La traición de Rita Hayworth*. 18 November 1971. Archivo General de la Administración, Alcalá de Henares.

Expediente de *Tres novelitas burguesas*. 12 May 1973. Archivo General de la Administración, Alcalá de Henares.

Expediente de *Tres novelitas burguesas*. 19 January 1973. Archivo General de la Administración, Alcalá de Henares.

Expediente de *Tres tristes tigres*. 8 October 1966. Archivo General de la Administración, Alcalá de Henares.

Expediente de *Tres tristes tigres*. 25 April 1968. Archivo General de la Administración, Alcalá de Henares.

Expediente de *Tres tristes tigres*. 29 January 1969. Archivo General dela Administración, Alcalá de Henares.

Expediente de *Tres tristes tigres*. 18 April 1969. Archivo General de la Administración, Alcalá de Henares.

Expediente de *Tres tristes tigres*. 17 December 1970. Archivo General de la Administración, Alcalá de Henares.

Expediente de *Tres tristes tigres*. 1 September 1971. Archivo General de la Administración, Alcalá de Henares.

Expediente de *Tres tristes tigres*. 15 December 1975. Archivo General de la Administración, Alcalá de Henares.

Expediente de "Vista del amanecer en el trópico." 16 March 1965. Archivo General de la Administración, Alcalá de Henares.

Expediente de *Vista del amanecer en el trópico*. 30 December 1974. Archivo General de la Administración, Alcalá de Henares.

Expediente I-326-67. 1967. Archivo General de la Administración, Alcalá de Henares.

Expediente I-1268-68. 1968. Archivo General de la Administración, Alcalá de Henares.

Expediente I-349-69. 1968. Archivo General de la Administración, Alcalá de Henares.

Expediente I-1764-70. 1970. Archivo General de la Administración, Alcalá de Henares.

Expediente I-1384-71. 1971. Archivo General de la Administración, Alcalá de Henares.

Expediente I-671-73. 1973. Archivo General de la Administración, Alcalá de Henares.

Expediente I-776-73. 1973. Archivo General de la Administración, Alcalá de Henares.

Expediente I-877-73. 1973. Archivo General de la Administración, Alcalá de Henares.

Expediente I-20-76. 1976. Archivo General de la Administración, Alcalá de Henares.

Ferré, Rosario. *El coloquio de las perras*. San Juan, PR: Editorial Cultural, 1990.

Foucault, Michel. *Discipline and Punish: The Birth of the Prison*. New York: Vintage, 1995.

Franco, Jean. "Narrador, Autor, Superestrella: la narrativa latinoamericana en la época de cultura de masas." *Revista iberoamericana* 114–115 (1981): 129–148.

Franqui, Carlos. *Diario de la revolución cubana*. Barcelona: Ediciones Torres, 1976.

Fuentes, Carlos. *La nueva novela hispanoamericana*. México: Joaquín Mortiz, 1969.

———. *El naranjo*. Madrid: Alfaguara, 1993.

García Márquez, Gabriel. *De amor y otros demonios*. Barcelona: Mandadori, 1994.

———. *Cien años de soledad*. Ed. Jacques Joset. Madrid: Cátedra, 1996.

———. *Cien años de soledad*. Buenos Aires: Sudamericana, 1967.

———. "Cien años de soledad." *Mundo nuevo* 2 (August 1966): 5–11

———. *Collected Stories*. Trans. Sj. Berstein. New York: Harper & Row, 1984.

———. *El coronel no tiene quien le escriba*. Mexico: Era, 1963.

———. *Los funerales de la Mamá Grande*. Xalapa, Mexico: Universidad Veracruzana, 1962.

———. *La hojarasca*. Buenos Aires: Sudamericana, 1969.

———. *La increíble y triste historia de la cándida Eréndira y de su abuela desalmada*. Barcelona: Barral, 1974.

———. "El insomnio en Macondo." *Mundo nuevo* 9 (March 1967): 9–17.

———. Letter to Cobo Borda. 1976. Papers of Juan Gustavo Cobo Borda. Firestone Library, Princeton University.

———. Letter to José Donoso. 13 (no month) 1968. Papers of José Donoso. Firestone Library, Princeton University.

———. Letter to José Donoso. 5 January 1968. Papers of José Donoso. Firestone Library, Princeton University.

———. Letter to Mario Vargas Llosa. 20 March 1967. Papers of Mario Vargas Llosa. Firestone Library, Princeton University.

———. *La mala hora*. Mexico: Ediciones Era, 1966.

———. *La mala hora*. Madrid: Gráficas Luis Pérez, 1962.

———. *Memoria de mis putas tristes*. New York: Knopf, 2004.

———. "La novela detrás de la novela." *El País*. 15 July 2001. 1, 31–32.

———. *Living to Tell the Tale*. Trans. Edith Grossman. New York: Knopf, 2003.

———. *Vivir para contarla*. Barcelona: Mondadori, 2002.

García Márquez, Eligio. *Tras las claves de Melquíades: Historia de Cien años de soledad*. Bogota: Editorial Norma, 2001.

García-Trevijano Garnica, Ernesto. *El silencio administrativo en el derecho español*. Madrid: Editorial Civitas, 1990.

Gil López, Ernesto. *Guillermo Cabrera Infante: La Habana, el lenguaje y la cinematografía*. Tenerife: Cabildo Insular de Tenerife, 1991.

Gimferrer, Pere. Personal Interview. 22 May 1998.

Goldchluk, Graciela. "Esquemas narrativos." Amícola, *materiales* 373–378.

Gómez, Andrés. "El retiro de la mítica Carmen Balcells." *La tercera*. 5 de mayo de 2000: http://www.latercera.cl.

Gómez, Lourdes. "Las galeradas de *Cien años de soledad* no tienen comprador." *El País*. 21 November 2002. 37.

González, Flora. *José Donoso's House of Fiction*. Detroit: Wayne State UP, 1995.

González Echevarría, Roberto. *La voz de los maestros. Escritura y autoridad en la literatura latinoamericana moderna*. Madrid: Verbum, 2001.

Goytisolo, Juan. "Manuel Puig." *El País* 27 July 1990: 9.

The Great Waltz. Dir. Julien Duvivier. Perf. Luise Rainer, Fernand Gravet, and Miliza Korjus. MGM, 1938.

Guillén Pérez, María Eugenia. *El silencio administrativo: el control judicial de la inactividad administrativa*. Madrid: Editorial COLEX, 1997.

Guillory, John. *Cultural Capital. The Problem of Literary Canon Formation*. Chicago UP, 1993.

Gutiérrez Mouat, Ricardo. "Aesthetics, Ethics, and Politics in Donoso's *El jardín de al lado*." *PMLA* 106 (1991): 60–70.

Harguindey, Ángel S. "Una nueva edición de *Tres tristes tigres* celebra los 70 años de su autor, Cabrera Infante." *El Pais*. 16 April 1999: http://www.elpais.es

Harss, Luis. *Los nuestros*. Buenos Aires: Sudamericana, 1969.

Henseler, Christine. *Contemporary Spanish Women's Narrative and the Publishing Industry*. Urbana : University of Illinois P, 2003.

Herralde, Jorge. *Opiniones mohicanas*. Barcelona: El Acantilado, 2001.

Herrero-Olaizola, Alejandro. "Consuming Aesthetics: Seix Barral and José Donoso in the Field of Latin American Literary Production." *MLN: Modern Languages Notes* 115 (March 2000): 323–339.

———. "Sujetos a la censura: Mario Vargas Llosa y el mercado literario de la España franquista." *Journal of Interdisciplinary Literary Studies* 9.1–2 (2003): 59–79.

Illán Bacca, Ramón. *Escribir en Barranquilla*. Barranquilla: Ediciones Uninorte, 1998.

Informe de la Oficina de Enlace ("Vista del amanecer"). 22 June 1965. Archivo General de la Administración, Alcalá de Henares.

Informe sobre el comercio exterior del libro. October 1963. Archivo General de la Administración, Alcalá de Henares.

Informes sobre las dificultades para la exportación a América de libros españoles. 1963. Archivo General de la Administración, Alcalá de Henares.

Internet Movie Data Base. "Rita Hayworth." http://us.imdb.com

Jansen, Sue Curry. *Censorship: The Knot That Binds Power and Knowledge.* New York: Oxford UP, 1988.

Jarque, Fietta. "*Cien años de soledad*, treinta años de leyenda." *El País.* 6 June 1997: 36.

Joset, Jacques. "Filología de un texto contemporáneo: las versiones de *La mala hora* de Gabriel García Márquez" *Bulletin of Hispanic Studies* LXX (1993): 337–349.

Joyce, James. *A Portrait of the Artist as a Young Man.* New York: Bedford Books, 1993.

Kerr, Lucille. *Reclaiming the Author: Figures and Fictions from Latin America.* Durham: Duke UP, 1992.

———. *Suspended Fictions: Reading Novels by Manuel Puig.* Urbana: U of Illinois P, 1987.

King, John. *Sur: A Study of the Argentine Literary Journal and Its Role in the Development of a Culture, 1931–1970.* New York: Cambridge, UP, 1986.

Klarén, Peter. *Peru: Society and Nationhood in the Andes.* New York: Oxford UP, 2000.

Kristal, Efraín. *The Temptation of the Word. The Novels of Mario Vargas Llosa.* Nashville: Vanderbilt UP, 1998.

Labanyi, Jo. "Censorship or the Fear of Mass Culture." *Spanish Cultural Studies.* Ed. Helen Graham and Jo Labanyi. New York: Oxford UP, 1995.

Levine, Suzanne Jill. *Manuel Puig and the Spider Woman: His Life and His Fictions.* New York: Farrar, Straus & Giroux, 2000.

Ley de 9/1975, 12 de marzo, del Libro. Boletín Oficial del Estado. March 14, 1975.

Ley de 18 de diciembre de 1946 sobre la mayor difusión del libro español, tanto en el interior como en el extranjero. Boletín Oficial del Estado. 19 December 1946.

Ley de Prensa. Boletín Oficial del Estado. April 23, 1938.

Libre. 1971–72.

Luis, William. *Lunes de Revolución. Literatura y cultura en los primeros años de la revolución cubana.* Madrid: Verbum, 2003.

———. "Exhuming *Lunes de Revolución.*" *The New Centennial Review* 2 (2002): 253–83.

Mac Adam, Alfred J. "The Boom: A Retrospective." *Review: Latin American Literature and Arts* 33 (1984): 30–36.

Machover, Jacobo. *La memoria frente al poder: escritores cubanos del exilio: Guillermo Cabrera Infante, Severo Sarduy, Reinaldo Arenas.* Universitat de Valencia P, 2001.

Magnarelli, Sharon. *Reflections/Refractions. Reading Luisa Valenzuela.* New York: Lang, 1988.

Manrique, Jaime. *Eminent Maricones: Arenas, Lorca, Puig, and Me.* U of Wisconsin P, 1999.

Manrique, Winston. "Colombia no participará en la subasta de *Cien años de soledad.*" *El País.* 18 July 2001: http://www.elpais.es

———. "Instituciones públicas y privadas pujan hoy por las galeradas de *Cien años de soledad.*" *El País.* 21 September 2001: 45.

Marcos, Jesús M. "Ningún postor se atreve a pujar en la subasta de las galeradas de *Cien años de soledad.*" *El Mundo.* 22 September 2001: http://www.elmundo.es

Martinetto, Vittoria. "*The Buenos Aires Affair*: anatomía de una censura." *Encuentro Internacional Manuel Puig.* Amícola and Speranza 212–223.

Martínez, Ezequiel. "El otoño de la Mamá Grande." *Viva: Revista de Clarín* 16 de julio de 2000. 63–68.

Martínez Alés, Rafael. "El final de un ciclo." *Cuadernos hispanoamericanos* 564 (1997): 31–35.

Meléndez, Priscilla. "Writing and Reading the Palimpsest: Donoso's *El jardín de al lado.*" *Symposium* 41 (Fall 1987): 200–213.

Mendoza, Mario. *Satanás.* Barcelona: Seix Barral, 2002.

Mérida Jiménez, Rafael. "Autores, agentes, editores y críticos." *Cuadernos hispanoamericanos* 582 (1998): 49–58.

Montero, Oscar. "*El jardín de al lado:* La escritura y el fracaso del éxito" *Revista iberoamericana* 49 (123–124) (1983): 449–67.

Mora, Rosa. "Generosa y terrorista." *El País.* 4 May 2000: http://www.elpais.es

———. "Mujeres del libro." *El País Semanal*. 23 April 2000: 38–49.

Moradiellos, Enrique. *La España de Franco, 1939–1975: política y sociedad*. Madrid: Síntesis, 2000.

Muchnik, Mario. "La mala salud de la industrial editorial española." *Cuadernos hispanoamericanos* 564 (1997): 25–30.

———. *Lo peor no son los autores. Autobiografía editorial, 1966–1997*. Madrid: Taller Mario Muchnik, 1999.

Mudrovcic, María Eugenia. *Mundo nuevo: cultura y Guerra Fría en la década del 60*. Buenos Aires: Beatriz Viterbo, 1997.

———. "*La tía Julia y el escribidor*: algunas lecciones prácticas en torno a la estética de lo huachafo." *Inti: Revista de Literatura Hispánica* 43–44 (1996): 121–34.

Neuschäffer, Hans-Jörg. *Adiós a la España eterna: la dialéctica de la censura*. Barcelona: Anthropos, 1994.

Nota informativa acerca de la obra "Pantaleón y las visitadoras" de Mario Vargas Llosa. 10 October 1973. Archivo General de la Administración, Alcalá de Henares.

Nota informativa reservada sobre actividades de republicanos y comunistas españoles en Cuba. 4 December 1959. Archivo General de la Administración, Alcalá de Henares.

Nota-Informe sobre las tarifas vigentes en España para el envío de libros a América y Europa. 1962. Archivo General de la Administración, Alcalá de Henares.

Nota sobre el libro "Amanecer en el trópico." Undated. Archivo General de la Administración, Alcalá de Henares.

Ordenación Editorial. Archivo General de la Administración, Alcalá de Henares, 1969.

Oviedo, José Miguel. *Mario Vargas Llosa*. Madrid: Taurus, 1981.

———. *Mario Vargas Llosa: la invención de una realidad*. Barcelona: Barral, 1970.

Papelera Española, S.A. 1958. Archivo General de la Administración, Alcalá de Henares.

Patterson, Annabel. "Censorship." *Encyclopedia of Literature and Criticism*. Ed. Martin Coyle. Detroit: Gale Research, 1991.

Paulhan, Jean. *Of Chaff and Wheat: Writers, War, and Treason*. Trans. Richard Rand. Urbana: U of Illinois P, 2004.

Pereda, Rosa María. *Cabrera Infante*. Madrid: EDAF, 1978.

Planes de Estados Unidos que van a afectar gravemente a la difusion del libro español en América. April 24, 1963. Archivo General de la Administración, Alcalá de Henares.

Pohl, Burkhard. *Bücher ohne Grenzen. Der Verlag Seix Barral und die Vermittlung lateinamerikanischer Erzählliteratur im Spanien des Franquismus*. Frankfurt am Main: Vervuert Lang, 2003.

Post, Robert, ed. *Censorship and Silencing: Practices of Cultural Regulation*. Los Angeles: Getty Research Institute, 1998.

Prensa e Imprenta. Madrid: Boletín Oficial del Estado, Colección Textos Legales, 1969.

Primera exposición itinerante del libro español en América. 1970. Archivo General de la Administración, Alcalá de Henares.

Puig, Manuel. *El beso de la mujer araña*. Barcelona: Seix-Barral, 1976.

———. *Betrayed by Rita Hayworth*. Trans. Suzanne Jill Levine. New York: Dutton, 1971.

———. *Boquitas pintadas*. Buenos Aires: Sudamericana, 1969.

———. *The Buenos Aires Affair*. Buenos Aires: Editorial Sudamericana, 1973.

———. "Losing Readers in Argentina." *Index on Censorship* 5 (1985): 55–57.

———. *Pubis angelical*. Barcelona: Seix Barral, 1979.

———. *La traición de Rita Hayworth*. Buenos Aires: Editorial Jorge Álvarez, 1968.

———. *La traición de Rita Hayworth*. Barcelona: Seix Barral, 1971 & 1982.

———. *La traición de Rita Hayworth*. Barcelona: Seix Barral, 1977. [*edición definitiva*]

———. "Writers and Repression." *Index on Censorship* 5 (1984): 28–33.

Radway, Janice. *A Feeling for Books: the Book-of-the-Month Club, Literary Taste, and Middle-Class Desire*. Chapel Hill: U of North Carolina P, 1997.

Rama, Ángel, ed. *Más allá del boom: literatura y mercado*. Mexico: Marcha, 1981.

Recomendaciones para tener en cuenta en la redacción de contratos de edición. Madrid: Instituto Nacional del Libro Español, 1965.

Recurso de Alzada (Seix Barral, "Vista"). 16 September 1965. Archivo General de la Administración, Alcalá de Henares.

Riera, Carme. "Carmen Balcells, alquimista del libro." *Quimera* 27 (1983): 23–30.

Robles Piquer, Carlos. Carta a Carlos Barral. 2 September 1963. Archivo General de la Administración, Alcalá de Henares.

———. Carta a Cabrera Infante. 3 March 1966. Archivo General de la Administración, Alcalá de Henares.

———. Carta a Vargas Llosa. 2 September 1963. Archivo General de la Administración, Alcalá de Henares.

Rodríguez Monegal, Emir. "Una escritura revolucionaria." *Revista iberoamericana* 37 (1971): 497–506.

———. Letter to Gabriel García Márquez. 12 December 1966. Papers of Emir Rodríguez Monegal. Firestone Library, Princeton University.

———. "A Revolutionary Writing." *Mundus Artium* 3.3 (1970): 6–11.

Romero, Julia. "De monólogo al estallido de la voz." Amícola, *materiales* 451–467.

Rostagno, Irene. *Searching for Recognition. The Promotion of Latin American Literature in the United States*. Wesport, CT: Greenwood P, 1997.

Saldívar, Dasso. "El rastro de las copias mecanografiadas." *El País*. 21 September 2001: 45.

———. *García Márquez: el viaje a la semilla*. Madrid: Alfaguara, 1997.

Santana, Mario. *Foreigners in the Homeland: The Spanish American New Novel in Spain, 1962–1974*. Lewisburg, PA: Bucknell UP, 2000.

Schiffrin, André. *The Business of Books*. London: Verso, 2000.

Serrano, Pío. "La agonía del pequeño editor." *Cuadernos hispanoamericanos* 564 (1997): 37–41.

Setti, Ricardo A. *Sobre la vida y la política: diálogo con Vargas Llosa*. Buenos Aires: Intermundo, 1989.

Smith, Barbara H. *Contingencies of Value: Alternative Perspectives for Critical Theory*. Cambridge: Harvard UP, 1988.

Sommers, Joseph. "Literatura e ideología: el militarismo en las novelas de Vargas Llosa." *Revista de crítica literaria latinoamericana* 1.2 (1975): 87–112.

Spacks, Patricia Meyer. *Gossip*. New York: Alfred A. Knopf, 1985.

Subastas Velázquez. *Cien años de soledad. Gabriel García Márquez*. Madrid: Subastas Velázquez, 2001.

Subcomisión del papel: informe sobre la evolución reciente, los problemas y las previsiones del sector. 1963. Archivo General de la Administración, Alcalá de Henares.

Works Cited

Telegrams between Lojendio and Castiella. January 1–9, 1959. Archivo General de la Administración, Alcalá de Henares.

Theiner, George. *They Shoot Writers, Don't They?* London: Faber, 1984.

Tittler, Jonathan. *Manuel Puig.* New York: Twayne, 1993.

Tola de Habich, Fernando and Patricia Grieve. *Los españoles y el boom.* Caracas: Editorial Tiempo Nuevo, 1971.

Torrealdai, Joan Mari. *La censura de Franco y los escritores vascos del 98.* Donostia: Ttarttalo, 1998.

Valenzuela, Luisa. "The Censors." *The Censors.* Willimantic, CT: Curbstone P, 1988. 24–31.

Vargas, Hugo. "Ser editor: disgustos y alegrías. Entrevista a Joaquín Díez Canedo." *Quimera* 116 (1993): 55–59.

Vargas Llosa, Mario. "Las aguafuertes excesivas de Ernesto Diera." October 1974. Papers of Mario Vargas Llosa. Firestone Library. Princeton University.

———. Carta al Ilustrísimo Señor Director General de Información. 8 July 1959. Archivo General de la Administración, Alcalá de Henares.

———. Carta a Robles Piquer. 17 July 1963. Archivo General de la Administración, Alcalá de Henares.

———. *La casa verde.* Barcelona: Seix Barral, 1966.

———. *Captain Pantoja and the Special Service.* Trans. Gregory Kolovakos and Ronald Christ. New York : Harper & Row, 1978.

———. "La censura y el cine." 16 December 1974. Papers of Mario Vargas Llosa. Firestone Library. Princeton University.

———. *La ciudad y los perros.* Barcelona: Seix Barral, 1963.

———. *La ciudad y los perros.* Barcelona: Seix Barral, 1996.

———. *Conversación en la catedral.* Barcelona: Seix Barral, 1969.

———. *Los cuadernos de don Rigoberto.* Madrid: Alfagura, 1997.

———. *La fiesta del chivo.* Madrid: Alfagura, 2000.

———. *A Fish in the Water: A Memoir.* Trans. Helen Lane. New York: Farrar, Strauss, Giroux, 1994.

———. *García Márquez: historia de un deicidio.* Barcelona: Barral Editores, 1971.

———. "The Genesis and Evolution of *Pantaleón y las visitadoras.*" Ed. Chang-Rodríguez, Raquel, and Gabriella De Beer. *The City College Papers.* The City College of New York, 1979.

———. *Historia secreta de una novela*. Barcelona: Tusquest Editor, 1971.

———. *Los jefes; Los cachorros*. Barcelona: Seix Barral, 1982.

———. "El jubileo de Carmen Balcells." *El País*. 20 August 2000: http://www.elpais.es

———. *Lituma en los Andes*. Barcelona: Planeta, 1993.

———. *Pantaleón y las visitadoras*. Barcelona: Seix Barral, 1973.

———. *Pantaleón y las visitadoras*. Barcelona: Seix Barral, 1995.

———. *El pez en el agua*. Barcelona: Seix Barral, 1993.

———. *The Time of the Hero*. Trans. Lysander Kemp. New York: Grove Press, 1966.

———. "The Writer in Latin America." 1984. Theiner, 161–71.

Vargas Llosa, Mario, introd. *El autor y su obra: Mario Vargas Llosa*. Salamanca: Hispagraphis, 1990.

Vargas Llosa, Mario and José Miguel Oviedo. "A Conversation." *Review: Latin American Literature and Arts* 61 (2000): 5–12.

Vázquez Montalbán, Manuel. "Carmen Balcells y las bellas artes." *El País*. 26 May 2000: http://www.elpais.es.

Villena, Miguel Ángel. "La demanda de libros se ha estancado en España, pese al aumento de títulos." *El País*. 12 April 2000: 27.

Viñas, David. "Pareceres y disgresiones en torno a la nueva narrativa latinoamericana." Rama 13–50.

Index

Abella Martín, Francisco, 2–3; and freedom of expression laws, 2
Abellán, Manuel, 2–3, 10, 32, 185 (n.2)
Alcoriza, Luis, 111, 116–117
Allende, Isabel, 31, 32, 200 (n.1); *La casa de los espíritus*, 174
Allende, Salvador, 24
Alzamiento Nacional, 136, 146
Amícola, José, 156–158, 160–161, 171, 198 (n.9), 199 (n.3), 200 (n.17)
Anderson, Danny, 14–15, 17
apertura, xiii, xv, xxiii, 1, 5, 9, 16, 31, 39, 44, 189 (n.5); and Barcelona, xxiii; and book circulation, 137; and censorship practices, 135, 178, 197–198 (n.3); culture of, xvii, xxiii, 37, 39, 44, 137; and economic development and expansion (*desarrollismo*), 2–3, 8, 16, 146; and economic prosperity, 37; market policies of, 16, 182; and relationship to Latin American literature, xvii; and Spanish-language book industry, 4, 11, 137. *See also* Franco regime, Spain
Archivo General de la Administración, xiv, xvii–xxii, 9, 31, 78, 129, 131, 178, 180, 185 (n.2), 197–198 (n.3); and *Asuntos Exteriores*, xxi; and *Cultura*, xxi; and *Comercio*, xxi; and decoding, xix–xxi;

Educación, xxi; and National Book Institute reports, xxi, 6; and personal experience at, xvii–xix; and relaxation of regulations, xxiii, xxiv; and research, xvii–xix, xxi, 2, 31
Arenas, Reinaldo, xiv; *El mundo alucinante*, xv
Argentina, 4, 6, 7, 19, 22, 34, 40, 83, 121, 122, 124, 134, 147, 148, 149, 153, 156, 159, 165, 168, 172, 180, 185 (n.3), 200 (n.1)
Arrabal, Fernando, 137
Asturias, Miguel Ángel, 12, 165–66
authoritarian regimes, 71, 72, 73, 79; critique of, 101. *See also* Franco, Castro

Balcells, Carmen, 22, 27, 30–31, 109, 119, 120, 122–123, 130, 183, 184, 188 (n.15), 200 (n.1); and Donoso, 174–175, 188 (n.15), 200 (n.1); fictionalized (as Núria Monclús), 24–29, 31; and García Márquez, 119–122, 175–177, 200 (n.1); as legendary figure (*leyenda Balcells*), 173, 173–177, 180 (n.15), 200 (n.1); and Vargas Llosa, 173, 174, 200 (n.1) 201 (n.4). *See also* Donoso, *El jardín de al lado*, *Historia personal*
Barcelona, 22, 24, 119, 134, 159, 190 (n.1); and *apertura*, xxiii; and

Barcelona, *Cont'd.*
architecture, 109; as auction site (for Subastas Velázquez), 109–110, 114, 115, 117; Big Mama of (Balcells), 173–174; and Catalan *modernisme*, 109; colony of writers in, 109, 125, 189 (n.5), 196 (n.9); intelligentsia of, 18, 20, 22, 109; as publishing site, xxiii–xxiv, 15, 17, 24–28, 31, 37–8, 79, 109–110, 118, 122, 124–5, 132, 137–138, 150, 153–154, 159, 167, 170–71, 174; and writers (see individual authors)

Barral, Carlos, xxiv, 2, 9, 10, 11, 13–22, 33, 34, 38, 39, 40, 44, 76, 78, 86, 88, 132, 176, 177, 180, 183, 189 (n.2), 192 (n.13), 201 (n.8); *Almanaque*, 73, 120; *Los años sin excusa*, 13–14, 49–51; *Años de penitencia*, 21; and appeals process, 90–92; and behind-the-scenes negotiations, 48, 58, 162; and Cabrera Infante, 73, 76, 78, 79, 86, 88, 89, 91–94, 104; and Catalan nationalism, 160; and censorship (rejection of), 40; and cooperation with censors, 38–70; correspondence with Cabrera Infante, 78; and correspondence with Cabrera Infante and Robles Piquer, 94–96, 98; and correspondence with Donoso, 30; correspondence with Robles Piquer and Vargas Llosa, 47–49, 50, 51; *Cuando las horas veloces*, 177, 187 (n.10), 201 (n.8); as "evil woman" (feminized), 165; as father figure (of the Boom), 176, 180–181; and García Márquez, 109, 119, 121–22, 124, 128, 131, 135, 175, 196 (n.9); and literary awards, 23–24, 38; *Memorias*, 18, 119–120, 124; and negotiations with censors, 91–92, 146, 162; and negotiations with Robles Piquer, 47, 48, 52–53, 96, 98; and oppositionality, 45; *Penúltimos castigos*, 29–31, 201 (n.8); and Puig, 142–143, 146, 148, 150, 153, 154, 160, 162, 170–72; and support of Cuban Revolution, 73, 89–90; and symbolic investment, 187 (n.10); and Vargas Llosa, 38–41, 43, 45, 46, 48, 49, 51 59, 60. *See also* Barral Editores, Seix Barral

Barral Editores, 14, 22, 30, 33, 123, 125, 187 (n.1), 188 (n.18), 189 (n.1), 200 (n.2)

Batista regime (*Batistato*), 71–72, 74–75, 77, 87, 91, 98, 101–103. *See also* Cabrera Infante, Guillermo

Baudelaire, Charles; "Au Lecteur," 191 (n.7). *See also* Cabrera Infante, Guillermo, "Lo que este libro debe al censor"

Benedetti, Mario, xiv, xv; *Gracias por el fuego*, xv

Benet, Juan, 167; and "El efecto Barral", 167

Bertelsmann Group, xv, 183, 198 (n.1). *See also* book trade

best seller, 15, 18, 39, 45, 47, 51, 53–4, 59–60, 151

Betrayed by Rita Hayworth. See *traición de Rita Hayworth, La*

Bioy Casares, Adolfo, xiv; *Diario de la guerra del cerdo*, xvi

Blasco Ibáñez, Vicente, 168; Hollywood adaptations of *Sangre y arena* (*Blood and Sand*), 168–69, 198 (n.10), 200 (n.16)

book trade, xiii xiii, xxii, xxiv; and alchemy, 178–179; and cultural dominance, xxii, xxiii, xxiv–xxvi; expansion of, 12, 20, 39–40, 182; global alliances (Bertelsmann Group), xv, 183, 198 (n.1); marketing strategies, xv, 5–6, 15–6, 26, 53, 128; statistics, 6–7, 185 (n.2); subsidies, xiv, 39–40, 178. *See also* market, Seix Barral, publishing houses, publishing industry

Boom (of Latin American literature), xv, xx, xxiii, xxiv, 4, 10, 12, 13, 15, 16–18, 40, 41, 56, 71, 73, 86, 108, 110, 124, 125, 126, 130, 136, 151, 165, 166, 178, 182; Big Mama of (Balcells), 173–177; bitching about, 22–34, 167, 184; and colonization of Spanish book market, 176; and commercial and aesthetic shifts, 28, 34; and economic/ideological tension, 144; economic profit from, xxiii; and *ediciones definitivas*, xxii; end of, 22, 24, 31; and exclusionary practices, 28–29, 32, 33, 34; and exiled writers, 109, 124; in fiction, 27–28; and globalization, 187 (n.9); and international context, 188 (n.16); literary distribution of, 4; and literary journals, 187 (n.9), 191 (n.6), 193 (n.19), 195 (n.7), 196 (n.8); male dominance in, 32–33, 167; massive distribution of, xxiii; marketing of, 16–17; modernization of the Latin American novel, 27; and *nueva novela*, 16–18, 22, 23, 28, 187 (n.9); origins of, 15, 46; post-Boom, 25; and publishing history, 173, 175; and politically and sexually explicit writing, 41; and Seix Barral, 4, 13, 14, 15, 31; and social realism, 52; success of, 56; and support of Cuban Revolution, 187 (n.9); and translations, 188 (n.16), 194 (n.1), 199 (n.11), 201 (n.5); and trends and Puig, 151; and stardom, 26–39, (as a Hollywood affair) 165–167, 172; and women writers, 25, 31. *See also* Cuban Revolution, names of individual authors, Seix Barral

Boom of Spanish American Literature, The: A Personal History. See *Historia personal del boom*.

Borges, Jorge Luis, xiv, 17, 32–3, 143, 165–6, 168; *El hacedor*, xvi
Bourdieu, Pierre, 5, 15–18, 22, 26, 100, 165; "Censorship and the Imposition of Form" (*Language*), 100
Bryce, Echenique Alfredo, xiv, 200 (n.1); *Huerto cerrado*, 4
Butler, Judith, 71, 190 (n.1)

Cabrera Infante, Guillermo, xiv, xv, 4, 20, 121, 142, 166, 191 (n.3, n.5, n.6), 200 (n.1); *Así en la paz como en la guerra*, 75, 104, 191 (n.4); and autobiography, 74; and Barral, 73, 76, 78, 79, 86, 88, 89, 91–94, 104; blacklisted, 72; G. Caín (pseudonym), 74; "Lo que la censura no ve," 81–82, 84; cooperation with censors, 77; correspondence with Barral, 78; correspondence with Barral and Robles Piquer, 94–96, 98; correspondence with Vargas Llosa, 97–98, 105; critique of Cuban Revolution, 77, 85, 107–108; critique of Castro, 79, 103; "Cronología," 191 (n.3); *Ella cantaba boleros*, 105, 106, 191 (n.2), 193 (n.18); "Epilogue," 73, 191 (n.2); "Lo que este libro debe al censor," 77–78, 94; *La España rebelde*, 192 (n.10); and exile, 73–79, 102–03, 106, 107; and explicit language, 193 (n.18); and fragmentation of narrative, 99–100, 103; *Infantería*, 81; *La larga noche de España*, 81; and *Lunes de Revolución*, 75, 80, 84, 85, 192 (n.10); *Mea Cuba*, 72, 84–85, 191 (n.5); "Metafinal," 73, 191 (n.2); and negotiations with censors, 90–94; *Un oficio del siglo XX*, 104; and opposition to authoritarian regimes, 71–79, 80–100, 102; and opposition to Franco, 79–81, 85, 102; political

Cabrera Infante, Guillermo, *Cont'd.* narrative in, 99–101; "Una posición: viente años de Franco", 80; and *Premio Cervantes*, 74, 104; as pro-revolutionary, 81, 85, 104, 193 (n.19); and residency in Spain, 72; "La respuesta de Cabrera Infante", 72; and "revolutionary writing," 106, 193 (n.19); and self-censorship, 100; and Seix Barral, 73, 74, 76, 96, 103, 104, 105, 191 (n.3, n.4); and Spanish literary market, 89; *Tres tristes tigres*, xv, xxii, 71–79, 84, 89–108, 119, 191 (n.2, n.3, n.7), 193 (n.15, n.17, n.18), 194 (n.21); "La última traición de Manuel Puig," 165–167; "Las vértebras de España", 81–84;"Vista del amanecer en el trópico," 76–80, 86, 89–108, 193 (n.16), 194 (n.20, n.22); *Vista del amanecer en el trópico (Relatos)*, 76–77, 194 (n.21)

Cabrera Infante, Sabá, 79, 80, 85, 88; "P.M." ("Pasado Meridiano"), 75–76, 79, 81, 84–85, 102, 191 (n.5)

Captain Pantoja and the Special Service. See *Pantaleón y las visitadoras*

Carpentier, Alejo, xiv, 12, 20, 89, 165–166; *El siglo de las luces*, xvi, 89, 192 (n.12); *El reino de este mundo*, 192 (n.12)

Casa de las Américas, xiv, xv, xxv, 7, 73, 79, 143

Casa Batlló, 109, 114, 135

Castellet, José María, 187 (n.11), 189 (n.2)

Castro, Fidel, 71–74, 83–85, 91, 103, 106, 122, 135, 143, 192 (n.9); Castro regime, 87–89, 94; and Revolution of 1959. *See also* Cuba

Castro-Klarén, Sara, 33, 190 (n.12)

Censorship, administration of new laws, 1–2; and betrayal, 171–172; and book covers, 62–65, 143–145, 162–164; and Book Inspection Services, 1; and Book Law of 1949, 179; breaking the code of, xiii, xxii; "censor figure," xx; as *censura oficiosa*, 50, 57, 130, 189 (n.6); citizen-initiated ("spontaneous censorship"; see Vernet), 128–30, 135, 138, 139; and commerce, 6–8; constitutive, xix; and *consulta obligatoria*, 9, 11; and *consulta voluntaria*, 9, 11, 186 (n.6); and cultural expansion 4–8; declassified, 144–146; and Department for Editorial Orientation, 1; and *depósito*, 9–10, 11, 12, 59, 104, 137, 153, 154; double censorship, 48, 74, 105; economics of, 4–6, 12, 21, 47–48, 134, 142, 144–146, 158, 160, 197 (n.2); elimination of (official censorship), 1, 3; and family ties, 39; flexibility, 41; of *gallegos* and Spanish immigrants, 156–158; gender-based, 31–34, 143–144; of historical events, 42, 96–97, 192 (n.12); history of (in Spain), 127; hyper-corrective, 128–130; implementation of, xviii; *lectores fijos* (official censors on the payroll), 185 (n.1); letters (in/of), 158–159, 170–171; and *Ley de prensa e imprenta*, 1, 59, 94, 185 (n.1), 185 (n.1); and *Ley reguladora de la jurisdicción*, 186 (n.5); and linguistic purity, xvi, 7, 12, 19, 41, 46–47, 48–49, 95, 128–130, 142, 151–152, 162–163; market-generated, xv, 31, 128; military (in/of the), 50–51, 56–57, 60–62, 70, 77; moral and political, 7, 59, 133–134, 136, 139, 142, 146, 147, 148, 152–153, 192 (n.12), 198 (n.4); 146; negotiated, xxiv, 24,

37–42, 44–45, 50–3, 58, 83, 94–98, 122–123, 125; new policies of, 20, 83, 146; and obscenity, 43, 137, 148, 154, 193 (n.15, n.18); official xiii–xvii, xxv, 40–43, 47–48, 50, 51, 69, 75, 83, 97, 108, 125,128, 130, 140, 143, 148; opposition to, 40–45, 47; post-production, 12, 58; practices of, 1–2, 7, 130, 144; productive, 71, 76–78, 101–103, 105, 106, 126–127, 186 (n.6), 190 (n.1); and profits, 47, 59, 146, 197; and proxy censors, xxiv, 134–140, 197 (n. 14, n.15); rationalization of, 2; regulatory, xiv, xviii, xxiv, 2, 9–13, 20, 50, 83; and relaxation of regulations, 3, 9, 39, 40, 42, 178, 179; and *secuestro* (sequestration), 10, 11, 12, 54, 59, 60, 138–139, 148–149, 153, 154; self-imposed (personal or internalized), xiii, xvi–xvii, 2, 74, 71, 77, 100, 105, 107, 108, 122, 125, 126, 147, 154, 155, 159, 199 (n.13); semi-official (see *censura oficiosa*); and *silencio administrativo* (official silence), 11, 20–21, 43, 56–58, 63, 81, 88, 89, 107–108, 154, 160, 186 (n,5), 192 (n.12); of sexual content, 60–3, 104, 122, 133, 139–140, 152–153, 162; shifts in/displacement of, 11, 44, 50, 60; "spontaneous" (citizen-initiated; see Vernet), 135, 138, 139; and strategies for Spanish book trade expansion, 2–3; and textual complexity, 100–101; theory of, xviii; and transatlantic exchanges, 79, 98–99, 105

censorship archive. See *Archivo*

Cervantes, Miguel de, xiv, 32, 33, 126–127; *El casamiento engañoso*, 32

Chambers, Ross, 44, 191 (n.7)

Cien años de soledad, xxii, 23, 109–117, 118–125, 123–125, 130–140, 175, 187 (n.14, n.15), 195 (n.3, n.4, n.6), 196 (n.9); and international success, 110, 119, 128, 130, 131; as school textbook, 136–139. See also García Márquez, Gabriel

Círculo de lectores, 38, 131, 181

ciudad de los perros, La, xxii, 18, 38, 39, 41, 44–59, 70, 89, 119, 153, 179, 189 (n.6, n.7), 190 (n.8). See also Vargas Llosa, Mario

Coetzee, J.M., xx

collective memory, 175, 183

Colombia, 125–127, 128, 186 (n.4), 196 (n.8)

coloquio de las perras, El (*Colloquy of the Bitches, The*), 32–34, 188 (n.17). See also Ferré, Rosario

community, 175, 180. See also Boom

Cortázar, Julio, xiv, xv, xxiv, 12, 25–26, 28, 29, 32, 52, 123, 165–66, 168, 190 (n.8); *La casilla de los Morelli*, xv; *Libro de Manuel*, xv, (censor's report on) xxviii; *Queremos tanto a Glenda*, 166; *Rayuela*, 123

Cruz, Juan, 174, 176, 177, 183, 200 (n.1)

Cuba; and Batista, 71, 75, 77; and Bay of Pigs, 192 (n.10); as book market competitor, 4, 7; Castro doctrine in, 80; and Castro regime, 71, 72, 79; and censorship, 74, 75; and publishing industry, 89; and regime, 71, 73–74; *fidelismo*, 79; Havana, 75, 76, 86, 90, 102; Hispano-Cuban relations, 86, 87; and Lezama Lima, 192 (n.9); and nightlife, 99, 102, 103; relations with Franco's Spain, xxi, xxiii, 88; Revolution of 1959 (Cuban Revolution), xxv, 4, 72–73, 75, 77–78, 83, 84, 87–89, 90–94, 98, 101, 106, 192–193 (n.9, n.10, n.19); Revolution ("Infantes of"), 79–89; Revolution in the novel,

Cuba; and Batista, *Cont'd.*
92–93, 97–101, 103, 106; and silencing, 89, 103, 106; and support from Seix Barral, 21–22
Cuban Revolution (of 1959), xxv, 4, 72–73, 75, 77–78, 83, 84, 87–89, 90–94, 98, 101, 106, 192–193 (n.9, n.10, n.19); and Barral's support, 73, 89–90; and "Infantes of," 79–89; and Cabrera Infante's critique of, 77, 85, 107–108; and Franco regime, 84–89; and *Lunes de Revolución*, 75–6, 78, 80, 84–85, 192 (n.10); in the novel, 92–93, 97–101; and Seix Barral, 21–22. *See also* Boom, Cuba

de la Cierva, Ricardo, 21
de Lera, Angel María, 12
Delgado, Héctor, 111, 117
desarrollismo, 2–3, 8, 16, 146. *See also apertura*
Diera, Ernesto, 190 (n.9). *See also* Vargas Llosa, Mario
Discipline and Punish (Foucault), 190 (n.1)
Donoso, José, xiv, xxiv, 4, 18–19, 20, 22–29, 30, 32–34, 180, 195 (n.7), 196 (n.9), 200 (n.1); and Balcells, 174–175, 188 (n.15), 200 (n.1); and Balcells/Núria Monclús, 24–29, 31; and correspondence with Barral, 30; correspondence with García Márquez, 195–96; *Coronación*, 23; *Donde van a morir los elefantes*, 29; *Este domingo*, 23; *Historia personal del boom*, 19, 22–23, 27, 166, 174, 180, 181, 188 (n.13), 201 (n.8); *El jardín de al lado*, xxii, 23, 24–29, 31, 174, 188 (n.14); *El lugar sin límites*, 23, 188 (n.15); *El obsceno pájaro de la noche*, 23, 24; and Seix Barral, 188 (n.15); *Tres novelitas burguesas*, 24

Donoso, María Pilar, "El 'boom' doméstico," 201 (n.8)

ediciones definitivas, xxii, 74, 189 (n.7)
Edwards, Jorge, 30
Echenique, Alfredo Bryce, xiv; *Huerto cerrado*, 4
EDHASA (Editora y Distribuidora Hispanoamericana Sociedad Anónima), 131–34, 137–39, 149–150. *See also* publishing houses
Ediciones Era, 116, 121, 131, 195 (n.7), 196 (n.10). *See also* publishing houses
Ediciones R, xxv, 75, 104. *See also* publishing houses
Editions du Seuil, 143. *See also* publishing houses
Editora Nacional, 201 (n.6). *See also* publishing houses
Editorial Alfaguara, xxii, 105, 174, 176, 177, 181, 189 (n.7). *See also* publishing houses
Editorial Anagrama, 180, 183; and Jorge Herralde (founder), 180. *See also* publishing houses
Editorial Anaya, 181. *See also* publishing houses
Editorial Ayacucho, 74, 77, 105, 193 (n.18). *See also* publishing houses
Editorial Joaquín Mortiz, 14, 22, 27, 33, 94, 149, 188 (n.15), 201 (n.4). *See also* publishing houses
Editorial Jorge Álvarez, 22, 146, 148. *See also* publishing houses
Editorial Iberoamericana, 128, 129, 130. *See also* publishing houses
Editorial Losada, 22. *See also* publishing houses
Editorial Planeta, xv, 183. *See also* publishing houses
Editorial Plaza & Janés, xv, 196 (n.10). *See also* publishing houses

Editorial Salvat, 181, 182. *See also* publishing houses
Editorial Sudamericana, xv, 22–23, 33, 110–11, 112, 116, 118, 120–24, 128, 131, 132, 137, 139, 146, 149, 151, 183, 195 (n.7), 196 (n.8, n.10), 198 (n.4). *See also* publishing houses
Editorial Verbum, 182. *See also* publishing houses
economic development and expansion (under Franco). See *desarrollismo*
Edwards, Jorge, 200 (n.1)
Emecé Editores, 11. *See also* publishing houses
Einaudi, 170, 171. *See also* publishing houses
Espresate, Neus, 116, 121, 122, 195 (n.7). *See also* publishing houses, Ediciones Era
exiled writers, 109, 124, 137

female literary agents, 201 (n.3). *See also* Balcells, Carmen
Ferrater, Gabriel, 121, 122
Ferré, Rosario, 31–32, 167; *El coloquio de las perras*, 32–34, 188 (n.17)
Foucault, Michel, 71, 186 (n.6), 190 (n.1). *See also* censorship (productive)
Fraga Iribarne, Manuel, 1–2, 9, 39, 50, 84, 137, 138, 140, 179, 185 (n.1), 192 (n.9); and Ministry of Information, 3, 6, 39, 59, 63, 134, 137, 140, 185 (n.1), 186 (n.4)
Franco, Jean, 27, 167, 177
Franco, Francisco, xiii, xv, 4, 5, 7, 15, 16, 20, 23, 38, 39, 40, 41, 44, 50, 52, 53, 56, 71, 72, 79–80, 81, 103, 105, 106, 124, 126, 135, 141, 142, 146, 156, 169, 170; and Cuban Revolution 84–89; death of, 73, 83, 154. *See also* Franco regime

Franco regime, xiii, xv, xvi, xvii–xviii, xxiii, xxiv, 4, 16, 37, 39, 76, 84, 127; and Argentina, 148; censors' reports and language, xvi–xvii, xxv, 141; and censorship, 23, 39, 40, 143, 188 (n.14), 189 (n.4); and Cuba, 80–87, 88; cultural dominance (during), 5–6; decline of 107; and *desarrollismo*, xxiii, xxiv, 182, 201 (n.6); and dominance of Latin American book trade, xxiv, 4, 178; *Francoism*, 79; *franquistas*, 146; and Editora Nacional, 201 (n.6); FET, 186 (n.4); and folkloric Spain/kitsch in Spain, 169; JONS, 186 (n.4); and liberalization of literary culture, 12, 16; and morality, 2, 5, 141, 142, 144, 146; and national unity, 157; and new rules for censorship and book production, 53; and official reports, xiv, xxv, 181; and official silence, 11; opposition to, xxiii, 21; *orden y concierto* (as expression of), 141, 143, 147, 151, 155; and overhaul of publishing industry, 180; and paper industry, 177, 178, 179; and preservation of Spanish language, 142, 150; and profitability, 142, 146; and promotion of pan-Hispanic culture, 4–5, 46, 56; and publishing industry, 38; and Seix Barral, 19–21; and transition to democracy, 4, 154; and theory of censorship, xviii; and unwritten regulations, xviii. *See also* censorship, Franco, Spain
Franqui, Carlos, 83; *Diario de la Revolución cubana*, 83
Fuentes, Carlos, xiv, xxiv, 4, 20, 25, 26, 28, 29, 32, 166, 200 (n.1); *Las buenas conciencias*, xvi; *Cambio de piel* (34); *El naranjo*, 29; *La nueva novela hispanoamericana*, 23, 187 (n.9); *La región más transparente*,

Fuentes, Carlos, *Cont'd.*
xvi, (censor's report on) xxix; *Los reinos originarios*, xvi

Galicia, 156; and *gallegos* (representations of), 156, 157, 160
Gallimard, 143, 149, 170. See also publishing houses
García Márquez, Eligio, *Tras las claves de Melquíades*, 110, 120–121, 123, 195 (n.7), 196 (n.8)
García Márquez, Gabriel, xiv, xvi, xxiii, 25, 104, 109–140, 175, 176, 194 (n.1, n.2), 195 (n.4, n.6, n.7), 197 (n.15), 200 (n.1); *De amor y otros demonios*, 200 (n.4); *El amor en los tiempos de cólera*, 176, 194 (n.1); and autograph galleys, 109–117; and Barcelona connection; 109, 118, 125, 196 (n.9); and Balcells, 119–122, 175–177, 200 (n.1); and Barral, 109, 119, 121–22, 124, 128, 131, 135, 175, 196 (n.9); *Cien años de soledad*, xxii, 23, 109–117, 118–125, 123–125, 130–140, 175, 187 (n.14, n.15), 195 (n.3, n.4, n.6), 196 (n.9); *Cien años* and international success, 110, 119, 128, 130, 131; *Cien años* as school textbook, 136–139; *El coronel no tiene quien le escriba*, 116, 124, 128, 131, 196 (n.10); correspondence with Donoso, 195–96; correspondence Rodríguez Monegal, 196 (n.8); correspondence with Vargas Llosa, 194–195 (n.3); *Crónica de una muerte anunciada*, 194 (n.1); *Cuando era feliz e indocumentado*, 196 (n.2); and economics of manuscripts, 112–114, 118; *Eréndira*, 125, 175, 176, 197 (n.15); and familiarity with censorship, 125–135; *Los funerales de Mamá Grande*, 131, 174, 176, 194 (n.2); *El general en su laberinto*, 176; and government censorship, 125; *La hojarasca*, 124, 128, 132, 194 (n.1), 196 (n.10), 197 (n.13); and journalism, 125–26, 128; and lack of censorship, 122; and magical realism, 133, 175: *La mala hora*, 116, 124, 128–32, 135, 194 (n.1), 196 (n.11); *Memoria de mis putas tristes*, 125, 126, 127; and missing manuscript, 116; "La novela detrás de la novela", 111–114, 116; and opposition to Franco regime, 196 (n.12); and original manuscripts, 109–113, 116; and press censorship, 126; and routine censorship, 125; and royalties, 176; and Seix Barral, 119, 121, 122, 123, 130, 132; and support for Castro Regime, 122, 135; *Vivir para contarla*, 110, 125, 126, 127, 128, 129, 194 (n.2), 195 (n.6)
Garden Next Door, The. See *jardín de al lado, El*
Garmendia, Salvador, xiv; *Día de ceniza*, 3
Gimferrer, Pere, 13, 186 (n.8)
Gironella, José María, 12
González León, Adriano, xiv, 34, 35
gossip, 175, 177, 181
Goytisolo, Juan, 142
Goytisolo, Luis, 187 (n.11)
Gráficas Luis Pérez, 128–30

Hamish Hamilton, 147, 170, 171. See also publishing houses
Harss, Luis, *Los nuestros*, 124
Hayworth, Rita, 159, 169–72, 200 (n.16, n.17); and *Blood and Sand*, 168, 200 (n.16). See also Puig, Manuel
Henseler, Christine, 210 (n.3)
Herralde, Jorge, 180. See also publishing houses
Historia personal del boom, 19, 22–23, 27, 166, 174, 180, 181,

188 (n.13), 201 (n.8). *See also*
Donoso, José
Hollywood, 197 (n.1), 198 (n.5, n.10); in relation to Boom, 165–167. *See also* Rita Hayworth

Instituto Nacional del Libro Español (INLE). See National Book Institute

jardín de al lado, El, xxii, 23, 24–29, 31, 174. *See also* Donoso, José
Joset, Jacques, 195 (n.4), 196 (n.11)
Joyce, James, 191 (n.8)

Kerr, Lucille, 31, 169, 199 (n.10, n.14)
Knopf, 147. *See also* publishing houses
Kristal, Efraín, 70

Labanyi, Jo, 9, 146
Latin American intelligentsia, 143, 168
Leñero, Vicente, xiv, 170; *Los albañiles*, 34, 89
Levine, Suzanne Jill, 143, 144, 147–149, 150, 165, 170, 198 (n.8)
Ley del libro (1975), 2–3, 179
Ley de prensa e imprenta, 1–4, 9–11, 59, 185 (n.1), 186 (n.5)
Lezama Lima, José, xiv, xv, 165–66; *Esfera imagen*, 192 (n.9); *Paradiso*, (censor's report on) xxvii, 192 (n.9)
Libre, 187 (n.9, n.10). *See also* Boom and literary journals
Living to Tell the Tale. See *Vivir para contarla*
López Llausás, 121, 122–24
López Llovet de Rodrigué, Gloria, 121, 123
Lunes de Revolución, 75–6, 78, 80, 84–85, 192 (n.10)

Machover, Jacobo, 81
Mairena, Ana, 33

Manrique, Jaime, 143, 165
Marcha, 187 (n.9). *See also* Boom and literary journals
market, and book production, xv; and cultural exchange/cultural commodities, 7; and expansion of Latin American novel, 27; and exportation policies, 4; and foreign exports, 6; and growth of Spanish book trade, 46, 136; Ibero-American, xxv; and import/export imbalance in Spain, 5; and increased competition with Cuba, 12, 89; and increased competition in Spanish-language book market, 142; and manuscripts as commodities, 110–11, 114, 116–17; profit losses, 46; and promotional tours, 89; and Spanish language, xxv, 7, 37, 142; statistics of book production (between 1959–1975), 6–7. *See also* book trade, publishing houses, publishing industry, Seix Barral
Mensa, Carlos, 63–64, 190 (n.1)
Mexico, 6, 7, 14, 22, 34, 40, 78, 86, 94, 102, 109, 111, 112, 113, 116, 121, 122, 124, 130, 147, 149, 170, 185 (n.3), 186 (n.4), 188 (n.15), 194 (n.1), 201 (n.5)
Molloy, Sylvia, 33
Muchnik, Mario, 181, 183
Mudrovcic, María Eugenia, 103, 200 (n.2)
Mundo nuevo, 103, 187 (n.9), 191 (n.6), 193 (n.19), 196 (n.8). *See also* Boom and literary journals
Mutis, Álvaro, xiv, 116; *Summa de Maqroll*, xv

National Book Institute (INLE, *Instituto Nacional del Libro Español*), 6, 8, 46, 51, 178, 185 (n.1), 186 (n.4)
neocolonialism, 19, 181–183; and postcolonialism, 175

Neruda, Pablo, 200 (n.1)
Neuschäffer, Hans-Jörg, 2

Ocampo, Victoria, *Sur*, 121
One Hundred Years of Solitude. See *Cien años de soledad*
Onetti, Juan Carlos, 32
Onganía Regime, 148
opening up (of the Franco regime). See *apertura*
oppositional practices/oppositionality, 44–45, 56, 58
Oviedo, José Miguel, 180, 190 (n.12); *La invención de una realidad*, 189 (n.2); interview with Vargas Llosa, 180

Padilla Affair, 22
Padilla, Heberto, 73
Pantaleón y las visitadoras, xxii, 37, 38, 39, 43, 44, 58–70, 189 (n.7), 190 (n.9, n.10. n.12). See also Vargas Llosa, Mario
Papelera Española, 178; Subcomission for Paper, 20, 178, 180. See also paper industry
paper industry, 177–180
Patterson, Annabel, xxiv
Penultimate Punishments. See *Penúltimos castigos*
Penúltimos castigos, 29–31, 201 (n.8). See also Barral, Carlos
Peri Rossi, Cristina, 31
Petit, Joan, 187 (n.11), 189 (n.2)
Picasso, Pablo, 81
Poniatowska, Elena, 31
Premio Cervantes, 43, 104, 121
Primera Plana, 72, 81, 187 (n.9), 196 (n.8). See also Boom and literary journals
Porrúa, Paco, 112, 121, 123, 124, 130, 149
publishing houses, 12, 84; Alfaguara xxii, 105, 181; Anagrama, 180, 183; Anaya, 181; Ayacucho, 74, 77, 105, 193 (n.18); Círculo de Lectores, 38, 131; EDHASA, 131–134, 137–139, 149–150; Era (Ediciones), 116, 121, 131, 195 (n.7), 196 (n.10); Gallimard, 143; Iberoamericana (Editorial), 128, 129; Einaudi, 170,171; Emecé (Editores), 22; Hamilton (Hamish), 147, 170, 171; Joaquín Mortiz, 14, 149, 188 (n.15), 201 (n.4); Jorge Álvarez, 22, 146, 148; Knopf, 147; lack of (in Latin America), 40; Losada, 22; Nacional (Editora), 201 (n.6); Planeta, xv, 183; Plaza & Janés, xv, 196 (n.10); R (Ediciones), xxv, 75, 104; Salvat, 181, 182; Seuil (Editions du), 143; Sudamericana, xv, 22–23, 110, 111, 112, 116, 118, 120–124, 128, 131, 132, 137, 139, 146, 149, 183, 195 (n.7), 196 (n.8, n.10); Random House xv; Verbum (Editorial), 182; Visor Libros, 148. See also Barral Editores, book trade, market, *Casa de las Américas,* Seix Barral, publishing industry
publishing industry, xii–xiv; in Argentina, 6, 7, 40; behind-the-scenes negotiations in, 142; control of, xiv, 46, 181–183; and competition, 26–28, 37, 167–168; in Cuba, 51; and Czech-Russian consortium, 7; and digital book production, 184; expansion of, xiv, xvii, xxiii–xxvi, 4–8, 18–19, 150; history of, 173; Ibero-American, 177; and market strategies, xiv–xv, 51; in Mexico, 6, 7, 40; and National Book Institute (INLE), 46, 178; and new printing and publishing law, 9, 59; and paper shortage, 8, 179–80, 201 (n.5, n.7); revisited, 173–179, 181–184; and rivalries between Spain and Latin America, 12; shift in control, xiv; Spanish-language, xiv, xv, xxv, 6–8, 10, 46, 90, 130, 142, 177;

and U.S. market, 8. See also book trade, market, publishing houses
Puig, Manuel, xiv, xv, 91, 122, 141–172, 148, 197–198 (n.3); and Barral, 142–143, 146, 148, 150, 153, 154, 160, 162, 170–72; *El beso de la mujer araña*, xxii, 143, 154, 159, 168; and betrayals, 142, 144, 146, 155, 158, 159, 165–166, 171–172; and Boom (exclusion from), 165; *Boquitas pintadas*, 143, 149–150, 151, 153; *The Buenos Aires Affair*, xxii, 149, 154, 159, 198 (n.4); and camp, 144, 152, 162; and Catalan name (Joan Manuel Puig), 197–198 (n.3); and censorship, 142; and critique of Castro regime, 143; and economics of censorship, 144–160, 172; and economic profit, 149; and "faggotry," 144, 146; and foul language, 152; and the gay novel, 143, 144; and heteronormativity, 148; and Hollywood, 165–172, 198 (n.5), 198–199 (n.10), 200 (n.16); and homosexuality, 147, 152, 153, 160, 161–162, 198 (n.4); and immorality, 148; "Losing Readers", 142–143, 149; and market competition, 148; and the modern/new novel, 165; and non-linear/fragmented narrative, 141, 147, 157–158; and omitted chapters/ sections, 155–165, 198 (n.9), 199 (n.11, n.13); and queerness, 152, 155, 172, 199–200 (n.15); and scrutiny in book market, 146; and Seix Barral, 142, 149–51, 154, 162, 170, 197–98 (n.3), 198 (n.7), 199 (n.11); and self-censorship, 155,158, 159, 162; and Spanish immigrants, 156–158, 169; and symbolic capital, 147; and textual economy, 155, 159–160, 199 (n.12); *La traición de Rita Hayworth*, xv, xvii, (censor's report on) xxvi, 141–44, 146–150 (importation of), 148–150, 151–168, 169–172, 197 (n.1), 198 (n.3, n.9), 199 (n.14, 15), 200 (n.17); and treachery, 155, 160;"Writers and Repression", 147

Radway, Janice, xv, 38
Rama, Ángel, 187 (n.9)
Random House, xv. See also publishing houses
Riensenfeld, Janet, 111, 117
Roa Bastos, Augusto, 26, 29, 200 (n.1)
Robles Piquer, Carlos, 39, 46–53, 57, 90, 94, 95, 96, 182, 189 (n.6), 192 (n.12); correspondence with Barral and Cabrera Infante, 94, 96, 98; correspondence with Barral and Vargas Llosa, 47–49, 52–53; correspondence with Cabrera Infante, 95–96, 98; in defense of censorship, 47, 49, 50, 51, 52; and negotiations with Barral, 47, 48, 52–53, 96, 98
Rodríguez Monegal, Emir, 147, 191 (n.6), 193 (n.19), 196 (n.8); correspondence with García Márquez, 196 (n.8); and cultural revolution and industrial boom, 187 (n.9)
Rulfo, Juan, 165–66

Sábato, Ernesto, xiv, 26, 29, 166; *Sobre héroes y tumbas*, xvi
Saldívar, Dasso, 116, 120, 121, 124; *Viaje a la semilla*, 124, 173, 195 (n.6)
Salvat, Santiago, 182. See also publishing houses
Santana, Mario, 12, 44, 52, 186 (n.7), 195 (n.6); *Foreigners in the Homeland*, 12
Sarduy, Severo, xiv, 166
secuestro (sequestration). See also censorship

Seix Barral, xxii, xxiii, xxiv, xxv, 3, 4, 13, 16, 38, 73, 135, 181, 186 (n.8), 187 (n.9); *Biblioteca Breve*, 13, 15, 17, 18, 19, 23–24, 38, 40, 41, 48, 52, 76, 80, 88, 89, 119, 120, 121, 142, 160, 170, 179, 180, 187 (n.11); *Biblioteca Formentor*, 13, 40; *Biblioteca Nueva Narrativa Hispánica*, 13; and book covers, 18, 35–36, 62–65, 180, 187 (n.12); and book trade expansion, 13; and the Boom, 4, 13, 14, 15, 31; and Cabrera Infante, 73, 74, 76, 96, 103, 104, 105, 191 (n.3, n.4); and Carpentier, 192 (n.12); and *Catálogo General de Publicaciones*, 4, 13, 19–21, 22, 33; and Donoso, 188 (n.15); foundations of, 13–14, 20; and Franco regime, 19–21; and García Márquez, 119, 121, 122, 123, 130, 132; and international prestige, 16, 17, 18; and literary journals, 187 (n.9); and literary prizes, 13–17, 188 (n.18); and literary prizes and women, 33; market-based diversification, 13, 18; market strategies, 20–22, 30, 38, 39, 46; new editorial policies, 13–22, 14, 31, 40, 44, 46, 51–3, 62–63, 89, 104, 186 (n.8), 188 (n.13); and pan-Hispanic literature, 19–20, 89; and *Premio de la crítica*, 41; *Premio Biblioteca Breve*, 15–6, 18, 23–24, 33–34, 38–39, 41, 48, 52, 80, 88, 89, 119, 120, 142, 160, 170, 179, 187 (n.12), 188 (n.18), 189 (n.2); prestige as avant-garde publisher, 15–16, 17, 19–20, 92, 171; *Prix Formentor*, 17, 22, 52, 187 (n.11); *Prix International de Littérature*, 17, 187 (n.11); pro-Cuba, 21; and promotion and distribution of Latin American Literature, xxiii, xxv, 27; and Puig, 142, 149–51, 154, 162, 170, 197–198 (n.3), 198 (n.7), 199 (n.11); and symbolic capital, 15, 16; and Vargas Llosa, 38–42, 59–70, 188–89 (n.1); and women writers, 33–34. *See also* book trade, market, publishing industry, publishing houses

Seix, Victoriano, 13, 14, 22, 177, 189 (n.2)

Serrano, Pío, 182; Editorial Verbum, 182. *See also* publishing houses

Skármeta, Antonio, 200 (n.1)

Spacks, Patricia Meyer, 175

Spain: and Catholic values, xvi, 179, 192 (n.12); Civil War (1936–39), xxv, 185 (n.1); and colonial past, xvi, xxv–xxvi, 87, 135; and colonial presence in the novel, 156; and expansion of book trade, 136; and history of cultural dominance (in Latin America), xxii, xxvi; and history of economic dominance (in Latin America), xxii, xxvi; and exiles in Cuba, 88; and exiled writers, 124; and Juan Carlos I, 181; and Latin American relations, 175; as *madre patria*, 176; and moral responsibility, 150; and neocolonialism, 19, 181–183; and paper industry, 177–179; and postcolonial cultural history, xxvi, 175; and profits from Latin American writing, 176; and regional nationalism, 157; and transition to democracy, 154, 188 (n.14). *See also apertura*, Franco, market, publishing industry,

Subastas Velázquez, 109, 115, 116, 117, 118, 132, 194 (n.1); and auction of literary works, 109–118, 194–95 (n.4, n.5). *See also* Barcelona

symbolic capital, 15–16, 18, 27, 147. *See also* Bourdieu

Tejera, Nivaria, 33, 36; *Sonámbulo del sol*, 33, 34, 39

Three Trapped Tigers. See *Tres tristes tigres.*
Time of the Hero, The. See *ciudad de los perros, La*
Traba, Marta, 33
traición de Rita Hayworth, La, xv; xvii, xxvi (censor's report on), 141–44, 146–150. *See also* Puig, Manuel
translation, 177, 188 (n.16). *See also* Boom
Tres tristes tigres, xv, xxii, 71–79, 84, 90, 94–108, 119, 191 (n.2, n.3), 193 (n.15, n.16, n.17, n.18), 194 (n.21). *See also* Cabrera Infante, Guillermo

Valentino, Rudolph, 168
Valenzuela, Luisa, 31–32; *Los censores*, xix–xxii
Valverde, José María, 52, 189 (n.2)
Vargas Llosa, Mario, xiv, xvi, xviii, xxiv, 4, 12, 18, 20, 22, 25–26, 28–29, 37–70, 142, 166, 173, 175, 176, 180, 183, 184, 189 (n.3), 200 (n.1), 201 (n.4); "Las aguafuertes de Ernesto Diera," 190 (n.9); and articles, 200 (n.1, n.2); and Balcells, 173, 174, 200 (n.1), 201 (n.4); and Barral, 38–41, 43, 45, 46, 48, 49, 51 59, 60; *Los cachorros*, 39, 43, 48–9, 59; *La casa verde*, 38 39, 41, 59, 70, 189 (n.7); "La censura y el cine," 189 (n.4); *La ciudad de los perros*, xxii, 18, 38–39, 41, 44–59, 64, 67, 70, 89, 119, 135, 179, 189–89 (n.2), 189 (n.6, n.7), 190 (n.8); and commercial success, 38; *Conversación en la catedral*; xvi, 38, 39, 41, 43, 49, 59, 61, 70, 189 (n.7); and cooperation with censors, 41–43, 45; correspondence with Barral and Robles Piquer, 47–49, 50, 51; correspondence with Cabrera Infante, 97–98, 105; correspondence with García Márquez, 194–195 (n.3); *Los cuadernos de Don Rigoberto*, 176, 188–89 (n.1); *La fiesta del chivo*, 177; *García Márquez: historia de un deicidio*, 42–43, 123, 188–89 (n.1), 200 (n.2); *Historia secreta de una novela*, 42–43; *Los impostores*, 48; interview with Oviedo, 180; *Los jefes*, 39, 41, 42; and military literature, 69–70; *La morada del héroe*, 48; and new narrative techniques, 69; and opposition to censorship, 40–44; and opposition to Franco regime, 43–44; *Pantaleón y las visitadoras*, xxii, 37–39, 43, 44–45, 58–70, 189 (n.7), 190 (n.9, n.10, n.12); *El pez en el agua*, 188–189 (n.1); *Premio Cervantes*, 43, 189 (n.3); and royalties, 176–177; and Seix Barral, 38–42, 59–70, 188–89 (n.1); Spanish naturalization of, 43–44, 189 (n.5); and writing under military rule (barracks writing), 45, 54, 55, 56–58, 59
Vázquez Montalbán, Manuel, 184, 200 (n.1)
Vera, Ernesto, 83
Vernet Mateu, José, 134–140, 146, 197 (n.14, n.15). *See also* censorship (citizen-initiated, "spontaneous")
View of Dawn in the Tropics. See *Vista del amanecer en el trópico (Relatos)*
Visor Libros, 148. *See also* publishing houses
Vista del amanecer en el trópico (Relatos), 76–7, 194 (n.21). *See also* Cabrera Infante, Guillermo
Vivir para contarla, 110, 125, 126, 128, 129, 194–95 (n.2, n.6). *See also* García Márquez, Gabriel